B

COMPASSION FOR WHOLENESS

A Call to Heal and Bless

Sylvanus N. Wosu

Compassion for Wholeness Copyright © 2014 by Sylvanus N. Wosu, Ph.D.

ISBN: 978-0-9746364-8-1 (Extended 1st Edition)
ISBN: 978-0-9746364-9-8 (Work Book)

The Library of Congress
United States Copyright Office
101 Independence Ave., S.E.
Washington, D.C. 20559-6000
202-707-3000

Original Cover design and publishing by Elohiym Publishing House, Inc.

For information contact;
KLI Publishing,
Kanmas Leadership Institute, Inc.
5100 Penn Avenue, Pittsburgh PA 15224
www.kanmasmasleadership.com

Printed in the United States of America
10 9 8 7 6 5 4 3 2 2

DEDICATION

Dedicated to all those who have extended and expended themselves in their deliberate acts of compassion to bring wholeness to me and others.

May the good Lord of compassion also bring wholeness to them all!

CONTENTS

PREFACE

Compassion reflects a practical response that emanates from a tender heart more than an emotional feeling or sympathy; compassion can be initiated out of personal concerns or sympathy. It occurs when there is a real need to care for another person. When you think about your relation to compassion, consider whether you have ever looked away from seeing the needs of the less fortunate, slighter privileged, the poor, or the marginalized. Do you often wait until they have told you their needs? Can you say that you are always aware or conscious of the states of suffering, hurt, loss, or despair of others? When you think about compassion, do you remember those who have impacted your life or walked through your wilderness-like state of despair? Let me share a few such moments with you to frame the context of this book.

When I Think of Compassion...

I remember the heart of compassion of Mama Paik, who turned her heart to perceive our state of needs and vulnerabilities, and chose to walk with us to uplift our spirits. She did not respond to want to meet those needs because we asked for her help or that we looked desperate. Rather, our hope was always on the love of God, and the fact that He had everything under His control. Hence, we always joyfully projected a sense of assurance that He would meet our needs. When Mama Palik opened her heart to be of use to God, God showed her what needed to be done. She did not have to ask us. She just did it, and she was always right. The encounter with Mama and the Lord's faithfulness transformed me forever. Her acts of compassion in labor showed me that, indeed, we are all created to serve God by caring for each other and the least among us.

How can I forget the selfless acts of compassion of people we never knew, at the time of the delivery of our child in the spring of 1980? While I was so excited about holding my first child, my wife was privately in despair as to how we would hold up financially. I refused to despair, and inwardly encouraged myself in the Lord, with an outbound assuredness and confidence that He would come through for us. My wife safely delivered Eliada, meaning 'who God Loves' – but continued to worry, and I continued to believe, pray, and hope. "Honey, we do not have anything in the house for the baby's needs, or money. What are we going to do?" she asked. "Do not worry, my wife, our God will supply," I assured her. From where was my assurance coming?

Well, I got home to witness the most uplifting act of compassion, and the greatest miracle of my Christian life. Before my very eyes were all kinds of baby items, which filled the house; everything my wife had wished and wept for, plus much more, were all in the room. All the brands were new. On my desk was $500 cash, wrapped with a white paper that read, "To Sylvanus and Enefaa." Beyond the gifts and the money, I felt an awesome presence of God that filled that room. As if that was not enough, a few days later, when my wife was to be discharged from the hospital, I went to the business office to sign a paper that was related to a payment arrangement for my wife's hospital care. I was told that the bill had been settled by someone who did not want to be identified. We are not sure if these two acts—the provisions in the house and the bill payment—were taken on by the same person or persons; we never could find out whom to thank, as there was no information anywhere to trace the source. These acts of compassion and the increased faith that resulted from them give me incomparable joy and emotions each time I remember them.

I remember Mr. Gaylord Wilkerson, a man very generous with his heart and a man who knew how to touch God's heart by seeing how he could meet the immediate needs of those around him. Gaylord was in a wheelchair most of his adult life after serving in the military. His acts of compassion would bring wholeness to those who were physically complete. Gaylord knew how to ask the right questions in order to explore more deeply into their hearts and to feel their needs. He was always obedient to doing whatever was required for anyone who he found whose heart needed healing.

A case to remember: we had been approved to submit application for permanent residency (Green) card. Brother Gaylord asked about the process and we excitedly informed him that all was going well. We casually mentioned to him that that application fee was $600. We never asked him for help, but on the Sunday after church, he asked us to join him for dinner in his house. As were about leaving after dinner, he handed us an envelope. "This will serve the need," he said. "Go back Monday and get it," he said as if giving a loving command. I looked at the money and said, "Brother Gaylord; the fee is $600 not $650." His very confident response was this: "The Lord impressed upon my heart to make it $650. I believe you are going to need it. Now go, and let me know how it goes." Knowing who he is and how God works, we thanked him. Without further question, he prayed for us and we left. On Monday, we proceeded to submit our application and was shocked that the total fee was $650 ($600 application fee plus $50 agent fee). Think about this! We shared the testimony with him as we returned and asked how he known exactly what we needed? He said, when he became aware of the need, he sort the face of God as to the real extent of the need, and the Lord impressed upon to make it $650, and he had to follow his heart. To me, Gaylord's acts of compassion-generosity to us and so many people remain indelible in our hearts.

I will not forget Brother Nsikak and his heartfelt conviction for compassion. On a cold Christmas Eve in Norman, Oklahoma, we did not have any groceries in the house, and were beginning to settle for having nothing for that Christmas. The winter was so bad that people were advised to remain indoors unless they had a good reason to go out. However, Brother Nsikak had such a reason to leave his house; he was moved with compassion to go meet what he was convinced was a need. His conviction for fulfilling this need overcame his fear for the inclement weather. "Brother Nsikak, why did you risk coming driving under this bad weather? Did you not hear the warning, not to go out?" I asked him as I opened the door to let him in with several bags of groceries. "Brother Sylvanus, I just could not choose not to come; I have this strong impression in my spirit that there was a need, and that would not let me have peace," he said. We had not talked to Nsikak about this, but somehow God had, and he answered—even though he was a student as needy as we were. He chose to open his heart to think about someone, and God directed his steps correctly. He made our Christmas complete and more joyful.

I will also ever remember Brother Peter's *empathetic* heart for compassion; he was another fellow student in Norman, Oklahoma. Our four-year-old first daughter's finger had just been unknowingly crushed behind a heavy steel door by her two-year-old brother. The finger was hanging by a little thread of flesh, and needed immediate surgery, or she would lose it permanently. We rushed her to the emergency room, and a few hours later, came back home rejoicing that we had not been rejected in our efforts this time, but were attended to with only a promissory note to pay. Brother Peter visited to see how our daughter was doing. We all rejoiced that she had not lost a finger. It was an act of compassion when, a few days later, Brother Peter called us to say, "Brother Sylvanus; I have been to the hospital, and you do not have to worry about that bill; it has been settled." Brother Peter, who at the time needed help for his school fees, had gone to this hospital and settled the bill of $357. In the 80s, that was a great deal of money for an international student working 20 hours per week, and at less than minimum wage. Nevertheless, when this Brother became aware of this need, he intentionally expended himself and shared not only joy to ease the girl's healing, but also sacrificed his own resources to settle the needed medical bill for the surgery, without being asked to, or in expectation of a reward.

I remember the cold winter night in Edmond, Oklahoma, and the intentional act of courage of an unknown driver who saved another brother and me as we almost froze to death in a stalled car. It was one of those unusually winter days. Brother Gilbert's car stalled on his way home from work at 7 PM, along route I-35. He walked to call me from a phone booth to come and help jump his car. Yes, in those days, we looked out for each other! The year was 1982, and there were no cell phones, in case you were wondering! I drove to meet him and, after several failed attempts to jump his car, my car's battery also ran down. From 9 PM till 5 AM, we were in my car with the car front hood opened, hoping that someone would stop to help us. Nobody came. By around that 5 AM, we were almost frozen to death because we did not have good winter coats.

I had just jumped into my car to rush to help, thinking that it would be an easy jump, so I had not dressed properly. It was an act of courage-compassion for an unknown driver to come to our aid. He saw us when he passed around 11 PM in the same direction with us, and then at 5 AM, returning on the opposite side of the road, saw us again. He reported that when he became aware that there were people in that car, his first thought was to see if they needed help; he was moved with compassion to empathize with us; he looked into that dead car, because he sensed that whoever was there must be in trouble and need help. He saw an urgent need that must be met, and rather than 'minding his own business', this 'Good Samarian' turned around to come check on what he could do to help in the situation. He found us almost dead. He immediately helped us into his car to take us to the hospital. On the way, we asked him to take us home to our wives, who by this time had alerted the police for two missing husbands. The wives were nursing a one month old and a six month old baby, respectively, at the time, and we were living in the same apartment complex.

I cannot forget Brother Lawrence Owoputi and his *heart of sacrifice* for the love of the brethren. This brother takes action whenever possible to meet the emotional, physical, and materials needs of people around him, with such a generous heart as I have never seen in anybody in my lifetime. In any situation, whether in sickness or health, you will always find this brother self-confident in himself; he has such an inner peace that it is almost contagious, and you can be sure to be comfortable around him.

When I think of compassion, I also remember my wife, Dr. Enefaa Wosu, and her big *care-giving* heart of compassion, in caring for me when I was sick, oppressed by outsiders, downcast, or weak in the spirit. She knew how to be on her knees to fervently pray to God to bring wholeness to me and the children. She was the family pathway to the gate of God's own heart. Even in my moments of unlovingness, she was loving, caring, and forgiving.

I appreciate the *Ministries of Compassion* of religious organizations such as the African Christian Fellowship, USA, which is all over Africa; the Compassion International, which works in Christian child sponsorship; the Assembly of God ministries all over the world; the National Catholic Ministry to the Bereaved; and many others.

In times of natural disasters, where many families and lives are lost or displaced, we remember the acts of compassion of ordinary citizens and non-religious organizations such as the Red Cross, which exhibit collective compassion to bring healing and wholeness to those affected, and also to the nations under duress.

When I think of compassion, I remember the *ultimate model of Compassion*: Jesus Christ. What He did and taught about compassion, and how He looked after people and still cares today. He cares when we are afflicted with a disease, pain, or suffering; He cares when we are grieving the loss of relatives. When we are broken-hearted for any reason, troubled in our spirit, or confused about the right path to follow, Jesus cares for us. When our best friends and loved ones mistreat, betray, or fail us, He can be trusted; when sin and the results of sin drag us down, or when we disobey Him, He grieves over our failures, and feels our pains; our infirmities touch him, and He readily forgives our sins. He does all this and more, because His love motivates His acts of compassion. We will list a few examples in the preceding section:

There are many more examples! What is compassion to you – caring, healing, showing concern, sharing yourself, comforting others, putting others above your need, etc.? Whatever you choose to do in light of compassion, it can be measured by the level of the intentionality in your actions. Such commendable actions are usually driven by the selfless love for others because of the indescribable love of Jesus for you. Compassion as demonstrated by Jesus is a dynamic act of practical response to whatever life issues you are aware of, or that are presented before you. These acts, like in the examples above, take many forms in changing situations. So I ask you, can you show compassion to others as a practical response and love for Jesus because He first showed you? (1 John 4:19). "We were by nature deserving of wrath. However, because of his great love for us, God, who is rich in mercy, made us alive with Christ even when we were dead in transgressions…" (Ephesians 2:3-5, NIV). When this mindset is in us, that we love because He first loved us, and that what we do to others

xviii   COMPASSION FOR WHOLENESS

is done unto Christ, then acts of compassion become not only practical, but a natural response to others' states of being.

About this Book

These acts of compassion, even as I recall them, are very emotional for my soul because we a society have become so apathetic and careless about what happens to others. I have always wondered why. When my family, friends, students, brothers, and sisters think about my compassion, will they remember anything I have done to bring healing to them? What about you? When you think about compassion, and this is aside from the compassion we experience in the love of Jesus, whom have you extended compassion to? How and why have you chosen to show compassion? Do you know what it means to show compassion that brings wholeness to another person? When was the last time you walked with someone in that person's wilderness state of suffering or in danger, as the account of the unknown driver above? What motivated you? These personal questions and much more will be explored in this book, in relation to modeling the hearts of compassion.

This book, *Compassion for Wholeness: A Call to Heal and Bless,* is the fourth in my series of books framed around the subject of leader as servant leadership. This volume addresses ways in which you as a leader-servant can develop a heart of compassion, and how you can develop self-awareness regarding states of sufferings, hurts, loss, or despair in others. Compassion is presented in the context of your intentional service leadership toward others, both within and outside of your family. It is about taking intentional actions, without been asked, to bring wholeness to another person's life. Compassion leadership must start from the family to the rest of the world.

My hope is that this book will converse with you, talk to you, and challenge you to become a better version of yourself in showing compassion for others. Even as the author, it has impacted me, just recalling these testimonies. One purpose of the book is to create some teaching moments and help you understand the key foundations and pillars to frame your attitude, relationships, skills, and success as a leader-servant in your acts of compassion.

For ease of reading, and unless otherwise specified for emphasis, the pronoun "he" refers to both male and female genders. Personal references to God and Jesus are capitalized, and other standard references to biblical terms are maintained for conformity. And for clarity of meaning, any reference to Servant Leadership is only with respect to the Leader as Servant Leadership concepts, and purely based on Biblical teaching.

A variety of Bible translations, from over 11,200 original Hebrew, Aramaic, and Greek words to about 6,000 English words, do exit with variations in meanings and emphases. I am not a biblical scholar, and do not pretend to be one; hence, I have avoided research into the roots of these words and personally prefer to use the New King James Version (NKJV). However, I have intentionally used other translations for three main reasons. First, this allows for increased impact and alignment of words to the most desired meaning, and emphasis in the concepts being addressed. Second, I wanted to find new and personal discovery of meanings from translations with which I have not been previously familiar. And third, I wanted to allow readers who may prefer translations other than the NKJV the benefit of their preferred translations. Hence, in addition to the NKJV, other translations used in the book include: the New International Version (NIV), the New Living Translation (NLT), the King James Version (KJV), the English Standard Version (ESV), and the Good News Translation (GNT). Unless otherwise specified, NKJV should be assumed.

Sylvanus Nwakanma Wosu, PhD

ACKNOWLEDGEMENTS

This book was inspired by the reflections on the acts of compassion, those of many with whom I have been associated in my life. To each of those, I want to especially express a special appreciation and say, thank you:

To Mama Paik, who turned her heart to perceive our state of needs and walked with us to uplift our spirits.

To those individuals whom we cannot identify, I say, thank you for your selfless acts of compassion at the time of the delivery of our first child in the spring of 1980.

To Mr. Gaylord Wilkerson, a man very generous with his heart, a man who knew how to touch God's heart by seeing how he could meet the immediate needs of others.

To Brother Iyo Nsikak and his heartfelt conviction for compassion that moved him to fulfill a need he was convinced was essential.

To Brother Peter Ayani for his empathetic heart, and for compassion and readiness to expend himself in bringing healing to our young daughter.

To the unknown driver whose intentional act of courage saved us from almost being frozen to death in a cold winter night.

To Brother Lawrence Owoputi: for his heart of sacrifice, and his love of the brethren, and the inner peace around him.

To my wife, Dr. Enefaa Wosu, for all her care and heart of compassion towards me and the children, sacrificing the best of her time to make us complete.

To all the Ministries of Compassion of religious organizations, such as the African Christian Fellowship USA, the Assembly of God, the Catholic Ministry, and others.

And to God be all the glory.

CHAPTER 1

ELEMENTS OF WHOLENESS COMPASSION

The framework of wholeness compassion is based on the leader-servant's willingness to serve in bringing a healing wholeness to others in different states of life's issues. Wholeness in this context means completeness, fullness, or acts of oneness. Hence, wholeness compassion can be defined as the unconditional love-motivated act or practical response of walking with someone in a state of brokenness or suffering, in order to make that person whole or complete again. In my previous work, *The Leader as Servant Leadership Model* (Wosu, 2014a), I positioned the Leader–Servant as a leader first, but not in the sense of projecting or lording his or her power and authority over others; instead, he or she is the person who leads the process of influencing desired changes in others by modeling the servant attitude toward others. He is a *leader-servant or a serving leader*, not *a servant-leader*. He leads as a servant by putting others' needs above his rights or position, to enable the acts of nurturing, strengthening, equipping, and developing other leaders who change their communities. The effectiveness of a leader to restore others to wholeness depends on the quality of his inner and outward attributes; the details are fully covered in my two books: *The Authentic Leader as Servant Part I (Outward) and Part II (Inner Strength): Attribute, Principles, and Practices* (Wosu, 2014b; 2014c) In this context, compassion is the quality of a leader's inner-strength and ability to know what matters most to others, and hence adapts appropriate behavior to add value to people's lives. As an inward quality, it is a selfless heartfelt concern of others, followed by a practical emotional response for their welfare. Outward compassion starts from a leader's internal humility and their ability to adopt appropriate disposition to be of service for the well-being and wholeness of those people. This chapter introduces compassion as a leadership characteristic, and focuses on the key dimensions of wholeness compassion with respect to the acts of a leader-servant.

The Elements of Wholeness Compassion

Wholeness compassion in all of its forms, as demonstrated by Jesus, is a love-based response practically directed to fulfill a need to make someone whole again from a state of brokenness. Wholeness compassion occurs when there is an intentional practical act to alleviate the suffering (pain, grief, distress, sorrow, etc.) of another person to make that person complete or whole again; it is a relevant impassioned response rather than just emotional feelings and sympathy (the practical action may originate from emotional feelings and sympathy, but must go beyond those). Suffering in this context can be caused by the pain from loss of a loved one; distress from the loss of employment, home, or property; pain from divorce, sickness, or poverty; or a lack for any reason, etc. At the core of the applicable response to the needs of others is the desire to answer the call for bringing wholeness healing and blessing to others in need. Answer to such a call takes self-awareness and personal perception of others, and being intentionally responsive to meet their expressed needs through compassion. The compassion that heals and brings wholeness requires us to share in someone else's brokenness with the goal of making that person whole again. The key elements of the acts of compassion, with respect to the wholeness and well-being of others, can be summarized below:

- **Acts of extending and expending yourself to share in another's suffering:** Compassion is generally referred to as sharing in someone else's suffering. This involves deeper engagement in the process of walking through the valley of a situation, through broadened experience and emulating God's empathy.
- **Acts of heart-felt response to meet a need or reduce suffering:** Compassion is more broadly an emotional response of sharing in the suffering of another person, along with an intentional desire to alleviate or reduce the suffering to make that person whole.
- **Acts of intense feeling that are followed by a personal healing-action:** Compassion is a direct healing-action motivated by a sense of deep emotional feeling to meet a need or alleviate the suffering of someone.
- **Acts of relating to others suffering through person concerns for action:** Compassion can also be referred to as the hearing and understanding of another person's suffering with an intention to help.
- **Acts of empathizing with direct action for wholeness:** Compassion is an element of empathy, and is often differentiated from the other elements of empathy by the intentional actions a

person with compassion performs to aid the person for whom he feels sympathetic.

- **Acts of intentional spiritual engagement:** Compassion involves intentionally engaging the transcendent aspect of empathy to help the receiver find healing, rest, and affirmation in God.
- **Acts of being self-aware of a need and practically responding to meet it:** Compassion happens when you become aware of the need and the state of suffering of others, and you allow your heart to move toward meeting the need. Jesus moved by that awareness and the sense of love He had for the sick and the lost.

Demonstration of Wholeness Compassion

Jesus' demonstrated **wholeness compassion** through the following acts. Note that in each case, the act was intentional, and designed to make the receiver complete or whole again:

- Jesus demonstrated *personal concern* as an element of compassion: when He encountered the man who was possessed by unclean spirits that made him to wander around unclothed with self-inflicted cuts (Mark 5), Jesus was moved and had mercy on him (Mark 5:19). Jesus was tender and acted to help this man out of the pitiful situation in which he was stationed.
- Jesus demonstrated personal *heart-felt grief* when He encountered a man with a withered hand (Mark 3) in a Hebrew synagogue on the Sabbath day. As the Jews suspiciously watched to see if He would heal the man on a Sabbath, to accuse him of violating the Sabbath by doing a good work, "He looked around at them in anger and, deeply distressed at their stubborn hearts, said to the man, 'Stretch out your hand.' He stretched it out, and his hand was completely restored" (Mark 3: 5, NIV). This is pure wholeness! Jesus was not only "grieved" over the heartless stubbornness of these Jews; His grief moved Him to compassion

as an example of good work. Another act of Jesus' compassion in this encounter was that He healed this man's withered hand in order to answer the question He had posed to them earlier: "Is it lawful on the Sabbath to do good or to do evil, to save life or to kill?" (Mark 3:4). His answer and lesson to them was that it was most legitimate on the Sabbath, or on any other day, to do the right thing and save life; His act of compassion to bring wholeness to this man was a fulfillment of that law of the Sabbath about which they were testing Him as he remained silent to His question.

- Jesus took *personal action* to make people whole as part of His ministry of compassion. For example, for a poor man who had leprosy (Mark 1:41), he demonstrated compassion as a practical (beyond emotional) response to the man's kneeling and begging: "If you will, you can make me clean." The Lord, moved with compassion, and said, "I will." "He touched the man, and he was instantly cleansed."

- Jesus' *self-awareness* of the needs of others served as the important face of compassion and practically responded to meet the needs he saw in His heart. However, even in His own personal grief for the beheading of John the Baptist, His Cousin, by Herod, Jesus showed compassion when he "saw a great multitude and was moved with compassion for them, because they were like sheep not having a shepherd" (Mark 6:34, NJKV). The disciples, on the other hand, did not have the same practical response. They asked that the crowd be allowed to go and "buy themselves bread" (Mark 6:36, NKJV). Jesus walked through the experience of this multitude running on foot to be with Him. Moved by that awareness and his sense of love for them, Jesus saw beyond the disciples' view, which this multitude needed to be fed before they were allowed to go home.

- Jesus' *heart went out* as an act of compassion to give life and wholeness to a heartbroken widowed mother. Jesus and His disciples went to a town called Nain with a large crowd following him (Luke 7:11-15). They met the funeral procession of a dead child, the only son of a widowed mother, being carried out in a coffin as they approached the gate of the town. The heartbroken widowed mother was crying over the death of her son. "When the Lord saw her, his heart went out to her, and he said, 'don't cry'" (Luke 7: 13, NIV). This was an act of compassion that brought life to her son, and completeness and wholeness to this mother. Can you imagine the completeness that this woman or anybody would feel when "Jesus gave him back to his mother"? (Luke 7:15, NIV).

- Jesus, through the parable of the Good Samaritan, showed that *extending love to all,* even your enemies, is a pattern of compassion: Jews had no dealings with the Samaritans, who they despised. Nevertheless, when an arrogant Jewish lawyer was asked by Jesus what he needed to do to have eternal life, he gave the right answer from the law: "You shall love the LORD your God with all your heart… and 'your neighbor as yourself'", but was not willing to make a response to it in practical terms. In an attempt to justify himself, he asked Jesus: "Who is my neighbor?" Jesus responded by telling the parable of the Good Samaritan, about a man who had encountered robbers and was left half-dead. The Jews—a Priest and Levite—who passed by, saw the man, but showed no concern. The despised Samaritan, when he passed by, saw the man and was "moved with compassion" to help this wounded man who was supposed to be his enemy (Luke 10:25-33).

- In the parable of the prodigal son (Luke 15:11-32), He showed that a father forgiving a rebellious child or forgiving those who intentionally abuse your love is an act of compassion. The foolish son had taken his inheritance and departed from his father into a distant land where he wasted it in reckless living until he became destitute. In his state of desperation, he reasoned he would be better off even as one of his father's servants in his father's house, and he resolved to return to his father. His father, seeing him from a long way off, was "moved with compassion" to run to and embrace his son, whom he'd thought was lost, and now was found. Here are the key lessons:

- **Compassion is an act of the unconditional love of a caring father.** Even when we turn away from Him, His heart of compassion yearns for us with unconditional love in which he yearns for us to return home to Him. He is always ready to receive us, so we too must be prepared to receive back any rebellious child. This must be the attitude of every earthly father. All a father must ask is for the child to come to his or her senses, repent, and turn away from whatever he or she has done.

- **Penitence moves the heart of compassion of a loving father.** Penitence unconditionally moves the heart of the compassion of an affectionate father beyond the defiant acts of a child. As rebellious as we have been, when we return with a penitent attitude, compassion for us moves our Father with greater joy, because we were on the path of destruction, but now by returning home, have brought wholeness back to the family. Mistakes do occur at every level, so the child must never allow the devil to use him or her for long, and without being ashamed or afraid to return to a father who is waiting for the return.

- **Compassion is a pathway to victory over the destructive vices of rebellion.** Rebellion is the devil's easy vice to steal, kill, and destroy our relationships with our earthly father, and to keep us away from our heavenly Father. It takes just a moment of reflection and remembrance of the abundance of the love and riches of God's mercy to come to our senses. A father must earnestly pray and yearn for his sons' victory over his rebellious mind. However, he must put aside his own disappointment and be ready, with unconditional love, to gain his child back. If he waits to be compassionate, for any reason, the end will be a shameful destruction for both, or sometimes may be the death of his son.

o **The proper way a father regains a rebellious child is through the reaffirmation of his love.** A father and members of his family need to understand that the proper way to receive an unruly child who comes to his senses and returns to godly principles is not by allowing any sibling jealousy, setting conditions and rules for better behavior, or showing feelings of disappointments for what the child has done. The first act of compassion is the loving embrace; this is a strong reaffirmation of love for everybody in the family, and a joyous celebration for his return. The celebration is not an acceptance of the child's disobedience, but a direct statement of total forgiveness by the family, and restoration of the child. To bring wholeness to a family broken by the rebellious act of a child, the acts of compassion must be understood to be a joint family effort centered on reconnecting the child's relationship fully back to the family.

o He modeled compassion for the lost as a demonstration of His love for them; even when we were yet sinners, He died for us. "For we have not a high priest that cannot be touched with the feeling of our infirmities, but one who has been tempted like as we are, yet without sin" (Hebrews 4:15). His self-awareness of the seriousness of the states that we find ourselves in precipitates His sympathy, emotional feelings, and practical responses toward people.

o Jesus demonstrated *personal concern* as an element of compassion: when He encountered a man who was possessed by unclean spirits that made him wander around unclothed and with self-inflicted cuts (Mark 5), Jesus was concerned and had mercy on him (Mark 5:19). Jesus, in tenderness, acted to help this man out of the pitiful situation in which he was wandering.

o Jesus demonstrated *personal heart-felt* grief when He encountered a man with a withered hand (Mark 3) in a Hebrew synagogue on the Sabbath day. Jesus was grieved, and said to the man, "Stretch out your hand." He stretched it out, and his hand was completely restored" (Mark 3:5, NIV). This is a pure restoration of wholeness! Jesus was not only "grieved" over the heartless stubbornness of these Jews who were watching to accuse Him of healing this man on the Sabbath, but went ahead in compassion for this man, and healed him. The man was made whole as an example of good works.

o Jesus took *empathetic actions* to heal people as part of His ministry of compassion. For example, for a poor man who had leprosy, He demonstrated compassion as a practical response (beyond emotional) to a man's kneeling and begging for wholeness: " 'If you will, you can make me clean.' Then Jesus, moved with compassion, stretched out His hand and touched him, and said to him, 'I am willing; be cleansed,' and he was cleansed" (Mark 1:40-42, NKJV).

o He taught compassion through the parable of the Good Samaritan as a *practical response* to the question of "who is my neighbor", asked by a certain expert of the law (Luke 10:25-32). A man encountered robbers who beat him and left him half-dead. The Priest and Levite passed by, and saw this wounded man, but showed no concern for his state of suffering. When the despised Samaritan passed by, he saw this man, like the other two had, but was "moved with compassion" to help the wounded man who was supposed to be his enemy. Concerning the "expert of the law," it is not enough to say that we know the law, or the Word of God, or say we love God with all our hearts, souls, and minds; we must demonstrate the love of God through our love for our neighbor, and in practical terms as a measure of our love for God.

o   In the parable of the prodigal son, Jesus here showed that even those rebellious children who have strayed deserve our unconditional love. It was an act of compassion that restored this prodigal son who had wasted his inheritance in reckless living, and when he returned home, he was forgiven, embraced, and welcomed by a loving father, with rejoicing at a lost son who had been found.

Authenticity in Compassion

Acts of compassion must be displayed with personal authenticity; otherwise, they could be perceived as mockery and could result in more hurt to the care-receiver. At the intimate level, acts of compassion are based on the inside-out love and moral leadership assets that can be related to the authenticity of a leader-servant. Authenticity has been shown to require self-awareness and objective self-identity in individual and social interactions with others. Authenticity means that the act of compassion a leader displays outside, especially in a personal or leadership life of service to others and the society, is based on the values the leader embraces inside

A key element of personal authenticity is that it is seen or measured in the context of societal, cultural, and organizational interactions. In that context, achieving personal authenticity becomes a challenge since it is influenced by social factors and the dispositions of individuals who usually depend on aesthetic and organizational realities. However, for leader-servant leadership, the leader can face those changing times by remaining focused on his key Biblically based principles or the Leadership Inner Value System. The first critical element of authenticity in practicing acts of compassion is the inside-out self-examination relative to the people served rather than the organization. The six essential characteristics of authenticity for the servant leadership process in compassion are shown in Table 1.1

Table 1.1a The Test of Essential Elements of Personal Outward Authenticity in Servant Leadership.	
Elements of Personal Outward Authenticity	Personal Outward Authenticity Assessment Questions (Answer YES/NO)
(1) Personal value-based outward behavior	1. Are your personal values and beliefs aligned with your acts of service and behavior toward others? 2. Do challenging situations threaten or strengthen your personal values? 3. Do you live-out your life according to your beliefs?
(2). Personal Self-Awareness	4. Do you have clarity of your personal vision and purpose? 5. Do what you know about yourself accurately describe what others say?

(3) Personal Outward Empathy-Compassion	6. Do you apply how you feel to what your followers need? 7. Do you lead from compassionate heart and sensitive to the plight and need of others?
(4) Personal Connection with followers	8. Do you feel deep, personal and spiritual connection with your followers? 9. Do you feel the followers' needs in your heart? 10. Does your outward act toward others reflect exactly your true intensions
(5) Outward Emotional Self-regulation	11. Do you have difficulty controlling your emotions to remain calm in a stressful situation? 12. Does your evaluation of your value of others agree with how they valued they feel?
(6) Personal Authenticity Feedback	13. Do your followers see your outward acts as true and honest? 14. Can your followers see other-centeredness in 70% or more of your attributes?

Table 1.1b The Test of Essential Elements of Personal Outward Authenticity in Servant Leadership.	
Elements Inner Strength Authenticity	**Inner Strength (Outbound) Authenticity Assessment Questions(Answer YES/NO)**

(1) Personal inside-out value-based behavior	1. Are your personal inside-out values aligned with acts of service and behavior outside? 2. Are you honest to yourself in relation to your inner strength and abilities?
(2) Inside-out Self- Awareness	3. Do have unbiased self-examination, and accurate self-knowledge of who you are inside-out? 4. Do know your inner strength and weaknesses relation to the good you want to outward attribute?
(3) Inside out Empathy- Compassion	5. Do you know and feel from your inside what you want for your followers? 6. Are you motivated to empathize with others based on your inside feelings?
(4) Inside-Out Connection with Followers	7. Do you feel deep, personal and spiritual connection with your followers? 8. Does what you say and how you act reflect how you feel when you relate to others? 9. Do you show affection toward feel despite their negative feelings toward you?
(5) Inside-out Emotional Self-regulation	10. Do you have difficulty controlling your emotion to remain calm in a stressful situation? 11. Are you always able to comfort yourself?
(6) Inside-out Authenticity Feedback	12. Do your followers see your inside-out value from you outside behavior? 13. Can your followers see other-centeredness in 70% or more of your leadership attributes?

	14. Will your followers feel that the abundant of your heart is in congruent with how you act or what you speak?

In my survey of 132 Christian leaders (Wosu, 2014a), 74% of them agreed that they always or frequently exhibit servant leadership attributes. Thus, passing the authenticity test means demonstrating 70% or more of these essential elements of authenticity (that is, a cumulative total grade, where your YES is 10 out of 14 of the assessment questions in Table 1.1 (a & b)).

Inner Value System

The Inner Value System (IVS) is the set of values, beliefs, character traits, principles, and convictions that forms the foundation of our external behaviors, reactions, and responses toward others. Your IVS is characterized by eight anchors that I will refer to as the *Personal Value System*. A value system is also foundational to compassion leadership because it secures the inner strength that allows a person to outwardly empathize with others. IVS is the mark of any leader, who aspires to be an inside-out transformational leader-servant. Hence, I have also referred to it as the *Leadership Inner Value System*. Your IVS is personal because its strength and completeness depend on your *diligence* to intentionally supply what is needed to make each anchor of the system secure. As Apostle Peter rightly pointed out, the eight values that make up the system are indispensable in the leader as servant leadership process (I Peter 1:8–11).

The two components of the inner value system, diligence referred to as the anchor builder and personal value system, are described below:

Diligence- The Anchor Builder

In developing the characteristics of a value system for fruitful growth, the active words in this passage (I Peter 1:8–11) are "diligence" and "add." Diligence here means to "make every effort" to add or supply to our value system the eight anchors of value , referred to below as the *Personal Value System,*, one at a time to secure our self-leadership. Diligence serves as an active catalyst that promotes and anchors the other elements of the system. The process is like that of laying bricks for a foundation, where a brick layer carefully and diligently measures, aligns, and lays each brick one at a time. The "brick" is each of the eight values. Misaligning one brick will produce a crooked wall, which will crumble very easily under the smallest load, beginning at the point of the weakest crack.

It is important to emphasize that each element is diligently supplied and aligned by the one preceding it. This is the image that Peter was trying to convey. Each value from Faith to Love is carefully and diligently positioned for secured foundation, and love bears, believes, secures, and sustains all of them; without love, all other aspects of the value system will fail to yield the desired result. (I Corinthians 13:1–13).

The diligence-attitude that initiates and completes a mission is its persistence and consistency in making every effort to take actions to accomplish the desired purpose. The attitude starts with the leader consistently working on himself—his character, values, weakness, and so on, in whatever area that needs improvement. We are to be diligent in our service to the Lord and business and must not be slothful in all that we do both in secular (Colossians 3:22-23) and non-secular works (1 Corinthians 15:58).

Obviously, diligence is very important in the life of a Christian, especially those who want to be used by God to serve others. How can we be diligent in spiritual work? Here are some elements of diligence to develop :

1. *Fervency*: Be fervent in spirit, that is, work with enthusiasm and a passionate attitude of mind as you labor in every work to the glory of God (Colossians 3:23).

2. *Self-motivation*: Understand that the leader's motivation is to serve the Lord by serving others. It is also the Lord that the leader serves even in secular, non-Christian work with sincerity of heart as servants unto the Lord (Ephesians 6:5).

3. *Obedience*: Remain obedient to people in authority over us "not with eye service, as men-pleasers" but as bondservants of Christ, doing the will of God from the heart." (Ephesian 6:7).

4. *Enthusiasm*: Serve wholeheartedly, as if you were serving the Lord, not people. We are to diligently serve with goodwill toward others, as unto to the Lord, and not to men (Ephesians 6:7-8).

5. *Uprightness*: Make every effort to be found by Him in peace, without spot and blameless (II Peter 3:14). That is, be diligent in your walk in Him such that He will always find you blameless and at peace with Him

6. *Readiness*: Be ready always to present yourself to God as one approved, a worker who does not need to be ashamed and who correctly handles the word of truth" [2 Timothy 2;15), That means be diligent to work to be approved by God in correct handling of the word of God

7. *Attentiveness*: Guard (protect) our hearts against those things (bad companies, teaching, thoughts)

that tend to distract us from our spiritual walk with God (Proverb 4:23).

8. *Christlikeness:* Diligently add each of the value above to your faith and make "every effort to confirm your calling and election." (2 Peter 1:10).

9. *Energetic*: Avoid being slothful (habitually inactive or reluctant to make effort) in the Lord's business. [Romans 12:11, Proverb 12:24].

Some words on the last element, slothfulness is the biblical opposite of diligence and can be shown to demonstrate apathy in the Lord's business; slothfulness gains nothing positive to a person. As diligence is anchor builder, so is slothfulness a time and anchor waster. You are slothful if you find yourself patient in spending too much time on less important issues that pertain to you but complain or are lazy about spending a few hours in the Lord's business.

A slothful attitude is a misdirected value that builds a lukewarm and apathetic attitude, something the Lord despises. For example, in the parable of the Great Supper, He taught that those who put personal pursuits first before the Lord's agenda would not enjoy or partake of the great supper with Him in Heaven (Luke 14:15-24). He also taught in the parable of the talents that that poor stewardship is a by-product of slothfulness (Luke 14:15-24) and being lukewarm is a by-product of slothfulness, which the Lord condemned in the church of Laodicea (Revelation 3:14–16).

To build the personal value system for leadership, we must overcome slothfulness by having goals and a vision for the service and high calling to which we are accountable... The Lord said, "I must work the works of Him that sent Me, while it is day:" (John 9.4a). This means that you must urgently step out in faith toward the work as if the deadline is now and you are accountable for the report or success of the finished work. This is what Paul was saying to the Philippians brethren, "I count not myself to have apprehended: but this one thing I do, forgetting those things which are behind, and reaching forth unto those things which are before, I press toward the mark for the prize of the high calling of God in Christ Jesus." (Philippians 3:13-14).

Personal Value System

A personal inner value system forms a solid foundation for compassion leadership. Personal leadership includes having a set of values (beliefs, skills, love, honesty, principles, and convictions) that the leader holds dear. It includes convictions placed on the worth of people, organization, concepts, or things. Here, we take beliefs to mean those deep-rooted principles and assumptions that the leader holds important about people, concepts, organizations, service, biblical teachings, religion, and so on. Value is a set of morals or beliefs that guide a person's action, reactions, behaviors, and decisions in life or "enduring beliefs that influence the choices we make among available means or ends" (Kernaghan, 2003). Your personal beliefs, thoughts and philosophy often will drive your behaviors and associated attitudes toward character, motivation, commitment, and attributes of service toward others.

The personal leadership inner values include what I have referred to as the personal anchors to secure the foundation on which to diligently develop to support your compassion attributes based on love are clearly evident in Paul's teaching: "Giving all diligence, add to your faith virtue, to virtue knowledge, to knowledge self-control, to self-control perseverance, to perseverance godliness, to godliness brotherly kindness, and to brotherly kindness love. For if these things are yours and abound, you will be neither barren nor unfruitful in the knowledge of our Lord Jesus Christ. For he who lacks these things is shortsighted, even to blindness, and has forgotten that he was cleansed from his old sins. Therefore, brethren, be even more diligent to make your call and election sure, for if you do these things you will never stumble" (2 Peter 1:5–10). The eight personal anchors are described below:

Faith. The meaning of faith is clearly stated in scriptures as "the substance of things hoped for, the evidence of things not seen. For by it the elders obtained a good testimony." (Hebrews 11:1–2 NKJ). Faith is the key starting point to foundational belief, values, and life existence of a Leader–Servant. Indeed, without faith, it is impossible to please God (Hebrews 11:6) or be an effective Leader–Servant. Faith is the confident belief in the truth, value, or trustworthiness of a person, idea, or thing—in this case, God and His written Word. Faith is the ingredient that distinguishes good leaders from great spiritual leaders. Faith as a confident belief does not rest on logical proof or material evidence. Organizationally, faith is a mental evidence, acceptance, conviction, or habit of placing trust or confidence in something not visibly seen. People exercise a measure of faith when they place trust in the value, competence, and experience in a new CEO or the new president for example. As the "substance of things hoped for," faith provides the support, ground work, confidence, subsistence, reality, and the essence of the leader's hopes. The hopes of a Leader–Servant, irrespective of his vision, must include destiny in his calling in God, future life in God, final rewards, to be like Christ, eternal life, and so on. And, "the evidence of things not seen" includes proof of invisible things, things of the Spirit, future things, His glory to be revealed, and the final salvation of his followers.

Virtue. To faith, must diligently add virtue. This means that our faith supplies our virtue. Virtue is the sum total of a leader's goodness and moral excellence. A leader's virtue consists of his assets (interest, talents, strengths, goodness), that make up his resources for purposeful life. Virtue is a by-product of values and faith that defines the quality and excellence of one's character. Virtue or goodness comes from meditating on things (true, noble, just, pure, lovely, good report, etc.)

that add value to one's life. Paul puts it very clearly: "Finally, brethren, whatever things are true, whatever things are noble, whatever things are just, whatever things are pure, whatever things are lovely, whatever things are of good report, if there is any virtue and if there is anything praiseworthy—meditate on these things." (Philippians 4:8 NKJV).

How can we live a life of virtue as Leader-Servants? A life of virtue is a life of walking with and working on God's agenda to please Him. Only Jesus was able to perfectly live such a life in behavior and attitudes of service to others. As we learned from Paul, having Christ in us is the primary way to live a life of virtue. "I have been crucified with Christ and I no longer live, but Christ lives in me. The life I now live in the body, I live by faith in the Son of God, who loved me and gave himself for me." (Galatians 2: 20, NIV). This means that being dead to myself, I can now by faith, depend on Him to control my life and develop a life of virtue in me through Him. To know if you are a virtuous leader, here are some characteristics:

- A virtuous leader seeks God's righteousness for the good of others first. He seeks to do the rights things to others as unto God and not for self- glorification, As Leader-Servants, we are to do the right things for the right reasons with no hypocrisy (Matthew 6:1–8). We are to seek and work toward the perfect plan of God by guiding our thoughts toward the bigger eternal agenda rather than our own plan. The Christ in him through faith produces a virtuous life in him for service to others that pleases God.

- A virtuous leader knows how to define his/her priorities. Too many priorities at the same time are tantamount to having no priorities. The Bible recorded that Solomon pursued too many things and toward the end of his life declared all to be vanity, to the Solomon, the wisest man that ever lived, virtue is to "fear God and keep His commandments, for this is man's all" (Ecclesiastes 12:13-14). Too many priorities can cloud a leader's vision from seeing the big picture in what matters most.

- A virtuous Leader–Servant's minimum requirement for service is to guide his or her thoughts to know not just what is good and acceptable but seeks for what is the perfect will of God in relation to the service purpose, the followers, and the community in which he serves; he prioritizes eternal things, not temporary things.

Knowledge. To faith and virtue, we are to diligently add knowledge, which the leader receives from the Word of God. Christ in me and my dependence on Him motivate me to want to know Him to become more intimate with Him. The resources of a leader for effective work come from God that sent him through His living Word. Leader–Servants depend on God for wisdom, knowledge, and understanding. Great leaders work in obedience and loyalty to the source of their calling. They are able to understand the difference between big and small things and expand their energy in what is most important. They do not sweat over things that distract them from the big picture. Rather, they seek what is most important as they seek God's agenda and purpose first.

Self-control. To faith, virtue, and knowledge, we are to diligently add self-control. This means that our knowledge of Him supplies our ability for self-control in our life through Him. Such total control provides us with the ability to control our emotions to face the daily challenges of the leadership process, including our temper, habits, worries, anxieties, agenda, and time. Self-control is also the ability of a leader to be self-disciplined in all things: in speech, emotions, actions, and responses to situations. Self-control is part self-regulation in self-leadership.

Perseverance (Patience). To faith, virtue, knowledge, and self-control, we are to diligently add perseverance. Perseverance is the ability to stay focused patiently on accomplishing a purpose no matter the challenges, discouragements, and barriers. Leader–Servants by nature of their calling do not quit serving; the sheep need to be cared for and cannot be abandoned no matter the draught. Leaders persevere to get results. Obviously, self-control sustains perseverance, but the critical elements of perseverance are patience and commitment to continue until the intended purpose is achieved. We can see several examples of this quality in notable leaders. James' epistle captures the attitude of the believers' perseverance: "My brethren, count it all joy when you fall into various trials, knowing that the testing of your faith produces patience. But let patience have its perfect work, that you may be perfect and complete, lacking nothing." (James 1:2–4, NKJV).

Godliness. To perseverance, we are to add the character trait of godliness—a spirit-filled lifestyle that reflects the Lord. It is a choice to be consistent with good works and to seek His holiness and righteousness. It is not as important to know why we need to add godliness to perseverance, but it is important to know and see how a spirit-filled, spirit-led lifestyle can increase one's faith and therefore produce a greater ability to persevere under the pressures of life and conflicting priorities.

Such godliness with contentment is a great gain, meaning that it will make the leader not just successful but very successful; not just a gain but a great gain resulting in growth. To be content is an attitude of choice and behavior that leaders must learn as Paul learned from the strength he derived from faith in Christ Jesus: "I am not saying this because I am in need, for I have learned to be content whatever the circumstances. I know what it is to be in need, and I know what it is to have plenty. I have learned the secret of being content in any and every situation, whether well fed or hungry, whether living in plenty or in want. I can do all this through him who gives me strength." (Philippians 4:11–13, NIV).

Brotherly Kindness. Brotherly kindness is the "kind affection" or act of compassion and care that we show to one another. Acts of kindness work to build relationships with readiness to forgive each other so as to be forgiven. Brotherly kindness is not just an inward quality but an outward quality of all the elements discussed thus far. This is very important as it is crucial to the spiritual growth and spiritual maturity from inside out in affecting how we relate to each other. Brotherly kindness is demanded of Leader–Servants because it is a direct reflection of one's love and understanding of Gods' love that motivate a Leader–Servant to choose to serve. Love for brethren is a distinctive Christian value. Hence, brotherly kindness in action serves as a visible demonstration of affection and unity among Christians and can be an effective way to draw others to Christ.

Love. The sequence of additions brings us close to Christlikeness; we slowly and consistently conform to the image of Christ in the predestined plan of God through the elements that grace supplies to us. Hence, the growth ends in love, and begins again in love. By all standards, this kind of love is the key motivator that enables a leader to selflessly sacrifice to serve others in a fellowship of brethren that share common values and purpose. Peter concludes with these assurances and the reasons these values are indispensable for a Leader–Servant or in the servant leadership process: "For if these things are yours and abound, you will be neither barren nor unfruitful in the knowledge of our Lord Jesus Christ. For he who lacks these things is shortsighted, even to blindness, and has forgotten that he was cleansed from his old sins. (I Peter 1:8–11) This means that if we develop and integrate these values as part of who we are, into our "leadership presence" and as part of our authentic self, we will increase in knowledge of the Lord and will not be blinded to what is required of us in any setting, whether it be secular or non-secular leadership. But when faith, virtue, knowledge, self-control, patience, godliness, brotherly kindness, and love are lacking in a leader or not incorporated in the leadership process of an organization, the leader is not only blinded but has no spiritual insight, no spiritual memory, and no vision for maximum productivity.

The critical element for the survival of any modern business is a value system that includes the credibility and integrity of its leadership and the trust of its customers. These core values of trust, credibility, and integrity are direct by-products of the LSL leadership value system. The Apostle Peter was saying that a value system such as this will guarantee fruitfulness and productivity in any organization that integrates these concepts and builds its operations on them.

Impact of Personal Inner Value System

The personal values system described above significantly impacts a person's relationship with others and the value one places on the welfare of people. Knowing the source of your personal value and how that is folded into acts of compassion are important. How can we build a secured, value-based compassion-leadership process that supports the ability to show empathy that impacts the wholeness of others?

Your personal value system impacts self-culture and your compassion leadership attributes in many ways. Specifically:

Personal inner value system shapes love-base acts of compassion. The scripture shows that Jesus at the beginning of His ministry based his vision-mission on His personal values. What are those values? Jesus was speaking to the leading religious men of his day, teachers and scholars, and famous people of influence when one of the experts of the law tested him with this question: "Teacher, which is the greatest commandment in the Law? Jesus replied: "'Love the Lord your God with all your heart and with all your soul and with all your mind.' This is the first and greatest commandment. And the second is like it: 'Love your neighbor as yourself.' All the Law and the Prophets hang on these two commandments." (Matthew 22:36-39, NIV) These scriptures clearly identify Jesus core values as Love of God (with all your heart, soul: mind, strength): and love for others we can also see love of humanity, humility to serve others, and oneness with the Father as other important values that defined his service. A leader's level of skills determines his or her competence, as his values determine his vision.

As shown in Figure 1.1, the highest value in the leadership value continuum is love for others. The highest impact of love and godliness on followers is in developing their Christlikeness and fruit-bearing capabilities. However, if a leader is high on love and godliness, but low on expressing acts of faith and virtue, the love will lack a strong foundation and authenticity. If a strong faith is missing, a virtuous life for service that pleases God will likely be missing and unsustainable. The result is that the leader will lack the consistent ability to set priories and meditate on things (true, noble, just, pure, lovely, good report, etc.) that add value to people's lives. To make a sustained high fruit-bearing impact, what is needed is a consistent effort to diligently ensure that most of the eight values are present or renewed in your leadership inner value system.

Personal inner value system develops a continuum of way of life. The personal value system described above in which we diligently add each value to another is illustrated as a continuum of way of life in Figure 1.1 from faith to love as we develop more Christlikeness. The continuum shows that from faith to knowledge, the impact is directed more on the self (personal leadership) than on others. These values are also more inwardly directed than outward. The values from self-control to love are directed externally more toward others than the self as we increase in Christlikeness. What happens to the outward impact if you are trailing behind at the low continuum of value, for example, such as expressing personal faith and having virtue, but lacking love and godliness? Your value for faith will probably have a greater benefit for you but not lead to love-based actions that impact others, and you will likely lack the ability to impact the lives of the followers through compassion; you will make little or no impact in the personal faith of the followers and small to moderate impact in developing servant heart in others because your faith without real works will question your authenticity.

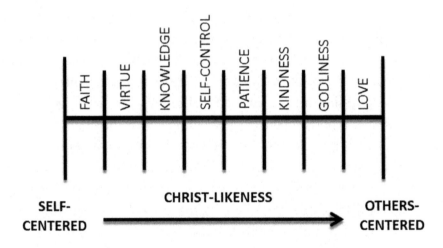

Figure 1.1. Continuum of the personal value system for the secured leadership foundation.

Personal value system has both inward and external impact on compassion leadership. Figure 1.2 illustrates Inner Value System Model with reference to external impact of compassion leadership. At the core of compassion leadership are value-based inward dimension comprised of the eight anchors that are built diligently for secured foundation.

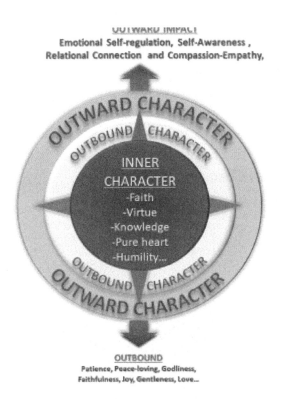

Figure 1.2. Inner Value System Model for compassion personal leadership

The growth increases outbound to impact the third outer dimension, which consists of the four external impacts: 1) Self-regulation, 2) Self-Awareness, 3) Relational Connection, and 4) Compassion-Empathy. In this framework, the first critical element of authenticity in acts of compassion is the level of self-regulation relative practical emotions in responding to where the people served are at any instant of time. That means being intentionally aware of the state of being of others.

Personal inner value system shapes your character. In general, character is defined as the set of qualities, such as quality of thought, emotions, habits, and behaviors that make someone distinctive. It forms the foundation that secures the leader's position in service. Character formation is a cyclic event that begins with the thoughts in the mind as the center of our personality as shown in Figure 1.3. "Our **thoughts** stir up our **emotions**; our emotions then influence our **desires**; and our **desires** are what produce our **actions**, and our actions, good or bad, create our **habits and attitudes**, and our habits and attitudes develop our **Character.**" (Missler, 1998))

Figure 1.3. The Mind Circle

A person's character is shaped by his habits and behavior. *Webster's Revised Unabridged Dictionary* defines character as the "Sum of qualities, by which a person or a thing is distinguished from others." It determines your personal leadership, who you are, how you behave toward others, and the predictability of your actions toward others in relational situations.

To understand how character is the complete product of habits, let us consider how these are shaped and related. Habit is an attitude that is frequently repeated, often with some degree of predictability. Hence, our habits are shaped by our attitudes, which are rooted in our thoughts. In his book, the *Seven Habits of Highly Effective People,* Stephen Covey defined habit as "the interaction of knowledge, skill, and desire...and to make something a habit, we have to have all three." (Covey, 2004)The habit of showing attitude of care to people in need comes from our knowledge of Christ's teaching and our collective responsibility to each other in love, which promotes the customs and desires to always show compassion to people as Christ did.

Our behavior is shaped by our habits, and it is the external mode in which we bare ourselves in the presence of others or act toward them. "Behavior is our manner of acting, reacting, about something or conducting ourselves under specified circumstances." (Missler, 1998) The three dimensions of character development shown in Figure 1.1 are described as:

1. **Inner Character**—forms the foundational traits that define the inner man. The inner character develops and projects itself toward the first outer dimensions of character. Elements of inner character include: faith, virtue, pure in heart, knowledge, self-control, godliness, perseverance, love, and all the innate characters that make up a person.

2. **Outbound Character**—directed toward humanity. It precedes or motivates the outward manifestation of the inside character toward others. Most of the fruit of the spirit can be classified as outbound toward humanity: patience, peace-loving, godliness, kindness, and love

3. **Outward (External) Character-** Visible external conduct emanating from the richness of the outbound and inside

character dimensions; it is the sum total of external manifestation of the inside person.

Personal inner value system shapes your leadership process. In a typical hierarchical, top-down power structure, rather than a value system as a driver, the leader follows a system of policies, procedures, and programs to influence the desired organizational productivity in a manner consistent with a defined strategic vision, goals, and objectives. Values may be mentioned in the strategic plan document but only for cosmetic value for the organization rather than for driving value. In general, one of the leader's functions is creating value for others or organization to follow, not necessarily for him to govern. The primary motive in these large organizations is maximum profit or benefit to leader or shareholders. In contrast, the servant leadership philosophy is a selfless shift toward followers with a bible-based value system better than any that can be created. The leadership value system is the central clue that holds the leadership together and shapes the characteristics of the leadership process; indeed, this directly determines the vision, behavior, activities, decision-making, and invariably the external reputation of the organization. Because the value system of a leader shapes his or her behavior and vision for service toward others, the values the leader holds dear matter very much if the followers or stakeholders are to be positively impacted. Rather than a value-creation mindset, the leader's focus is on value integration. His function is primarily to diligently integrate the eight biblically-based elements of the value system described above into his strategic vision, mission, goals, and objectives. He also instills the same mindset in followers, who are usually quick to measure the leader's authenticity and behaviors in line with those stated values.

While the value system in the LSL model when followed well will meet most of the desired results expected in the traditional leadership value system, the opposite is not true. The value system of a hierarchical, top-down power structure is ineffective in the servant leadership process. A biblically based value system is the surest way to yield desired results in service of others in servant leadership. "For no one can lay any foundation other than the one already laid, which is Jesus Christ. If anyone builds on this foundation using gold, silver, costly stones, wood, hay or straw, their work will be shown for what it is, because the Day will bring it to light. It will be revealed with fire, and the fire will test the quality of each person's work." (I Corinthians 3:11-13, NIV).

Of course the comparison is clear. A foundational layer based on virtue, knowledge, self-control, patience, godliness, brotherly kindness, and love that comes from grace through Jesus Christ is secured as gold, silver, and precious stone when tested with the challenges of leadership. It will survive the test of trial more than that built with wood, hay, and straw. The personal inner value systems reminds us of the process of **fruitful** growth in the faith. The strong value system not only shapes the leadership process, it gives meaning to personal leadership vision so as not to be shortsighted and blinded to stumble.

Personal inner value system determines your actions and reactions. Your value system includes your values and beliefs, your love for humanity, your fruit of the spirit. Jesus sets a clear value system to guide His disciples. The Apostle Paul had a clear set of value-based principles to guide his behaviors in service of others. A Leader-Servant must have a well-defined code of conduct and expectations that must measure and determine his reactions and actions. No external pressure or emotional experiences should be allowed to devalue your servant leadership principles. This means that we must know what is most important and self-regulate our emotions to conform to those important qualities. A leader is a steward of the mission and the sheep

God has given to him; therefore, he must have the sense of accountability for his actions on and reactions to emotions.

An easy way to lose control of an emotional situation is by reacting impulsively, expressing the emotions verbally or on paper or via email without much thought. Instead, take time to think over your thoughts if you have to talk, then let the conversation be one-on-one first with a calm and controlled spirit with the assumption that you are acting as the "servant." So, you assume no rights to be served even though you are the "boss." You put the follower's right to be healed or happy above your own right to be obeyed. Do not be too quick to react to a situation. Rather, give yourself time to heal and evaluate the impact of any action you want to take. If there is a remote possibility that the action or reaction you intend to take will compromise your value system or expectations, or if it will not build up the other, then it is a risk not worth taking. Compassion leadership is not about you, but it's about the others you serve.

Personal inner value system influences your behavior. A leader's predetermined value system influences his or her behavior and his priorities. This is because the inner values of a leader shape his or her character, which in turn impacts the leader's motivation, activities, decision-making behavior, and reputation. King David (Psalm 15:1–5) described the value of a leader and the behaviors that result from those values. If a leader values dwelling or walking with God, then that walk with God shall be of so much worth to him that he will be careful to do the following: Leads a blameless life and does what is right; speaks the truth from a sincere heart; refuses to gossip or harm his neighbors; speaks no evil of his friends; honors the faithful followers of the Lord; keeps his words even to his own hurts; not greedy at the expense of others; takes no bride from any one; and works with strong sense of character.

Defines your commitment and philosophy. A leader's value system defines his or her leadership commitment and philosophy. Commitment is one's personal promise to complete an agreed upon task or meet an obligation requires values that are aligned to a defined purpose. A leader that has high value for missions work, for example, will commit to the work of missions by budgeting for it. Show me your budget, and I will measure your commitment by the budget on the line items. Your value to your education can be measured by how much you invest in education such as your children's schooling. A leader's value for the welfare and growth of followers can be measured by his acts of compassion and sacrifice to walk along with them in their states of needs. The salvation of the world had a high value to God, so He allowed Jesus to commit His life to it. The parable of the rich, young ruler is a good example of a leader who placed so much value on his possessions that he failed to commit even to love others in order to inherit eternal life (Luke 18:18–23). His commitment to his temporary wealth was so high that he could not be inspired to see the benefit of eternal life. Your value system defines not only your commitment but your motivation. Over the many years in my leadership role as dean for diversity, I have learned that when leaders value the diversity of the talent pool in the organization, they are able to commit resources and intentional efforts to improve their diversity.

Shapes the organizational culture. "A leader's personal values are known to have great impact on the resulting culture and unity in purpose of an organization." (Smith, 2005) In general, the culture of an organization is defined by the system of shared beliefs, assumptions, goals, and values of its members, as influenced top-down by the leader. Leaders can influence and instill in followers the values, positive or negative, they espouse and exhibit in the organization. His values can serve as a major source of influence for bringing about the desired change (Smith, 2005). In today's culture and political system, where self-centered leaders lead from their personal negative perception of people that do not look them, have different world view from them, and do not generally agree with their philosophy, or worse, where the leader feels so insure in reaching out to others outside his or her base, developing authentic compassion leadership is one pathway such leaders can follow in their inner self-transformation to enable them empathize and walk along with all people to positively impact their wholeness.

CHAPTER 2

THE NATURE OF COMPASSION

A measure of a leader's compassion is the empathic engagement in a follower's experience and state of well-being, beyond just expressions of feelings and concerns.

How can we make compassion a human and spiritual nature? How can a leader develop and make compassion a part of who he or she must be? This chapter highlights the spiritual and human nature of compassion as driven by a leader's heart of humility; the chapter will also explore how to further develop the heart of compassion that impacts followers and communities.

Humility: Intrinsic Driver for Compassion

Intrinsic humility sets the leader's mind on the needs of others. A humble leader-servant's disposition to set his mind on the needs of others above his own rights and position cultivates the heart of compassion. He humbles himself, and by developing appropriate attributes based on a sound foundation, chooses to sacrifice his rights to serve others, as well as inspire them to gain more rights and personal growth. For example, Jesus clearly showed that humility is not a sign of weakness, but a source of strength for a leader. It is a mark of authenticity and pragmatism without which there is no compassionate empathy or willingness to serve. Humility allows a leader to admit his weaknesses and show his own need for renewed power. We also see the attitude of humility in Paul, exampled when he defended his teaching and leadership to the Church in Corinth, in the midst of false teaching and doctrines, spiritual immaturity, and carnality (II Corinthians 1:12). Paul responded with absolute humility, without defending himself, rationalizing his feelings, or addressing the accusation as one would have expected. Rather, he redirected his energy to introduce a culture of responsibility, honestly pleading and sharing his heart. As with Jesus' example, Paul saw the work as much more important than himself. Leader–servants humble themselves enough to see the broader perspective, and see their wrongs without projecting their personas or defending their moves, or making excuses for their failures. Only self-effaced leaders see beyond their own self-worth without feeling trampled.

The humane and spiritual nature of humility is a catalyst for compassion. Stephanie Slamka, in her paper, "Humility as a Catalyst for Compassion", discussed several topics related to the mortal and transcendent nature of humility in connection to compassion. Highlights of her discussions are summarized below (Slamka, 2010):

- Humility is considered the death of the self, ego, self-importance, superiority, and selfishness. When a person is not concerned with the self and the self's desires, he is more apt to recognize others and recognize them on the same human level as himself.
- Humility is the way we serve others and our reality. It is what links us to oneness, equality, nothingness, and divinity all at once.
- Humility assists us to receive empathy by helping us to see others by removing us from self-desires, our individual ego,

and our own perceptions, long enough to see, hear, and sense what others feel and suffer.

- Humility acts on reflection in empathy, because it helps us to listen. We close the doors on our inner chatter enough to read body language and actively hear the messages others are providing.
- Humility helps our intent of well-being in empathy by reminding us of equality, sameness, and oneness.
- Humility begins to act on the verbal and nonverbal behaviors between interpersonal relationships—reflection becomes more accurate and deep.
- Humility allows us to recognize others and see them as equals; allows us to be open-minded, decreases our sense of pride, and helps us serve others by listening.
- Humility extends itself to empathy by opening our perspectives with assistance from the Divine.
- Humility destroys the ego. Humility has key points—it is immaterial and spiritual in nature, is innate, and requires interpersonal experiences to be recognized and used.
- A humble person brings himself to an identical level with other persons, and meets them on an equal playing ground. This could mean adapting to accommodating the culture of others.
- Humility acts on the feelings, thoughts, and behaviors of someone else.

Developing the Heart for Compassion

Developing the heart for compassion is having the same care for another. This means that there is no partiality, no preferential treatment, and no discrimination of any kind. Having the same care for another also means that we must not choose one over the other. All members are equally important. This is critical for parents, to show same care for their children and not to prefer one child over another, while recognizing that each child is uniquely created for a well-defined purpose.

Developing the heart for compassion involves suffering with all members who hurt. The ability to walk with each other through any state of suffering is a critical element of compassion. Suffering with each other means bearing with anyone who is hurting or emotionally down. You bear with each other when you visit the hurting and act in ways that help to bear each other's burdens. These actions may include such things as listening to empathize with those that hurt, enduring the pains caused by people, forgiving each other, and tolerating the weakness of each other. Within the family, temperaments are different, and bearing with others is accepting and learning to work with diversity within the family.

Suffering alongside anyone who is going through something also means sharing in that person's pain, which is accomplished through intentional actions. Such actions include sharing in the work and services within the family or fellowship. It means not allowing the member to carry the load of service, but having the willingness to extend your personal life and share in some of the load. To share and bear with one another, we are called to be kind, tenderhearted, and forgive one another, even as God in Christ forgave you (Ephesians 4:32).

Developing the heart for compassion also involves rejoicing with a member who is honored. This is an act of showing oneness in the family, and encourages the honoree. When we share in another's state of rejoicing, we show that we care for that person. That sense of caring creates positive emotions which bring wholeness. Here are other ways we can develop the heart of compassion:

Seek out the good works that grow others.

How much does your work impact others? An example of good works is seen in God's work of salvation as cited earlier. That work impacted humanity and reconciled humanity to God. Does your work yield Christ-like fruits that impact people around you? A direct measure of our good works in servant-leadership is the growth of the followers, and the excellent fruit that results from their work or service to others. The goodness of the work a leader does depends on the depth and quality of services rendered, and the depth of our service reflects our humility, breadth of compassion, and love to those being served. One can think of several leaders in our local fellowships or churches who have served so selflessly. What we remember most are the nature of the services, and the impact those services had on the people ministered to, instead of hero-worshiping the person serving. Here are some ways we can impact others through compassion:

Build relationships through brotherly kindness

The act of brotherly kindness is one direct way of extending compassion to others. Brotherly kindness is the "kind affection" or act of compassion and care that we show to one another. Acts of kindness work to build relationships with a readiness to forgive each other so that we too can be forgiven. Brotherly kindness is not just an inward quality, but an outward quality of all the elements discussed thus far. This is very important, as it is crucial to the spiritual growth and maturity from the inside out in affecting how we relate to each other. Brotherly kindness is demanded of leader–servants because it is a direct reflection of one's love and understanding of Gods' love that motivate a leader–servant to choose to serve. Love for brethren is a distinctive Christian value. Hence, brotherly kindness in action serves as a visible demonstration of compassion, affection, and unity among Christians, and can be an effective way to draw others to Christ.

Develop the Acts of Affective Compassion

Affective compassion is care-giving devotion given through acts of kindness or benevolence. The compassion we show to others can be a measure of our affection. Through compassion and love for others, we can impact others' lives by helping them come to Christ to receive the gift of salvation (John 14:12). Here are two ways we can develop or show compassion affection: first, use empathetic compassion to give affection. The Acts of affective compassion are to help someone in need to survive through suffering, and, in doing so, work to build relationships with a readiness to forgive each other and receive forgiveness in turn. Born from empathy and commitment to alleviate hurt, affection from empathetic compassion is illustrated by the Good Samaritan: he showed affection through his act of empathy, he took direct and personal steps, and he "went to him and bound up his wounds, pouring on oil and wine" (Luke 10:34, KJV). He provided the needed help—beyond just sympathy—for the other person to survive. This is a pure articulation of affective action in servant leadership. His emotive actions resulted in the ultimate survival of the suffering man.

Give affection with authentic emotions

The emotions we give or receive from affection can be referred to as effective signs. These are things such as a genuine smile, acceptance, commitment, a promise of support, greetings, positive emotional gestures, and so on, or any action we take to communicate support and commitment to help others. However, I must caution here that it is better not to communicate any commitment to help a person who is in the state of survival than to promise, and then not follow through. It is also better not to smile at someone in a state of suffering, than to give a smile that is not genuine and authentic; broken promise or the lack of a smile can be more hurtful than helpful/affective.

An affective sign has the power to help activate a positive emotional response. For example, a follower in a state of suffering or survival mode hearing a declaration such as "How can I be of help?" will recognize this statement as the beginning of the help, showing of intentions to help in the healing process. In such cases, though, we must not promise what we are not able to deliver or not guarantee delivery so that the person would not build high expectation. You can say, "I will see what I can do but not promising any guarantees." But let him know as soon as you know you cannot deliver on the promise.

Know the needs of your followers

Your followers are all those who follow in where you go and what you do. They may not even be your supporters. Your followers could be your disciples or members of your family—your children, your wife, your servants; they could be members of your staff, etc. Your disciples are usually the closer few of your followers who are intimately committed to your mission and are willing to submit to your teaching or mentorship. Thus, a disciple is always a follower, but a follower is not always a disciple.

Most of Jesus' acts of compassion were based on life situations, and He used every one of them as a teaching moment. That was very effective because He used the little that people knew and the questions they asked to teach them what they did not know. He used the questions He asked to expose their emotions and to teach them the critical truth they needed. For example, Jesus led Peter to discover his pride when He refused to let the Lord wash his feet (Luke 10:28). He made the woman in the well know what the "living water" was (John 4:10), and gave out the need to seek and desire for that which will last for everlasting life: to the young lawyer's question: "Teacher," he asked, "what must I do to inherit eternal life?" (Matthew 19:16, NKJV).

Practice and grow in the act of compassion

Commissioning disciples is a way of encouraging them to apply what they have learned in order to make other disciples for the Kingdom's business. Disciples are also to live out what they preach. Jesus concluded the Parable of the Good Samaritan with the words, *"Go and do, likewise"* (Matthew 10:37 NIV). He was telling the disciples that, now that they knew who a good neighbor was, and could see His complete compassionate empathy in sharing in the suffering of others, they should follow the same example. He called the Pharisees "hypocrites" because they did not practice what they preached in reciting the laws of Moses (Matthew 23:2-7). In the same way, Paul encouraged his followers to "Keep putting into practice all you learned and received from me—everything you heard from me and saw me doing. Then the God of peace will be with you" (Philippians 4:19, NLT). To put teachings into practice means to live out the example of what you have been taught, and to educate others. The learning is of no effect and will not be retained for long unless the disciple increases in knowledge and is willing to apply that knowledge to new situations. When Jesus sent out the 70, He wanted them to use what they had learned. In the words of John C. Maxwell, "preparation positions your talent" and "practice sharpens your talent" (Maxwell, 2007). You become perfect in using your talent or skill by continuously practicing that talent in different contexts.

Expend yourself by sharing with those in need

This is a critical part of the compassion-generosity attribute. Leader-servants must be highly committed to meeting followers' needs. The leader demonstrates this quality by actually sharing in the suffering and well-being of the followers. In the case of Jesus, he did not just share in the need; He completely took on the suffering of humanity from God's wrath, and died to reconcile man to God. He also demonstrated his compassionate heart for the people's needs, as shown in His feeding of the four and five thousand. Paul practiced the same principle of sharing in people's needs though his ministry. He wrote, "For Macedonia and Achaia were pleased to make a contribution for the poor among the Lord's people in Jerusalem..., for if the Gentiles have shared in the Jews' spiritual blessings, they owe it to the Jews to share with them their material blessings" (Romans 15:26-28).

Share with others freely, and without grudge. The disciples showed practical love toward each other through their benevolent acts of giving: "For all who were possessors of lands or houses sold them, and brought the proceeds of the things that were sold, and laid them at the apostles' feet; and they distributed to each as anyone had need" (Acts 4:35). Some other ways we can be generous and others-centered include: intentionally making sacrifices to forego certain comforts so that others can have some; sharing thoughts, words, deeds, and emotions; developing a sense of other's insufficiency, and offering to meet those needs as much you can. You can also develop a sense of sharing with people without expecting a reward, and committing daily to relate to your actions as giving offerings to God. This yields a sense of intimacy with your followers, and a sense of importance towards kind affection. Think of things you can express to make someone feel improved —an enhanced way to talk, a better control of your emotions, and the sharing of testimony with others in a state of suffering, in order to encourage them.

Seek compassion as a call to wholeness-healing.

Wholeness-healing care is an attribute in servant leadership. It is the ability as a compassionate care-giver to comfort and make others emotionally and spiritually whole, irrespective of the leader's feelings (good or bad) toward the care-receiver. In Proverbs 6:25 (NIV), we read: "If you have been trapped by what you said, ensnared by the words of your mouth…go and humble yourself; press your plea with your neighbor! Allow no sleep to your eyes, no slumber to your eyelids...Free yourself…like a bird from the snare of the Fowler." This is an imperative call for action for healing of the victim and offender, and requires humility and boldness. Be an imitator of Christ, who was an empathetic healer through reconciliations.

My recent survey of 132 leaders shows that 42% of the leaders agreed that they regularly assessed their actions and the impact of their actions, and were always able to bring wholeness to people.[1] This agreement is low, which is a reflection of the leader's tendency to put his or her feelings and interests above those of the followers, or a tendency to want to hold on to his or her own rights above those of the followers. The healing attribute is characterized by the leaders' acts of forgiveness, reconciliation, compassion, and empathy, including the following:

1. Seeking self-healing for wholeness in you.
2. Empathizing with followers' wholeness.
3. Taking intentional actions that contribute to wholeness.
4. Taking care of people who depend on you.
5. Being an authentic forgiver. True forgiveness is an act of love whereby the offended puts aside or does not count a mistake, hurt, discourtesy or debt by an offender, and in a way that glorifies God.
6. Readily reconciling with others to bring healing. Reconciliation is the act of bringing together two old enemies or a broken relationship into a new friendship or relationship. How do you as a leader reconcile relationships? Here are some actions:
    *   Help the offender to deal with the state of regret, repentance, and forgiveness.

- Help the offended deal with the state of pride, anger, and forgiveness.
- Work together to rebuild each other's strengths, trust, and emotions.
- Empty the hurt to reconcile and bond again.
- Be a reconciler of your followers not only to God but to each other, confessing faults one to another in order to bring healing and wholeness to the body.
- See apology as God's command and as a part of repentance and reconciliation to bring healing.

CHAPTER 3

THE CALL FOR COMPASSION

A call for compassion is a command to serve and bless others. To serve is to render a help or aid to someone who needs help. The service is the work, favor, or duty rendered as the action of a servant while serving others. The service is designed to bless others; which is, to exalt or to lift others up.

It is easy for ministers to think that service is limited to ministering at the pulpit as a pastor, going on the mission fields, or being a deacon or deaconess, and so on. For a CEO, the mindset might be that service is about influencing a big change in their organization. These thoughts are important; however, service is just as consequential when one is rendering a small act of kindness or personal care to another individual in need. Such little things are significant to God. Jesus said, "Assuredly, I say to you, in as much as you did it to one of the least of these My brethren, you did it to Me" (Matthew 25:40, NKJV). In your localized fellowship, when was the last time you saw someone in need and felt compelled by compassion to render some service? Are there widows and widowers in your local church or fellowship? When was the last time you volunteered to go and help a single sister mow her lawn, pick up her children from school, reduce the crushing weight of an adversary, work with someone in need alongside a path of suffering, or be a part of someone's testimony?

The U.S. military is one organization that has exemplified service, and often refers to itself as "the Service." It is *selfless service* as a means of doing what is right for the nation, the army, the organization, and subordinates. In general, service is what we do unto the Lord to lift up someone else's burdens, and service leadership is the process that gets us there. As a working definition, service can be defined as the sum of the leader's *good works and self-less love* for the growth of others, *delivered* through the process of service leadership to produce good works in people and for the people. Service leadership as *good works* for others and in others is motivated by love:

Love of followers is both the starting and ending point of compassion through service leadership. First, God's love of mankind was the attribute that defined the work of salvation and His reconciliation of mankind to Himself (John 3.16). Understand how to model personal compassion by an appropriate emotional response of sharing in the suffering of others with a desire to alleviate or reduce the suffering to make that person whole. The Apostle Peter demonstrated how we can show compassionate love in our attitude of service to each other (1 Peter 3: 8–13). For example:

> *"Husbands, likewise, dwell with them with understanding, giving honor to the wife, as to the weaker vessel, and as being heirs together of the grace of life, that your prayers may not be hindered. 8 Finally, all of you be of one mind, having compassion for one another; love as brothers, be tenderhearted, be courteous; 9 not returning evil for evil or reviling for reviling, but on the contrary, blessing, knowing that you were called to this, that you may inherit a blessing" (1 Peter 3:7-9, NKJV)*

Compassion: A Call to Dwell with Understanding

Compassion is a call to dwell or walk along with others with understanding. Husbands are especially commanded to dwell with their wives with understanding, by giving them honor as the weaker vessel. The passage is more about emotional strength instead of physical strength. It is a show of compassion, which is walking through with the weaker vessel (a compassion process). The husband is wired to be emotionally stable and stronger, and he gives emotional strength and firmness to the emotionally softer wife (1 Peter 3:7). Such practical response is to the mutual benefit of husband and wife as "heirs together of the grace of life that your prayers may not be hindered" (1 Peter 3:7).

Compassion: A Call to Love as Brethren

Compassion is a call to love as a brother or sister. We are to be tender-hearted, readily forgiving each other and repaying evil with blessings. To love as a brother means to love each other as if from the same family— parents and blood. "Finally, all of you be of one mind, having compassion for one another; love as brothers, be tender-hearted, be courteous" (I Peter 3:8). Three important lessons can be learned here about compassion from the act of love:

Compassion love-action is to bear with one another. It is a call to bear with one another, knowing that we belong to each other. Bearing with one another is one way of empathizing with and showing practical love to each other. We must build wholeness of the brokenhearted within and outside of the family and the fellowship, and this depends on our intentional efforts to bear with each other in love.

Compassion love-action is to be of one mind. Unity of mind is the unity Christ had with the Father; this same unity of spirit and mind is what He expects from all of us. If we are in one mind, then we will feel the heart of each other, understand each other's needs, and be more willing to act in times of need. Having one mind will also reduce conflicts that tear down relationships.

Compassion love-action is to be courteous and tender-hearted as the measures of our love-affection. The compassion we show to others can be a measure of our love-affection toward that person. We are to be unified in purpose, to love just as Jesus and the Father have loved. Through compassion and love of others, we can impact others by helping them come to Christ to receive the gift of salvation (John 14:12). Affection is given and received only in the atmosphere of compassion. Without an authentic heart of compassion, "I love you" means nothing in these hard days in which we struggle to live.

Compassion: A Call to Bless and be Blessed

Compassion is a call to selflessly bless others first, and in return, receive our blessings for our labor of love from God. As people of Christ-like values, we are not to return evil for evil or reviling for reviling, but instead we are to bless in order to obtain our blessings (1 Peter 3:9). From one dictionary definition, to revile someone is to "criticize that person in an abusive or in an angry and insulting manner." The reviling of people openly is often disliked by any community which has moral values. If such an act is directed at you, you are called by your act of compassion to bless that reviler because you are to be a blessing and not a reviler. Most importantly, we must understand that our call to receive blessings and the answer to prayers is based on our obedience to the command to show compassion to all, notwithstanding those who do evil toward us.

When my kids were growing up, as I left the house to go to work, I would see my wife with the broom, sweeping and mopping up after the children's mess. On my return from work, I would see her in the same way, trying to clean some more. However, instead of empathizing with her and appreciating her, and responding lovingly to her, "Honey welcome home," I would ignore her greetings and would often say instead, "Why is this house so dirty" or "What have you been doing all day?" You would see her completely broken, as she would respond with statements like, "Honey, you really do not love me." I knew, deep down, that I loved her more than anything, but she was not feeling it. It took God to show me how inconsiderate I was. I was not a blessing to the one person I was supposed to honor and bless. It breaks my heart with godly sorrow to remember those moments today. My healing and lessons from those days drove me into family ministry, to use those aches to bless couples facing similar challenges.

Compassion: A Call to Sustained Abundance

Compassion is a call to make our day and someone's day whole. Peter goes on to command that, to make our days good and to be able to continue to love the benefits of life, we must restrain our tongues from speaking deceit (1 Peter 3:10). Why? "Death and life are in the power of the tongue, and those who love it will eat its fruits" (James 3:5-8, ESV). To "eat its fruit" means you will reap the negative reward of what the fire of the tongue can do. The Scripture says that the "tongue is a fire, a world of unrighteousness...It is a restless evil, full of deadly poison" (James 3:5-8, ESV). While we use the tongue to praise God, bless, and bring compassionate healing to others, it remains one of the most powerful and untamed weapons the devil uses to destroy the work of compassion. "The tongue that brings healing is a tree of life, but a deceitful tongue crushes the spirit" (Proverbs 15:4). To make your days pleasurable for you and others through your work of compassion, you must control your tongue because, if "you claim to be religious but don't control your tongue, you are just fooling yourself, and your religion is worthless" (James 1:26). The love that compassion can build in 24 hours, the tongue can destroy in a second.

Compassion: A Call to Manifest Strength

Compassion is the manifestation of an inner strength, which adds value to what matters to people. A positive attitude for compassion is a direct manifestation of the fruit of the Spirit—kindness, goodness, faithfulness, gentleness— and a measure of the quality of the spiritual work of a leader toward others. Consider the command: Since we live by the Spirit, let us walk and keep in step with the Spirit. (Galatians 5:22–26) This means that the Spirit of God in you, as a husband or wife, should yield the fruit of the Spirit to drive a heart with compassion toward others. This, in turn, should produce fruits and affect the people served. A husband as the leader of his household can only produce in his wife or children the identical fruits he already has inside and has displayed outwardly. In other words, how much love, joy, and peace your work brings to others is the measure of how much of the same you can demonstrate. To explore your inner strength more deeply, answer the following reflective questions:

1. Are you joyful in your work?
2. Do the people you serve feel loved and joyful?
3. How forbearing and kind are you when you contribute to work in the home or office?
4. Does your work manifest goodness and faithfulness to your spouse and others?
5. In rendering your service, how much gentleness and self-control do you show?

How did you do in the questions above, or in reflecting on each of the attributes of love delineated in I Corinthians 13:4-8? Your love of others is defined by what your acts of love do for others' emotional responses—do they feel loved, joyful, uplifted, forgiven for an offense, respected, honored, etc.?

CHAPTER 4

DEVELOPING OUTWARD COMPASSION

Compassion must not end with family and close friends, as we discussed in the previous chapters. It must be extended outwardly to others. How can you be "everything to all people" for their well-being and wholeness? The primary pathway for outward compassion is through empathy-compassion. This chapter discusses key wholeness acts, compassionate across gender, marital status, social status, etc., including how to share in the challenges faced by people who are different from us. For example, how can a married man show compassion to an unmarried single woman, a Christian show compassion to a Muslim, or how can you show compassion to your enemy or those who revile you, as we saw in previous Chapter in 1 Peter 3:8-9? How a leader walks along with someone experiencing a "wilderness" state of suffering, or in times of danger, is motivated by his selfless love to that person. Whether it's in your church, your business, your institution, or in your community, this chapter provides a comprehensive biblically-based discussion on the role of the leader as a servant in empathy-compassion to those whom he leads. This is a practical chapter that attempts to discuss what we must be in order to develop a compassion ministry within and beyond our own organizations and communities. It will encourage us to cultivate a compassionate fellowship and share some learning outcomes on how to improve in these areas of need.

Characteristics of the Empathy-Compassion Attribute

Empathy is an innate personal caring act in which an individual gives undivided attention to someone else's experience, and in a way that makes the other person feel that they both share and understand the essential elements of an experience. You feel empathy when you've "been there." Here, I refer to empathy as personal empathy: an inner strength quality of a leader-servant that gives him or her the required sympathy, compassion, and responsiveness to care for a follower in a way that builds that person up from and within that experience. Self-awareness is an important element of empathy because you can only project a personality you know you have, and can control.

Personal empathy involves a deeper level of emotional experience. The functional element is the ability to emotionally feel or be self-aware of what the person is going through, because you have experienced the same or similar, or you can somehow relate to that encounter. This is the experience of an event where one can make valid sense by projecting oneself into the experience or sharing in a close experience.

Empathy sympathy is the kind of sympathy that leads to empathy. Empathy sympathy is not showing pity; it is the beginning of concern that moves to the level of empathy. Sympathy is feeling concern and care that the needs of others are not being met. Empathy and sympathy have similar uses, but are very different in meaning and application. One's level of sympathy depends on the varying state of needs, pain, vulnerability, and danger the sympathetic object feels. While sympathy involves expressing feelings and concerns for the well-being of another person without sharing any precise impassioned state, empathy involves self-awareness, understanding, and sharing a specific emotional state with another person.[6] The emphasis in sympathy is awareness, or an understanding of another person's situation that deserves attention because of an element of pain, suffering, or loss that the person is experiencing.

Empathy-Compassion is another characteristic of the leadership empathy attribute; it is the perceptive engagement or responsive stage of empathy. Empathy-compassion is the action level of empathy that occurs when one shows feelings and concerns (sympathy), shares deep emotional experiences with a care-receiver (empathy), and takes further action (compassion) to meet the needs of or ease the person's suffering. Compassion as an empathetic dimension involves putting oneself in the other person's shoes and taking action to help ease their pain, not just feeling or showing concern. Researchers on human emotions generally agree that compassion is a feeling in response to another person's state of suffering, and one which motivates action to relieve that suffering.

God is our ultimate Empathizer, because He knows us more than we know ourselves. David said, "For He knows our frame; He remembers that we are dust" (Psalm 103:14, NKJV). How comforting it is to know that God records all our tears as we struggle in our lives! "The LORD is close to the brokenhearted and saves those who are crushed in spirit" (Psalm 34:18, NIV). This is David's way of expressing God's total empathy toward His children. Paul also uses some comforting words of sympathy: "Praise be to the God and Father of our Lord Jesus Christ, the Father of compassion and the God of all comfort, who comforts us in all our troubles, so that we can comfort those in any trouble with the comfort, we receive from God" (2 Corinthians 1:3-4). The abundant comfort we receive from Lord emanates from our inside and enables us to comfort others (2 Corinthians 1:5). All three levels of emotions: sympathy, compassion, and empathy relate to feelings, but at different levels.

A leader-servant must be able to demonstrate empathy-compassion. The Apostle Peter said, "Compassion for one another; love as brothers, be tenderhearted, be courteous...." (1 Peter 3:8, NKJV). The Apostle Paul recommended similar sentiments when he exhorted fellow Christians to "Rejoice with those who rejoice, and weep with those who weep" (Romans 12:15, NKJV). This means to project oneself into the experience of those who rejoice, weep, or sense others' feelings. From the above background, and as shown in Figure 4.1, a five-stage integrated inner strength elements of empathy-compassion emerge:

1. **Emotional experience**—the presence of past or present situation that expresses needs or state suffering in which one shares heartfelt emotion toward the person in need;

2. **Self-Awareness**—in which one becomes aware or understand the emotional experience or state of suffering of someone.

3. **Empathy-Sympathy**—perceiving and expressing feelings and concerns for someone's emotional state (sadness, grief, worry, or hopelessness) of which you became aware, it is often expressing understanding of the situation at a personal level and desiring to practically help heal the hurting person.

4. **Empathy-Self-regulation)**—the ability to "stay in control" of your own emotions and feelings as you walk in others' experiences to practically extend comfort to bring wholeness to the broken hearted.

5. **Empathy-Compassion** (Practical response)—being practically responsive to the needs of another with a focus on easing the pain or suffering of that person.

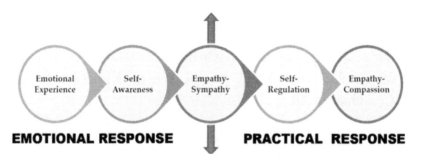

Figure 4.1. Five-stage integrated inner strength elements of empathy-compassion

The first two stages in Figure 4.1 are obviously emotional responses, requiring no direct practical reaction. The readiness to extend practical help starts at end of the stage that one becomes aware of the presence of emotional experience. The level of understanding the situation defines the beginning stage of sympathy and desire to act. Some people may sympathize with the situation but fails to practically walk along the person. Hence, sympathy can be both emotional and practical responses. The rest two stages after sympathy are purely practical, culminating in personal empathy-compassion, walking the walk generated by the first four stages.

A Case for Wholeness-Compassion

What are some of the challenges we face in extending compassion outside of families, to strangers or even our enemies, in places outside our usual comfort zones? What are some barriers that a married woman, for example, faces in showing compassion to a single or unmarried woman or man? What actions do we need for the unattached individual, widows, divorcees, or children, native and foreign, to feel complete and whole in a fellowship as brethren? What about the disabled children of God among us? How do you show compassion to them? What did Apostle Paul mean when he said, "To the weak I became weak, to win the weak. I have become all things to all people so that by all possible means, I might save some" (1 Corinthians 9:22).

Barriers to Compassion

Self-centeredness

The key barriers to compassion, as we will see in the Scriptures, are evolved from self-centeredness. Self-centeredness paralyzes acts of compassion by blinding a person's heart from seeing or feeling beyond the self. The story of the rich young ruler illustrates a case where compassion was lacking. He came to Jesus, passionately seeking knowledge of the truth concerning everlasting life and how he could obtain it. Jesus said, "'Honor your father and your mother,' and, 'you shall love your neighbor as yourself.' …. Go, sell what you have and give to the poor, and you will have treasure in heaven; and come, follow Me." (Matthew 19:16-21, NKJV) The young ruler lacked compassion because he could not understand how he could love his neighbor as much as he loved himself. Such a disposition will impede any action to walk alongside another person in a state of suffering or poverty. Several important lessons can be derived from this negative example of empathy, which reflects self-centeredness:

- **Improper perception and self-awareness.** The young, rich ruler was aware of who he was and what the law said, but he could not see how he could love his neighbor more than his material possessions. Furthermore, he did not have a correct understanding of who Jesus was; he thought that by doing the "good thing" and keeping the commandments, he could inherit eternal life. Hence, he had no emotions or feelings for the poor, beyond being self-absorbed in his own world.

- **Lack of commitment to love.** The young ruler failed to understand the full meaning of the commandment, "You shall love your neighbor as yourself" (Matthew 19:19, NIV). This is where he completely lost any sense for empathetic compassion, and only showed interest in personal gain and involvement with no one other than himself.

- **Self-centeredness and blindness.** The young ruler had an incorrect perception of what was most important. He knew that he had many possessions, but he was unwilling to sacrifice the temporary things for the eternal things he was seeking. His self-awareness of his position and wealth resulted in self-centeredness, and blinded him from seeing a better future. What a tragedy!

- **Tightfisted feelings and Pride.** He was unhappy at the end primarily because he could not part with his possessions to extend love to others. "He went away sorrowful, for he had great possessions" (Matthew 19:22, NKJV). It was important to Jesus for the rich young ruler to deal with his love for his possessions before he could correctly perceive the real meaning of Jesus' mission in order to follow Him.

Lack of trust from Outsiders

Fear of outsiders (people outside your family), people that you want to reach, and their perception of your intentions, can impede your motivation and passion to be of help. Good intentions can easily be misunderstood, and often rejected due to a wrong perception of people you want to reach. Some years ago, walking down a street in New York, I saw a disabled veteran in a wheelchair. I had just finished shopping and had a few dollars to spare. As we both were stopped at the traffic light, waiting to cross the street, I reached out to hand him the change, and offered to help him push his wheelchair across the road. He rejected my offers and became so upset with me that he literally reached into his undercoat for something I thought for sure was a gun. My impression was that he did not want my sympathy, or had been robbed or taken advantage of before, and was ready to defend himself. There are many who hate any sense of sympathy being extended to them. Nevertheless, sympathy is the first emotional response toward a genuine act of compassionate empathy, as we will learn in the chapters that follow. The above example might not be common, but it did have a negative effect on me. The fear of such an encounter paralyzed my usual desire to reach out to another unknown person in a wheelchair on any busy street.

Fear of the pain and sacrifice for compassion

The act of compassion, through mission work to the poorest places of this suffering world, requires a good measure of sacrifice and endurance. Many missionaries have exposed themselves and their families to danger, and some have lost their lives in the mission field. Others have come back physically and emotionally sick from the experience. People familiar with these experiences are often paralyzed by the fear that the same could happen to them.

Fear of your convictions being compromised

Walking into unfamiliar territory can often be uncomfortably unpredictable. Some of these fears are born out of a lack of security. Apostle Paul demonstrated the fact that we must not be ignorant of the devices of the enemy, even in those areas where we try to help. "To the weak I became as weak, that I might win the weak. I have become all things to all men that I might by all means save some. Now this I do for the gospel's sake, that I may be partaker of it with you" (1 Corinthians 9:22-23, NKJV). How can you be "all things to all people" outside of your immediate family? Paul was very specific as to what motivated him—in the hope that others might partake of the gospel through him. He became as weak, meaning that he adapted his behavior to the appropriate and visible behavior in their environment of weakness, though he was not weak himself; he was self-secured in himself. There will always be the expectation of fear and the awareness of danger in these places. However, how we handle these fears determine our capacity to move with compassion in such cases. For example, how could you as a married minister extend compassion to that beautiful single sister, or a sister of that handsome unmarried brother, without ungodly attraction beyond the convictions of the Word of God? How do you convince even your wife or husband that you will be safe in the hands of that other person you want to help? These are real fears and challenges that need to be overcome, and must be dealt with. Otherwise, we will be depriving some key members of the fellowship of the benefit of partaking in the full fellowship of the brethren.

Suppose a sister or brother is single because he/she lost a spouse or was divorced from an abusive marriage? What is our responsibility, as a fellowship, to be a part of the healing or wholeness? Usually, such brethren would feel isolated or even oppressed in response to the perceived fear of others. Some completely lose the sense of identity with their community. We cannot afford to be people of God who "shrugs their shoulders, and stop their ears so that they could not hear" the cry of others (Zechariah 7:12); nor can we afford to act in ways that make anyone feel oppressed or feel unloved (Zechariah 7:10). We cannot afford to define any among us by their own perceived and unjustified fears, for whatever reasons.

Apathy in the lives of people

Apathy in the lives of people who are different from us, and the lack of being able to understand their needs, are other common barriers to compassion. A heart of compassion is motivated by self-less love and a heart of service to others. Obviously, a low sense of value or the worth of the people could cloud our judgment and our ability to extend ourselves to others.

Unresolved cultural differences

Cultural differences present a silent barrier to compassion. Have you ever been in a church that is culturally different from yours, and suffered the loss of a loved one or experienced some state of pain? They will readily announce the dead of someone in the church, but when it comes to the death of a close family member on a far continent, they cannot seem to relate. I have often wondered why it is difficult for them to know that death is death and will always carry emotions beyond culture. In a typical African community of brethren, you do not have to tell someone that an extension of compassion is needed in sharing the pain of the loss. You do not ask, "what can I do?" You just do what you can do. I find that different in some other cultures, especially in the U.S.A. They ask you, "What can I do?" Out of respect, a typical African will often play the usual religiosity with, "please pray for us." However, no, you often need more than praying. You need some hands and boots on the ground, doing and walking with the hurting person.

Division in the family

Division, strife, conflicts, unforgiveness, etc. in a family unit or any organization of people are human factors that can readily paralyze any acts of compassion. Compassion within the family or fellowship of brethren is effectively extended when there is no division and all members are working on the same mission of caring for one another. The Apostle Paul makes clear the function of compassion in showing concerns, sharing suffering, honoring, and rejoicing together in a body of Christ: "But God has put the body together, giving greater honor to the parts that lacked it, so that there should be no division in the body, but that its parts should have an equal concern for each other. If one part suffers, every part suffers with it; if one part is honored every part rejoices with it" (1 Corinthians 12:24-26).

Overcoming Barriers of Outward Compassion

How can we overcome the barriers discussed above to be able to show compassion to those outside our family? Here are some strategies to consider:

Walk along in others states of suffering

How can a leader make a lasting positive impact in the lives of those he or she leads? Daniel Coleman, a leading American psychologist, listed empathy as one of the five elements of emotional intelligence, and defined it as "the ability to understand and manage both your own emotions, and those of the people around you" (Coleman, 1997). Coleman shows that people with a high degree of emotional intelligence usually know what they're feeling, what the emotions mean, and how their emotions can affect other people.

Other elements of emotional intelligence include self-awareness, self-regulation, motivation, and social skills.

Cultivate the habits of adaptability-compassion

The key to overcoming barriers to compassion is your adaptability of attitude. How you can be of service people outside of yourself depends on your acts of adaptability-compassion. Adaptability-compassion is the leader's inner-strength, and their ability to know what is worth loving or dying for and adapting appropriate behavior to add value to people's lives with self-confidence. Compassion is a key element of the adaptability attribute because it provides the passion that allows the leader to be flexible in adapting his or her behaviors or personal assets to be or service to people. Here are some actions to consider:

Be engaged to know people's needs. The key element of adaptability-compassion, with respect to outsiders, is empathy for the suffering of others, and selflessness in taking appropriate action to alleviate that suffering for the well-being of that other person, irrespective of who he or she is, or the circumstance. Thus, compassion is at the top of the pyramid of adaptable leaders and serves as an inner driver for the leaders' passion to take action in ministering to others. Some of Jesus' models of adaptability can be seen in his methods of healing people. He adopted healing physical touches for the sick in the areas where they were hurting, whether it was their ears, eyes, or hands. In some cases, He allowed the sick to touch Him, "And as many as touched Him were made well" (Mark 6:56). In other cases, He heals by compassion, speaking the Word of God, and being alone with the sick or dead, as He did when He raised Lazarus from the dead. He continuously gauged people's needs and adapted to the appropriate method for accomplishing the mission or impacting people the most.

Place a high value on people. The level of compassion you show to people can be measured by your sense of value of them, more than their feelings toward you. People in an organization, no matter who they are and how different they may be from you as the leader, are the essence of the organization and that legacy you want to leave behind; they are more valued in the sight of God and man than that product you want to develop or the name you want to make for yourself or the organization. When you make intentional efforts to get to know people, you will find that there is more that can bind you together than that which can separate or scare you away. Most people outside your family are afraid of you or do not trust you because you have not given them the opportunity to see your caring heart, or to see that you can be trusted with their feelings.

Understand the challenges of the outsiders

Another key to overcoming the barriers for compassion to others, different from us in any form (gender, singleness, marital status, or societal status), is to make intentional efforts to learn and understand each other. In developing compassion across this group or groups, the following strategies have been proven to work:

Be a compassionate care-giver. This strategy can be sculpted after the Stephen Ministry model where brethren are trained to be caring or compassionate givers, with sisters visiting and ministering to sisters, and brothers to brothers, in atmospheres of absolute confidentiality and trust. Here, a trained sister or brother can share completely with another sister or brother, and seek appropriate healing and emotional support.

Have a heart for the singles' ministries. These are ministries already existing in most churches where singles (male and female) have joint fellowships. Such singles' ministries create a healthy and controlled environment where the adults can interact, and may find each other and relate for a genuine godly relationship that can lead to marriage.

Cultivate the desire for compassionate empathy

Compassionate empathy is the empathy that communicates passion to care for the suffering of followers or others without compromising your convictions. An adaptable leader-servant will expend his care, cultivating the desire to alleviate another's suffering by adopting an attitude for empathetic perception. He must be compassionate enough to enter and walk with the care-receiver through the hurting experiences.

Compassionate empathy allows us to adapt our temperament and sensitivity to ease the hurts of others for their well-being; the leader can bring appropriate healing without adding to the hurt. Compassionate emphatic leaders are consistently empathetic, and can easily adjust their attitudes to forge positive connections with others in need, even if that other person is a negative person. Adaptable leaders are compassionately flexible; they are able to create a bridge to ease the suffering of others.

Compassionate empathy allows leaders to be "high on people" and it enables them to make appropriate adjustments to serve anyone. The leader-servant needs to be sympathetic and empathize to adapt appropriately in order to serve all of the people in need.

Cultivate the desire for compassion-selflessness

Compassion-selflessness is a people-centered disposition for concern for the welfare of others. Rather than spending themselves and their energies on their own needs and comfort, compassionate leader-servants spend their efforts—and make whatever sacrifice is required— to meet the needs of others. Selfless acts are born of compassion instead of just feelings or sympathy. Compassion-selflessness attitudes equip leader-servants in developing people-centered missions with the mind to give their lives to a purpose that counts. This is the essence of Paul's ministry.

To have compassion-selflessness, a leader must have the sense that the work they do is bigger than they are, and that it matters to God. They must see a loving God in suffering hearts and commit to be the person to heal that hurt. The leader-servants' depth of satisfaction comes from knowing that the mission is accomplished, and that others have gained from their selfless sacrifices.

Cultivate the heart of generosity-kindness

Generosity-kindness is an act of compassionate affection whereby you extend yourself and readily do all you can to offer what you have to care for others' needs. It means showing kind action toward caring, comforting, and extending emotional healing to others, especially the fainthearted. Kindness is the practice of being or the tendency to be sympathetic and compassionate (show consideration and caring). 'For whoever gives you a cup of water to drink in My name, because you belong to Christ, assuredly, I say to you, he will by no means lose his reward' (Mark 9:41). The giver of generosity kindness expects nothing in return.

Create opportunities for compassion

Compassionate opportunity is a change-driven concern that allows the leader to see peoples' situations as opportunities for change. This is accomplished by creating sympathetic opportunities to understand and deal with peoples' situations through proactive acts of service, and without compromising any norms and values. The leader is passionate enough to give up his rights and personal preferences in order to become an agent of change to turn various situations into opportunities for growth in the other person, and to serve as an agent to influence change in the present situation of the follower. The leader's mission is to influence specific behavioral change. It may be to serve the person's health needs, spiritual needs, or material needs. For example, the need might be homelessness due to a natural disaster, or servant ministries to widows, and so on. A leader-servant as an agent of change must first identify the specific need or change he wants to influence, and then adapt his resources and frame of mind to meet those needs as much as possible within his limitations. His primary influence is to change the person's wholeness—physical, mental, emotional, and spiritual—and well-being.

CHAPTER 5

DEVELOPING EMPATHY ATTRIBUTE

"…The empathic engagement in a follower's experience and state of well-being beyond just expressions of feelings and concerns."

Outward compassion can also be developed through the effective empathy attribute. The empathy attribute is defined as the act of projecting one's individuality and experiences into another person's thoughts, emotions, direct experience, and position. However, it is not only *having* the ability, but *using* that sensitivity toward the wellness of another individual. The empathy attribute is the sum of the actions you take to walk through that other person's experience in a particular position. In all cases, the end goal is the well-being of another person. The empathy-principled attribute is defined as the *"combined acts of projecting oneself and one's experiences into another person's thoughts, emotions, and experiences to give needed care for that person's state of well-being"* (Wosu, 2014b). Developing effective empathy attributes requires developing each of the levels of empathetic characteristics. It requires humility at its core, as demonstrated by Jesus. All five elements of empathy work in stages and are driven purely by humility at the different levels to establish the groundwork for compassion. As a principle of the empathy attribute, a direct measure of a leader's compassion is *"the empathic engagement in a follower's experience and state of well-being beyond just expressions of feelings and concerns"* (Wosu, 2014b). This principle and attribute are modeled in Figure 4.1 as a progression of intentional actions leading to total empathy and expressed as a function of the characteristics:

SELF-AWARENESS + SYMPATHY + SELF-REGULATION+ COMPASSION = EMPATHY

This principle means that empathy results when a leader, as a caregiver, intentionally engages himself to walk alongside another person to extend care. The leadership empathy attribute is effective in building up or healing a follower; usually the follower can sense the impact of the leader walking along in the experience. Thus, an important measure of effectiveness is whether the care-receiver or follower senses that the caregiver is relating empathetically with him or her. It is not enough to say that you have related emphatically to a person unless that person senses a direct impact from your action.

Figure 5.1 shows it is possible to have cross-interaction among the levels. For example, one can move from self-awareness to emotional self-regulation without passing the sympathy level, or move directly from sympathy to compassion. Bruna Martinuzzi, the President of Clarion Enterprises Ltd., noted in her book, *The Leader as a Mensch: Become the Kind of Person Others Want to Follow*, that "Some people… are naturally and consistently empathetic—these are the people who can easily forge favorable connections with others. They are people who use empathy to engender trust and build bonds; they are catalysts who are able to create positive communities for the greater good" (Martinuzzi, 2009). Despite the nature of empathy, Martinuzzi agreed that empathy can be developed and enriched.

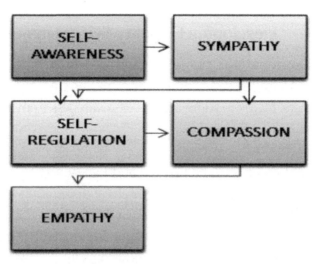

Figure 5.1: A four-stage Progression Model of the Servant
Leadership Empathy-attribute

Stephanie Slamka, in her paper, "Humility as a Catalyst for Compassion: The Humility-Compassion Cycle of Helping Relevance to Counseling," discussed how humility, wisdom (similar to awareness or knowledge), and empathy are all related to compassion, and made the following key observations (Slamka, 2010):

- Empathy is comprised of several facets, upon which all of humility acts. These facets include a developmental level, reception, reflection, mutuality, and intent for well-being.
- Empathy, humility, and compassion can be cultivated, developed, and improved in various ways.
- Empathy progresses through various steps, just like wisdom, to build on the developmental level of compassion.
- The degrees of humility, empathy, and compassion are different in each individual, as everyone is inherently unequaled in their unique context.
- We are born with empathy and humility, and these concepts grow as the individual develops, moving in stages of increasing abilities.

Developing Empathy-Self-awareness

There are several examples of self-awareness in the Bible, as seen in the lives of Adam, Moses, Joshua, Abraham, Joseph, David, Jesus, Paul, and others. Here are some acts of self-awareness from a few of these leaders:

1. **Adam and Eve:** When Adam and Eve sinned against God, they initially became aware of themselves, discovering that they were unclothed. Their first response was to try to cover their nakedness (Genesis 3:7-9). Here we see self-awareness as an intentional effort to discover something new about ourselves, or know ourselves better.

2. **David's walk with God:** David's walk with God was so important to him that he was frequently working on his inner self, always being self-aware of his emotions as a way to gain strength and clarity in his walk. David said, "Why are you downcast, O my soul? Why so disturbed within me?" (Psalm 42:5,11, 43:5) Whatever David was feeling, he wanted it out of his system in order to walk better with God. We see the importance of self-awareness here, when one wants to walk with the Holy Spirit and desires to positively clear his or her mind in the presence of God or before the people he serves. David was self-aware of his sin against God. He said, "For I know my transgressions, and my sin is ever before me. Purge me with hyssop, and I shall be clean; wash me, and I shall be whiter than snow. Create in me a clean heart, O God, and renew a right spirit within me. The sacrifices of God are a broken spirit; a broken and contrite heart, O God, you will not despise" (Psalms 51:3, 7, 10, 17, ESV).

3. **Jesus' examples of self-awareness:** Jesus told his disciples, "If anyone would come after me, let him deny himself and take up his

cross and follow me. For whoever would save his life will lose it, but whoever loses his life for my sake will find it" (Matthew 16:24-25). Jesus was calling these leaders to partake in self-denial and to know what is most important in their walk with Him. You can only self-deny what you know you have; you make choices according to the scale of preferences and priorities you know. Jesus is calling leaders for commitment to put Him first above all else, and make all sacrifices to put God's agenda above their own. Jesus was self-conscious about who was in His encounter with Satan and used that knowledge for victory over all the temptations. His rebuke of Satan, "Away from me, Satan," is an authority based on His power and knowing who He is. When Jesus said to Satan, "You shall not tempt the LORD your God" (Matthew 4:7, NKJV), He was reminding Satan that He was God. He was also self-aware from His own declarations that He was the True Vine, the Son of God, the Son of Man, the Living water, the Light of the World, the Light of Life, the Master, the Friend, the Teacher, the fulfillment of the scriptures, and others, and clearly communicated those qualities to His disciples and others, then and now, throughout the Gospels.

4. **Teachings from Apostle Paul:** The Apostle Paul said, "Examine yourselves, to see whether you are in the faith. Test yourselves. Or do you not realize this about yourselves, that Jesus Christ is in you?—unless indeed, you fail to meet the test" (2 Corinthians 13:5 ESV). Here, Paul is suggesting we examine ourselves to be aware of ourselves—our faith and the depth of Jesus in us. He also instructed them, saying, "For by the grace given to me, I say to everyone among you not to think of himself more highly than he ought to think, but to think with sober judgment, each according to the measure of faith that God has assigned" (Rom 12.3, ESV). Again, Paul is telling us to think carefully to see ourselves exactly as we are. We need to be self-aware of who we really are: "and so,

you also must consider yourselves dead to sin and alive to God in Christ Jesus. Do not let sin therefore reign in your mortal body, to make you obey its passions" (Romans 6:11-12).

Based on the above discussions and scriptural references, the leader-servant's self-awareness can be defined as the self-consciousness of one's personal identity (values, inner strengths, weaknesses, etc.) that fosters deep perception and sensitivity in relating to others. We can state that self-awareness is a function of self-examination (self-assessment), inner perceptions, and experiential learning (what experience has taught you about yourself). Self-awareness determines the core qualities of the empathy attribute and is developed through practices that focus on enriching four critical areas: (1) self-assessment, (2) perception of inner personality, (3) external perceptions, and (4) experiential learning (see Figure 5.2).

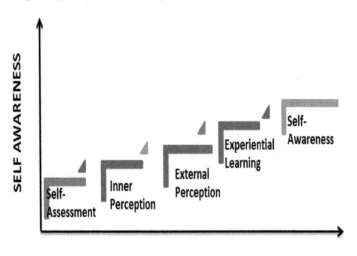

PERSONAL DISCOVERY

Figure 5.2: Self-awareness Model: Increasing self-awareness through a three-stage personal discovery process.

These practices lead to effective growth in the empathy attribute only when they are used. Because awareness of your emotions enables you to have better control, negative thoughts that result from these emotions will cause you to respond differently and, in turn, nurture good relationships. A clear perception of one's thoughts, possible reactions, and behavior patterns is at the core of good and empathetic communication and relationships.

Develop self-awareness: self-assessment

Continuous self-assessments require a leader to frequently assess his actions, reactions, and general attitudes toward people in relation to others' perceptions. If the peoples' perceptions of their leader's behavior toward them is opposite of what the leader feels, there may be something wrong with the way the leader's "good work" is shown or perceived. For example, people feel most valued when they are respected and included, when they feel empowered to engage in high productivity. Such respect and inclusion may be more valued by a worker than the fat raises the leader assumes to be a measure of his or her value of workers. Through self-assessment, and by asking tough questions about his or her behavior and getting answers through honest feedback, a leader can test how behaviors should change through an awareness of the areas of focus in his or her development as a leader. A leader-servant must arm him or herself with this basic character, as much as Christ suffered for us in the flesh (1 Peter 4:1). A leader's awareness allows him to perceive the impact of his actions and of people's needs.

Develop self-awareness: inner perception

Perception of inner personality refers to possessing a clear perception of one's personality (strengths, weaknesses, thoughts, beliefs, motivations, and emotions). Correct perception increases a leader's understanding of his or her character in relation to followers' feelings or difficulties. Knowing your strengths allows you to use that strength to help others; knowing your weaknesses humbles you to identify with the weaknesses of others; knowing your emotions gives you better control when communicating with others. If you are aware that you have problems with anger, you can prepare yourself more effectively to control that anger when dealing with people. If you know that you have the tendency to raise your voice when you speak with people, you can work on controlling your tone of voice when you talk. Perceptions of personality as a part of self-awareness are about discovering your internal self and your God-given inner makeup. This allows you to give more of yourself to others without a sense of servitude. This will improve empathy, authenticity, and your relationship with others via these strategies:

Increase the perception of your personality. Self-awareness as an inner dimension of empathy is the perception of one's personality. Self-awareness is the starting point of empathy that allows a person to understand and experience another person's emotional state in a given situation. One must differentiate self-awareness from self-centeredness, in which a leader makes his or her life the center and primary focus in all that he or she does.

Gary van Warmerdam, a consultant and trainer in techniques of developing self-awareness as a "Pathway to happiness", referred to self-awareness as "having a clear perception of your personality, including strengths, weaknesses, thoughts, beliefs, motivation, and emotions. It allows you to understand other people, how they perceive you, your attitude and your responses to them in the moment" (Warmerdam, 2013). Self-awareness provides the following elements as the starting point in the process of empathy:

- *Clarity to choose* whether you express emotions of love or express emotions out of reactions of fear.

- *Possibilities to catch yourself* in the moments prior to saying something destructive or thinking and believing a negative thought.
- Means to identify *your unconscious patterns* and raise them in your consciousness, so they can be changed.
- Pathways to identify *the underlying core beliefs* that drive destructive behaviors and create happiness.

Understand and use the positive nature of self-awareness. Self-awareness is an innate quality God created in us and can be used for both good and bad. An excellent example of positive self-awareness can be found in the life of Nelson Mandela, who became the first South African President after 27 years in prison. Attending the inaugural service with many dignitaries, presidents, and world leaders, were three prison guards whom Mandela had personally invited to attend. During his address, President Mandela looked up and asked the three guards to stand up to be recognized. He explained that he wanted to recognize and thank them personally because they had treated him with dignity. He also noted that not forgiving those that hurt him during those years would amount to still being in prison. His inserting their acts into his speech shows how self-aware forgiveness was a part of his healing process. That was empathy. Mandela described it this way (Mandela, 1994):

> *I always knew that, deep down, in every human heart, there are mercy and generosity. Even in the grimmest times in prison, when my comrades and I were pushed to our limits, I would see a glimmer of humanity in one of the guards, perhaps, just for a second, but it was enough to reassure me and keep me going. Man's goodness is a flame that can be hidden but never extinguished.*

His self-awareness allowed him to perceive the guards' responsibilities, and yet appreciate that their actions were different in the way they treated the prisoners with dignity. Harsher actions might have been justified or had no real negative consequence due to the prevailing political culture.

Develop self-awareness: external perceptions

External perceptions are those outside the inner personality described above. Exterior perceptions include observations outside of yourself and observations of changes around you, as described below:

Increase perception outside of yourself. The perception outside of you refers to the way a leader is observed on the outside, by others. The way followers perceive and respond to a leader's ability to improve his self-efficacy (his ability to produce the intended result) in a variety of situations can help a leader understand his or her strengths and weaknesses, and be aware of the things previously outside of his or her consciousness A follower's perception of a leader exercising his or her leadership role can also help reveal attitudes of which the leader is not sensitive. Reactions to, and perceptions of, a leader's normal behavior in pursuing desired results can easily provide a mirror through which a leader can understand him- or herself. Thus, there is a need to pay close attention to how people perceive the leader or even themselves in the company of the leader. For example, people's fears of a leader may reveal a leader who is not kind or pleasant. Understanding followers' lives, what motivates them, what they are sensitive to or what makes them feel energized or valued, can provide valuable feedback that can improve a leader's self-awareness.

The leader's ability to perceive his environment increases his effectiveness in using teams in decision-making. A team leader must sense and understand the viewpoint of everyone around the table by taking the time and listening to everyone in the group, directing the team in way that bring everyone together, encouraging people to speak more openly about their frustrations, and raising and handling constructive complaints during meetings. The result is heightened collaboration.

Increase perception of changes around you. Having an awareness of what you want in life reveals what you need to change to achieve a purpose. How you define success in your life determines the path you'll take to get there. It may be that you need to start by refining your definition and attitude toward success. This begins with re-examining perceptions of your thought process, and having a clear sense of your thought process and how to best direct it.

Self-awareness through perception of changes around you assists the leader in identifying areas of his life that need to be transformed in order to impact the desired change on the outside. One such area is attitude. Attitude determines a leader's effectiveness, and it is an impact factor in achieving success. It is commonly stated that a leader's "attitude determines his altitude" in leadership. Attitude is formed by habits, and those habits are formed by thoughts. With effective self-awareness, a leader can change his or her thoughts and interpretations, and this will affect emotions positively. One simple change that can be made is toward better communication in relationships.

Develop self-awareness: experiential learning

The common sayings that "experience is the best teacher" and "practice makes perfect" are very fitting as the pathways for exploring the leader's inner strengths and weaknesses, and for discovering new solutions in numerous situations, challenges, environments, companies, and expectations. How can CEOs and leaders with several years of experience in a variety of situations deal with life and corporate challenges better than those with limited experiences? The "wilderness life experiences" of these leaders have prepared them to understand how to deal with new challenges more effectively. Good leadership training intentionally includes simulations and scenarios of such experiences as coaching strategies. Such training is a way to motivate and encourage people to explore new and unknown roles or situations. Questions and feedback from such learnings are a very powerful way of helping the leader know him- or herself, gain an accurate self-perception, and develop the ability to analyze an experience for growth and self-awareness.

Talking about wilderness life experience, how did Jesus Christ start his ministry, and his leadership journeys on earth? He first gained some wilderness experience. In Luke 4:1-13, we learn about the "role of wilderness" in a leader's life. Jesus allowed himself to undergo this important experiential learning for 40 days and 40 nights. He was purposeful and determined to go through it. What exactly did He expect to learn about Himself in terms of self-awareness?

What can we gain from a wilderness experience? Let us consider the following lessons from Luke's account:

The wilderness-need is a source of inner strength. The wilderness-need is a source of inner strength to focus on and understand God's provision. In those 40 days, the wilderness provided no food. Jesus intentionally ate nothing, but disciplined His body. At the end, he was hungry. Knowing His vulnerability for instantaneous gratification, the devil tempted Him with His idea of an immediate and legitimate answer to His need to "command this stone to become bread" (Matthew 4:3), but His answer was "man does not live by bread alone but by every word of God" (Matthew 4:4). In other words, the devil wanted Jesus to show off His position and power as the Son of God, to meet the need rather than waiting. Jesus was aware of who He was and of the devil's clear devices. Leaders can lose focus of who they are and who God is by concentrating on their own needs. Wilderness needs can be the source for renewing your inner strength, rather than a place of your weakness.

The wilderness-discipline yields dependence on God. The wilderness-discipline yields dependence on God to keep the mission alive. In His answer to the devil's first temptation, Jesus reminded the devil that the Word of God was an alternative to food, and gratification to a leader, and had the potential to help the leader grow. He showed that He must depend solely on God for sustenance, and believe God would provide all that was needed. Can you imagine what would have happened to Jesus' ministry and God's purpose if the devil had succeeded in this temptation? Discipline learned from real-life experience provides a leader with full awareness of the source of his strength. Depending on God is most expedient for the mission.

The wilderness-power and authority are from God. The source of the wilderness-power and authority is from God. The devil stated, "All this authority I will give You and their glory; for this has been delivered to me, and I give to whomever I wish. Therefore, if You will worship before me, all will be Yours" (Matthew 4:8-9, NKJV). James C. Hunt, in his book, *The Servant*, defined power as "the ability to force or coerce someone to do your will, even if they simply chose to do it because of your position" (Hunt, 1998). We can notice the devil's lie in his statement, claiming the glory and power that belong only to God. How can the devil think he could give to Jesus the power he does not have? It is easy to see the content of the devil's temptation: "you will get authority and glory if you worship me." In Jesus' time, and even in today's secular world, power and control are important, as is a desired glory as seen in the self-righteousness of the Pharisees. The devil knew this and saw the opportunity. This is always possible in the wilderness state of suffering. The Wilderness walk forces you to either see your vulnerability or know how the power of God can be perfect in those vulnerabilities. The choice is yours! We can learn from Jesus' response: He deflected the temptation and showed that power and authority belong purely to God, and He used His authority to command the devil, "Away from me, Satan. You shall worship the Lord, thy God and Him only you shall serve" (Matthew 4:10, KJV). A leader seeking power and control, self-promotion, and self-glory cannot be humble and, therefore, cannot be an effective leader-servant. However, a leader must be aware of the power he has in service, even in the most daunting circumstances, and use that power wisely to the glory of God that extends that power to him.

The wilderness-battle is won by your identity. The wilderness-battle is won by knowing your identity, and the power and authority you have in God to be victorious as a part of self-leadership. The devil tried, even by misquoting the scriptures, to convince Jesus to use His position as the Son of God. In all these experiences, the devil wanted Jesus to prove He was the Son of God to self-promote His own power over the power of God. Jesus answered, "You shall not tempt the Lord, thy God" (Matthew 4:5, NKJV). Here again, Jesus recognized His own authority over the tempter, and asserted Himself above the devil. Jesus first led Himself well to overcome the temptation.

The wilderness-suffering is a season of preparation and revival. The wilderness-suffering is a season of preparation for extended growth. It is a season of knowing that, indeed, the weapons of your warfare are "mighty in God", and perfect in your weakness. In the several years of my own wilderness journey as a graduate student with a wife, four children, and working full-time on my PhD and having financial support only from two part-time jobs to support the family and my education, life was a challenge. We appeared to be suffering. But it was a period of "suffering" through which I chose to walk. Hence, I made the supporting choice to depend solely on God It was a period of "financial woes" as one of my friends called it, but also of no lack in God's timing. There were periods when we had little food to eat, and some Christmases were celebrated without gifts. And yet, it was a period of utmost stillness in God's presence, a period of increased faith, and, yes, the best period of my joy in the Lord. In the "suffering," God provided opportunities for growth. His strength was indeed made more than perfect in my weakness, for I saw nothing in me but that which was focused fully on Him. God came through for me then. I have since wondered why I was much happier in my weakness than now in my assumed strength. The answer is simple: then, my dependence was fully on God more so than in today's thinking that a fat paycheck can make it for me. A lasting joy cannot be based on external sources. The joy then was purely inward, and based on the sufficiency of God and knowing that even in the wilderness drought, God was in control. Yes, the wilderness-suffering was a season of preparation, spiritual renewal, and revival for growth.

The wilderness-perseverance provides a focused mission. The wilderness-perseverance is the capacity to endure in suffering and challenges in a purposeful mission. At the end of his wilderness experience, Jesus returned endowed with power and anointing to begin His ministry with focus and few distractions. He gained a complete sense of self-awareness concerning his mission. The source of our strength, the inner and external battles we must win, and the source of our power as leaders, creates in us diligent perseverance to focus on finishing whatever God has set before us. Experience is the leader's best teacher in self-leadership.

Developing the Acts of Empathy-Sympathy

The third action in developing outward compassion is the act of empathy-sympathy. Empathy-sympathy is an expression of feeling a concern toward others' emotional states based on our perceptions and interpretations of their condition. According to A. J. M. Djiker writing on "Perceived vulnerability as a common basis of moral emotions", he referred to sympathy as "based on the principle of the power to help the vulnerable," (Djiker, 2010), and noted that it is usually driven by the instinct to want to care for the person. Arthur J. Clark, in his research paper, "Empathy and Sympathy: Therapeutic Distinctions in Counseling", noted that sympathy acts in a way that provides a means of understanding another person's experience or situation, good or bad, with a focus on their individual well-being"(Clark, 2010). Specific conditions that must occur in order to experience sympathy include the need to give attention to the care receiver, when we presume that the person needs help. Particular characteristics of any given situation can create the state of need. Without proper undivided attention to the specific situation and need, the care receiver cannot experience sympathy.

There are several biblical situations where sympathy was expressed. David said, "From the end of the earth I call to You when my heart is faint; Lead me to the rock that is higher than I" (Psalm 61:2, KJV). This is reminding us that God is the rock of salvation and is to be trusted when our heart is sorrowful. Jesus said, "Come unto Me, all who are weary and heavy laden, and I will give you rest" (Matthew 11:28, KJV). This is an expression to reinforce the promises of God's peace in all circumstances. Jesus also gave a very specific message to grievers: "Blessed are those who mourn, for they will be comforted" (Matthew 5:4, KJV). "Do not let your hearts be troubled. Trust in God; trust also in me" (John 14:1). These verses and many like them are ever-present reminders that God's peace is available to troubled hearts.

These scriptural messages have some key elements in common: they are providing comfort to vulnerable people who may be having some type of challenge in their lives; people who are grieving the loss of someone; or alternatively, people who are simply yearning for encouragement for various reasons. You can always find these situations in our lives and in the lives of those we lead.

Sympathy consists of the perceptive feelings and concerns that begin the third stage in the process of empathy. However, sympathy only stops at the level of feeling and concern; empathy turns the sympathy feelings to a desire to act; compassion takes the feeling and desires toward the practical action, which is built to meet those needs or feelings.

These feelings result from self-awareness and are expressed and used effectively through the level of our ability to communicate them. The defining elements for developing sympathy for an effective empathy attribute are affectionate listening and communication to foster a leader's ability to correspond with the feelings and concerns in the care-giving relationship.

Developing Empathy Self-Regulation

As an element of outward compassion, emotional self-regulation is the capacity to regulate and control one's emotional sympathy in order to channel attention and to comfort another person. This is the stage above just feelings and concerns for the presence of emotional experience. It involves controlling your emotions that allow you to want to enter and walk through that person's heart-warming state by applying the deeper perspective of the care-receiver's experiences. Broadened experiences of the care-giver usually help in regulating one's emotions effectively. Psychologists generally agree that "emotions are specific and intense psychological and physical reactions to a particular event. These emotions can be the result or reaction to an event or experience, the subjective individual expression of feelings, the physiological response (fight-or flight reaction), or expressive behavioral actions such as facial expression, tone of voice, restlessness, or other body language. Our primary emotions that need regulating include feelings such as joy, fear, love, hatred, sadness, surprise, and anger. Sympathy, self-awareness, and compassion are all critical elements that complete empathy in servant leadership. Without the capacity to control and channel one's emotion to the benefit of the other person, however, empathy will not bring the needed healing to others.

Self-regulation means having a good understanding and control of how one can relate to others, and an ability to adjust one's behavior to relate positively to people or mange others' emotions and weaknesses. You can only change a behavior that you know! A leader who has an understanding of what can anger him- or herself will have the ability to improve his or her self-control as an important part of disciplining the body. Jesus' self-awareness of His mission and how significant the mission was to the Father dictated all His actions and responses to issues. Our awareness (not ignorance) of the devices of the enemy equips us to handle the devil's subtleties better, which are otherwise intended to draw us into ungodliness. Increased emotional capacity is required to lead people effectively in the presence of difficulties, and can be developed through the following strategies:

Paul, in training Timothy on self-regulation in leadership, had this to say: "And a servant of the Lord must not quarrel but be gentle to all, able to teach, patient,²⁵ in humility correcting those who are in opposition, if God perhaps will grant them repentance, so that they may know the truth" (2 Timothy 2:24-24).

Express and channel your emotions directly to God. As found in the Scriptures, David and Paul, for example, know how to express and channel their emotions straight to God, gaining empathy and comfort from the Lord. David expressed his different feelings and usually found comfort and empathy from God's promises. He said, "And why should you moan over me and be disquieted within me? Hope in God and wait expectantly for Him, for I shall yet praise Him, my Help and my God" (Psalm 42:5, NKJV). These scriptures also suggest ways to control these emotions, including putting our hopes in God, prayer, and supplications.

Be sensitive and considerate of others' feelings. A careful understanding of including those feelings expressed in decision-making increases people's security and confidence in communicating their feelings, and thereby help a leader improve his empathy attribute. There may be introverted people in the organization who by nature are people of few words, or extroverted people with too many words and too much energy to express them. These two personality traits express feelings differently, and intentional effort must be made to be sensitive, giving distinctive responses to the same experience. Some people are encouraged to express more of their feelings to a leader when the leader is seen paying attention through such gestures as nodding, smiles, or looking at them directly in affirmation.

Know the correct perceptions of yourself to increase emotional capacity. Having a clear perception of yourself means that you can better control your life as it affects those you serve, and also your ability to choose the appropriate response for a given situation. A sense of how one perceives him- or herself is at the core of one's quality of life. How one perceives him- or herself often determines self-esteem, self-confidence, and attitudes in several aspects of life. If you perceive yourself as a child of God, your attitude will reflect the values of a child of God; if you perceive yourself as a leader-servant, you will adopt key behaviors that reflect humility and servanthood; if you perceive yourself as a failure, you will always and quickly act as a failure. Importantly, a failed attempt in a venture does not make one a failure. A sense of failure is a false sense of perception; if you perceive yourself as an achiever, you will work to develop the attitude of an achiever. These are simple facts of life!

A correct perception of yourself increases the leadership ability to lead others, because perception as an element of self-awareness allows you to identify those things you want to change and improve. In self-leadership, you are the only person who has the power to influence change in yourself. We have discussed the importance of value systems (faith, preference, self-control, love, beliefs, etc.) in Chapter 1. When we have a correct perception of how we come across when we communicate with others about our feelings and attitudes, we can enter and walk through someone's experiences, and bring them appropriate healing without adding to their hurt.

Apply your emotional intelligence to empathy. Mayer et al's (2001) proposed ability model of emotional intelligence is based on the assumption that individuals vary in their abilities to deal with information of emotional nature, and in their abilities to relate their impassioned processing to a wider level of cognition (Mayer et al, 2001). These authors defined emotional intelligence as the "The ability to perceive emotion, integrate emotion to facilitate thought, understand emotions and to regulate emotions to promote personal growth." In the literature, there is a disagreement, as to whether the ability model actually measures ability that can be related well with the notion of emotional self-regulation (Bradberry, 2003). Emotional intelligence, according to the ability model, includes four types of abilities as summarized below (Adler et al, 2001).

1. Perceiving emotions – the ability to detect and decipher emotions in faces, pictures, voices, and cultural artifacts—including the ability to identify one's own emotions. Perceiving sentiments represents a basic aspect of emotional intelligence, as it makes all other processing of emotional information possible.
2. Using emotions – the ability to harness emotions to facilitate various cognitive activities, such as thinking and problem solving. The emotionally intelligent person can capitalize fully upon his or her changing moods in order to fit the best task at hand.
3. Understanding emotions – the ability to comprehend emotional language and to appreciate complicated relationships between emotions. For example, understanding emotions encompasses the

ability to be sensitive to slight variations between emotions, and the ability to recognize and describe how emotions evolve over time.

4. Managing emotions – the ability to regulate emotions in both ourselves and in others. Therefore, the emotionally intelligent person can harness emotions, even negative ones, and manage them to achieve intended goals.

Developing the Acts of Empathy-Compassion

As it has been defined earlier, compassion in servant-leadership is about caring for, helping healing, and blessing others. It takes self-awareness, the ability to perceive feelings, and expressing concern to responsively meet manifested needs through compassion. The leader-servant extends his power to help ease pain actively, and is not contented with just feeling or showing concern. It is the last stage that puts all the first acts toward affecting the desired wellness of a person through empathy. From the above elements, compassion-empathy is the act of compassion given, beyond just sympathy and self-regulation, to bring wellness to a person. A leader walks along with someone in that individual's state of suffering or danger through these four stages of empathy. It is only with compassion, motivated by selfless love, that empathy will result in a greater effect on the wellness of a person. Here are some strategies to help us develop compassionate empathy:

Humility maximizes empathy-compassion

Practice humility to maximize empathy-compassion. As we are humble before others, we can care for them more as an example of being Christ-like. Following the model developed by Slamka (2010), based on the idea of humility as a catalyst of empathy and a constant assistant to compassion as an individual develops in personal leadership, so do empathy and compassion develop at differing levels.[4] Acts of humility at each level of developing empathy build the foundation for compassion and help us be more other-centered in service leadership. At this stage of awareness, we can see ourselves at an equal human level. Consider the following model scenario:

Practice 1: Imagine Person A is walking down the street. She is humble and, therefore, open to seeing others in her reality. Her humility allows her to see people on the human level she occupies; no one is greater or lesser than she is.

Practice 2: Person B, who is also carrying the capacity of humility, crosses paths with Person A, and sees Person A as just a human possessing the same qualities. They mutually and equally recognize one another. Neither shares any desire to become superior nor powerful over the other; neither wishes to become submissive. They just accept each other as they are—humbly equal.

Practice 3: Imagine now that Person B is in a state of suffering. Person A, seeing Person B suffering, still recognizes and judges both of them as equal, despite Person B's state. How do they hear each other and share their suffering together? Here's an example:

Person A sees Person B as the same and can reflect her suffering with the attitude of "we are the same, humans that can feel pain alike one another." Person A sees B busy trying to start her car and tearing up. Person A says, "Friend, is everything alright? It appears you are having trouble starting the car, do you need help?" This shows an inclined expression of concern and an open, caring body posture (signaling recognition and awareness).

Person B answers, "Yes, I am troubled because I am about to go late to work and now my car would not start; I have been warned that I would lose my job if I ever come late to work. I am anxious and worried because I just cannot do not know what to do."

Person A follows with the deeper reflection of suffering, saying "I see you are upset," with the intent of assisting in Person B's well-being. Person A then says "Do I get it right that the car would not start but you anxiously need to get to work on time?" (This is an empathetic reflection to show understanding and care).

After B responds in the affirmative, then A offers to help: "I understand. Can I help you by driving you to work? That way you can fix the car when you return from work?" (Exhibiting compassion and suffering shared).

The greater the degree of humility, the stronger it acts to build and sustain empathy, and the more advanced a leader becomes in expressing empathy in service to others. In the above example, humility-listening translates into empathetic listening to express: "Your suffering means something to me, because we are the same. I do not wish to feel pain nor do I wish to be different than you." On the other hand, it can translate to "Let me help ease your suffering so that we are the same again and are both at peace." The very nature of humility is to provide the open door for well-being, which is at the core of empathy and compassion. When someone is humble, like Person A, he or she does not feel the need to be superior to another person; Person B in suffering and is also modest, and does not feel inferior. They do not engage in power struggles during interpersonal experiences; they do not need to have the last word, and so on. A person who is feeling humble thinks to bring themselves to the same level of the other, and meets the individual on equal footing. This could mean adapting to meet the other's different culture.

Empathy-compassion is sharing and caring.

A call for compassion is a call to bless someone in need by sharing and caring for that person. The element of empathy allows you to walk in that person's experience to show care. The apostle Peter exhorts Christians, individually and collectively, to have compassion for one another in humility and tenderness of heart: "Finally, all *of you, be* of one mind, having compassion for one another; love as brothers, *be* tenderhearted, *be* courteous" (1 Peter 3:8). Apostle Paul has a similar message and call for compassion through sharing and caring for one another without division: "The members should have the same care for one another. And if one member suffers, all the members suffer with it; if one member is honored, all the members rejoice with it" (1 Corinthians 12:25-26, NKJV). To the Ephesian believers, Paul also wrote that all must "be kind to one another, tenderhearted, forgiving one another, even as God in Christ forgave you" (Ephesians 4:32).These leaders, including the Apostle James, demonstrated that a call to compassion is an intentional and practical response to walking in service in the suffering of the most vulnerable of God's children. "Pure and undefiled religion before God and the Father is this: to visit orphans and widows in their trouble, and to keep oneself unspotted from the world" (James 1:27, NKJV).

Emulate the empathy of God

Jesus in a human form experienced mortal temptation and was, therefore, able to empathize with what we go through. He became humanity's chief advocate in the presence of God: "For we do not have a High Priest who cannot sympathize with our weaknesses, but was in all points tempted as we are, yet without sin. Let us therefore, come boldly to the throne of grace, that we may obtain mercy and find grace to help in time of need" (Hebrews 4:15-16, NKJV). This presents Jesus as our compassionate High Priest to model our lives after. Through Jesus, then, God is revealed as one with both the capacity and power to enter all humane experiences. In several miracles Jesus performed, and through the temptations he endured, he identified with the human experience, battling the diseases and afflictions of others, pain, suffering, and death (2 Corinthians 5:21).

Consider the following four strategies of developing relational empathy:

1. **Imagine experiencing the other's suffering.** Imagine that a loved one is suffering. Something terrible has happened to him or her. Now try to imagine the pain the person is experiencing. Imagine the suffering in as much detail as possible. This means that you should experience the other person's suffering or emotions from that person's frame of reference, as if you are in that person's shoes. Jesus, in observing the widow who lost her only son as she was going to bury him, sensed the woman's pain and approached the funeral procession, and then resurrected her son. "And when the Lord saw her, he had compassion on her and said to her, 'Do not weep.' Then he came up and touched the bier, and the bearers stood still. And he said, 'Young man, I say to you, arise'" (Luke 7:11-16, NIV).

2. **Practice the act of kindness.** Imagine that you are Person B in Practice 2 (from the Practice Model above), and are suffering. Now imagine that another human being would like your suffering to end. What would you like that person to do to end your suffering? Now reverse roles: you are the person who desires for the other person's suffering to end. What would you do to help ease the suffering or end it completely? Practice doing something each day to help end the suffering of others, even if in a tiny way. The door of a leader's heart for love and kindness is opened to the level of his empathy attribute. It allows us to be better aware of the need to ease someone else's pain. "Rejoice with those who rejoice, weep with those who weep" (Romans 12:15).

3. **Practice relieving others' suffering.** Imagine the suffering of a human being you've met recently. Reflect on how happy or relieved that person would feel if you can, or are able to, act to help that person. That's the feeling you want to develop. With constant practice, that feeling can be grown and nurtured. A study by the Forbes group suggests that the more you meditate on compassion, the further your brain reorganizes itself to feel empathy toward

others.[25] This is also illustrated in the scriptures: "But whoever has this world's goods, and sees his brother in need, and shuts up his heart from him, how does the love of God abide in him?" (1 John 3:17). A measure of our love of God is in our practical acts of love and care toward others, especially our action to meet the needs we know people have, rather than ignore them.

4. **Take a personal interest in people.** Show people by real actions, not feelings, which you care about them in some way in order to share in their experiences and in their lives. These experiences can be explored further through intentional efforts to get to know individuals, asking questions about their daily activities, lives, hobbies, challenges, and families. Show that you value people as people first, before you value them as employees in your workplace. One can show private interest in human beings by being authentic, and recognizing and affirming people with genuine praises, and making oneself approachable. Effective empathetic leaders pay attention to what people are doing, not to punish or micro-manage them, but for the primary purpose of affirming them with specific praise for those things, or for sharing in their challenges. When you give praise or share in the struggles, make your genuine words memorable: "I share your pain in the loss of your _____; you can take some time off to get some relief." Compassion occurs when you do more than simply recognize the pain, but make some sacrifice to relieve the pain.

A Case of Complete Empathy: Compassion

A case of complete empathy is about compassion being extended to others outside of your family. Recall the definition of personal empathy as the inner strength quality of a leader-servant that affords the required sympathy, compassion, and responsiveness to care for the follower in a way that builds that person up in that experience. Such personal empathy leads to compassion through direct intimate involvement in alleviating suffering. The accounts of the feeding of four thousand and the Parable of the Good Samaritan clearly illustrate the kind of complete sympathy, self-regulation, and compassion in the process of personal and spiritual empathy toward others. Jesus said:

> *A man was going down from Jerusalem to Jericho, and he fell among robbers, who stripped him and beat him and departed, leaving him half dead. However, a Samaritan, as he journeyed, came to where he was, and when he saw him, he had compassion. He went to him and bound up his wounds, pouring on oil and wine. Then he set him on his own animal and brought him to an inn and took care of him. And the next day he took out two denarii and gave them to the innkeeper, saying, 'Take care of him, and whatever more you spend; I will repay you when I come back.'* (Luke 10:32-35, ESV).

We can identify five key elements of complete compassionate empathy in this Parable:

1. **Emotional connection.** Here we see the presence of emotional experience. The man was beaten and hurting in a poor impassioned state; he was a "sheep" in a state of suffering and needed help. Empathy-compassion is initiated by a heart-felt emotional connection or the presence of a situation that drives all the other four dimensions of compassion.

2. **Empathetic awareness.** The Samaritan looked and saw him in the situation; when he saw him, he understood a person in such a state as he needed help (awareness); he was aware and took action to engage him fully to help.

3. **Empathetic sympathy.** His self-awareness moved his inward feelings to want to help. The Samaritan showed concern and feelings of pity toward him; he came to where he was (sympathy). Indeed, the Samaritan cared and shared in his feelings.

4. **Empathetic regulation.** The Samaritan took intentional steps to control his emotions; instead of focusing on how this man must have been beaten to the point of death, feeling just sorry for him, or being paralyzed by fear, his self-regulation allowed him to be calm enough to think. He could control any element of fear for his own safety.

5. **Empathetic compassion.** He reached full compassion: he took direct and personal steps. He went to him, gave him first aid, disinfecting and bandaging his wounds. Then he lifted him onto his donkey, led him to an inn, took care of him, and made him comfortable (Luke 10:34, ESV).

He personally walked into the experience to meet the man's immediate needs; he was shocked, obviously, but proceeded first to control the man's immediate emotion of pain, feeling the pressure as he got fully involved in the experience. He shared the suffering of the man by relinquishing the right of his time, donkey, and money, and brought him to an inn, where he committed to additional care. This is a pure illustration of loving humanity and an example in Leader-Servant leadership.

The critical element of compassion is that it must lead to personal and practical action to ease the state of suffering of another individual. According to Pastor Lance Lecocq of the Monroeville Assembly of God, "The heart of compassion is to consider the needy, be personally involved in caring for them with whatever we have, and have a positive 'sheep-attitude' toward them. We need to look for opportunities for the sheep to experience God's love."

In the Bible story of the feeding of four thousand (Matthew 15:30-35), we find the same elements of empathy leading to compassion fully illustrated in the emotional experience of a multitude that was weary and hungry, and Jesus' awareness of the situation: "I have compassion for these people. They have already been with me three days and have nothing to eat. I do not want to send them away hungry, or they may collapse on the way" (Matthew 15: 33, NIV). Jesus' expression of concern and feeling toward them (sympathy), and willingness to provide for them with both his emotional control of the situation and his intentional steps (compassion) to ease their pain, was exampled with food and comfort: "They all ate and were satisfied" (Matthew 15:37, NIV).

These exemplify the elements of empathy in servant leadership. These words mean that Jesus' ultimate goal was to heal the people's spiritual weariness and, in an act of compassion, He took personal steps to accomplish that. He saw the followers were not only weary, but scattered, lost, helpless, and without a shepherd to guide them. The awareness of these elements drove His emotional feeling to the highest level of compassion.

To answer our beginning question as to what motivates a leader to empathize with a follower, we can see that love-motivated selfless compassion is the ultimate driver for empathy. A leader trapped in self-centeredness is often unwilling to give up positional rights in order to show real compassion for others. Lack of compassion is borne out of lack of humility, lack of feeling commitment to love others, and an unwillingness to take personal responsibility for the well-being of others. Can you imagine yourself or anyone exhibiting these four qualities? At what level will you begin to develop the correct attitude of compassion? This young ruler missed the first level of a required level of self-awareness of another's needs. Without intentional effort to understand people's state of needs, you cannot build any feelings or emotions toward the situation.

A Case of Sharing Self in Empathy-Compassion

One personal experience comes to mind that demonstrates the point of sharing one's self in empathy-compassion. It was a rainy evening in New Orleans; we received a call from a couple of friends of ours of several years. We will call our Brother Dr. A, and his wife, Sister B, both in job jobs. Both are seasoned and respected children of God, married for more than fifteen years and doing well financially.

At the other end of the phone line was a frantic plea from Sister B: "Bro Wosu, your Brother A and I are through; I cannot handle this anymore. I have packed my stuff and am ready to go with my children and never to return to this marriage."

As my wife and I wondered what could have gone wrong with this loving couple, we reflected on their beautiful relationship, their work in the faith, and their four beautiful children.

The time was 9:15 P.M., and the couple lived three hours away. My wife and I immediately gathered a few changes of clothing and jumped into our car, and headed to meet the couple. About 30 minutes from their house, our old sport Jaguar stalled in the middle of the road at a traffic light, and under a heavy rainy storm. For the next several minutes, with no umbrella or rain coat, I tried to figure out what was wrong with a car that had had no problems before this night. We did not really know what to do but pray. After some few minutes of prayers, miraculously, as if the car had heard our rebuke, the car started without any real intervention beyond my shaking the battery cable. One wonders why this car stopped in the middle of the road after two hours of highway driving, and stopped at the first traffic light as we exited toward their house. We leave that for the Lord; however, we arrived at our friends' home at just before 12:45 A.M.

The brethren were waiting; they were weary after several hours, or maybe days or weeks, of quarrels. This friendly couple who we knew so well looked so down that the joy that usually defined them was not there; it was replaced with hurts, sorrow, and brokenness.

There was no time for pleasantries. We immediately changed our wet clothes and sat down to talk. The couple, especially the husband, Dr. A, who is naturally the quiet type, was not ready to talk. For the next four hours, there was neither understanding nor agreement. The tension was too high, and both were determined that their marriage was over.

At about 3:45 A.M., I called a time-out for everyone to have a quiet moment to pray or rest for 15 minutes. We resumed a few minutes later. At this time, I felt the Lord prompting my spirit to change the approach. My wife and I now started sharing both our personal experiences on the specific issues with which they were battling. We validated their different hurts and shares of the responsibilities in their conflicts; we tried to separate the major issues from the minor issues, and shared how we had worked together to resolve our similar issues effectively. We were shamelessly transparent and honest in the sharing. We shared with them how what they saw as a major issue was really the accumulation of the unresolved issues amounting over several years, and that no one seriously wins in the conflict, other than the devil himself, whose major goal is to destroy their partnership. We related the enemy's plan to destroy or impede the work of God to our car experience. We got some laughs over that, for the first time. There was a breakthrough. We all walked through the same experience with the car to see that it was the devil that was at work. The enemy had tried to stop us in the middle of the road to block us from reaching them. By relating the encounter about the car, they could see, in reality, how the devil can be at work to destroy the children of God, even marriages. Could this be why God had allowed this car experience? I am not sure. However, what followed convinced me that the empathy we are talking about could be an effective way to bring healing to hurting souls.

Now the time was 5:15 A.M., when our brother Dr. A, who before this time had been mostly closed to any suggestions for agreement, began to open up and ask questions. There were some tears. We saw healing, and a new beginning started to occur; apologies were rendered and accepted. They shared with us how they had gone through several rounds of counseling in two states on these issues, and nothing had impacted them more than the experiences; we shared our ability to understand and walk beside them. They were humbled that even we had gone through such experiences. That empathy produced a change in them and led to their willingness to allow healing. Today, this couple remains the best of friends to one another, and still cannot believe that it all actually happened.

CHAPTER 6

WHOLENESS - HEALING COMPASSION

Comforting others in any trouble, with the divine strength with which we are soothed by God, brings wholeness-healing.

Effective leadership begins with an emotionally and spiritually healthy leader, who can reconcile and bring comfort and healing to the followers, irrespective of followers' feelings (good or bad) toward the leader. The healing attribute and personal security complement each other. You must have the capacity of self-healing and individual security if you are to meet others' comforts, and for several reasons. First, insecure leaders cause their organizations to plateau, and people to be hurt. Personal security provides the infrastructure to support leaders in adversity and heal others who are hurting. Second, insecure leaders can hardly empower and develop secure followers. A leader's or a group's success is measured by the strength of the weakest member or follower. A leader-servant has the ability as a care-giver to comfort and make others whole both emotionally and spiritually.

Healing is one of the most abstract and mis-understood leadership attributes, and yet, in my estimation, it is one of the most important. Why? It crosses over most of the other outward and outbound attributes—empathy, responsibility, accountability, etc.

To understand the deeper dimensions of compassion outwardly directed toward others, we need to look at the wholeness that compassion can bring through healing care. What healing-care means in practical terms to you as a leader is the subject of this chapter concerning what we can learn from biblical teaching about bodily healing and health.

A Case of Compassion Wholeness-Healing

Many years ago, my two children, Emi and her brother HeCareth, had a motor accident that changed the life of my daughter Emi. Her brother was driving her back to her campus in Johnstown in January, which is known to be one of the most dangerous months in which to drive to Summerset, Pennsylvania. The road was so bad that people were advised to stay home unless they absolutely had to travel. Well, Emi had good reason to go because she had exams and projects to complete. Precisely four miles before the Summerset exit leading to Johnstown, their car skidded uncontrollably off the road, went off a cliff, and plunged to 150 feet below, landing a few feet from the Alleghany River at the bottom. Some trees prevented the car from plunging into the river. Fortunately, an 18-wheeler truck driver had observed them sliding down and stopped to call the police. For 45 minutes, however, my children were at the bottom of the valley where they landed. They managed to emerge from the car, but were faced with two feet of snow. Emi had lost her shoes and had to stand on her brother's toes for warmth. He was hurt more badly than she was, but he still took extra steps to see that his frightened sister was well, and tried to keep her awake. He was showing healing-care! She was in danger of falling into a coma. Before the police and ambulance arrived, they were almost frozen to death. Yet, they came out alive with only minor bruises. According to police, they were not supposed to have been able to survive that accident. A similar accident had happened the year before, one that was not as severe, and all four people in the car died. In response, Emi said, "Daddy, God gave me a second chance to live again." Unfortunately, for years after the accident, Emi was afraid of driving.

The news of the mass killings and deaths all over the world often make a compassionate heart cry. In the wake of recent killings in Nigeria, we received emails and calls about a family friend whose brother and his nephew are both in Nigeria, and their children were slaughtered in the Northern city of Maiduguri overnight. Obviously, the brother's heart was broken. What do you do with such news? How do you handle the news when all members of a family have perished in an accident, except the youngest infant child? How do you respond to bring wholeness, other than to pray? What is needed is the collective compassionate act of wholeness for healing care.

In the aftermath of the September 11, 2001 tragedy, what was needed the most was cooperative healing for the families who had lost loved ones, given through care and compassion. Several people and groups found good reason to be united in a common goal to bring healing to the suffering. Such collective responses result when organized action is taken to foster compassionate wholeness healing or restoration. According to Kanov et al (2004), compassion can be enabled through three processes: collective noticing, collective feeling, and collective responding.[21] Collective noticing occurs when people, during a difficult time such as the September 11 incident or mass shooting or killings, become aware of the incident and volunteer to seek out those who need help. Such actions usually bring the community together, and they will move to achieve a purpose with a common desire to express compassion toward bringing wholeness to the broken-hearted. The community coming into unity will result in the next level of a unified feeling where the people collectively express and share their feelings and emotions through planned public events. Based on those meetings, the act of compassion can move to the level of combined responding, such as writing letters to the government, lobbying for changes in laws, or peaceful demonstrations. It can also occur when the President of an organization or the pastor of a congregation sends out emails or messages to the general memberships, announcing a bereavement or urgent need in the fellowship; everybody responds to meet that specific need as an act of collective compassion. All these three levels work together to foster a climate of compassion.

Let us identify the key distinguishing characteristics of wholeness healing care, and formulate a working definition and principles of the leadership healing-care attribute as based on those characteristics. Each characteristic will be discussed in detail, with emphasis on strategies of how they can be further developed or practiced by a leader-servant as part of the servant leadership process.

Characteristics of the Wholeness-Healing Attribute

God desires not only for us to prosper in good health and sound mind, but also He desires for us to have wholeness as humans. This is what is required by a leader-servant, that is, the desire to see wholeness in all of his or her followers. This includes commitment and working with God to ensure that the followers are cared for. John desired that his followers be whole. He assured them when he said in 3 John 1:2, "Beloved, I pray that you may prosper in all things and be in health, just as your soul prospers."

Wholeness healing has four critical elements: *physical, emotional/ psychological, relational, and spiritual healing.* All these elements are additive and intertwined in wholeness; this means that issues with one element can cause issues in the others. The mind, body, soul, and spirit are entirely connected, so emotional trauma such as anger and sadness can cause depression, which can itself be linked to physical illness from the resulting stress. In most cases, human emotions are responses to experiences, or imagined situations in the past or present, which a person has gone through... For example, the memory of a serious car accident experienced in the past, in which someone died, can create an impassioned fear of driving in the present. Yet, the life that was spared in that same accident can also increase our faith and love for God.

Basic human emotions can be traced to some degree to heart-felt love-based, fear-based, and spirit-based sources. Examples of loved-based emotions include such feelings as desire, pleasure, contentment, acceptance, peacefulness, excitement, patience, self-esteem, assertiveness, and generosity. Fear-based emotions include anxiety, contention, envy, anger, selfishness, sorrow, bitterness, jealousy, depression, irritability, rejection, and aggression. A few examples of spirit-based emotions include faith, love, hope, peace, faithfulness, gentleness, patience, and all fruits of the spirit (Galatians 5:22-23).

From the above introduction, we can deduce that wholeness-healing requires *emotional and spiritual* wellness, along with capacities for healing *physical* diseases and the mental health of followers. All of these elements must be considered for absolute wholeness, even though a leader may not be professionally equipped or trained to handle all four dimensions. However, it is part of a *caring* attitude to understand these dimensions and to provide recommendations for attention when needed. We know that our human thoughts can stir up emotions, and our ability to regulate our responses to those emotions can determine our wholeness.

Our wholeness depends on our physical, relational, emotional/mental and spiritual (psychological) states. Although emotional behavior is a condition or feeling of the heart, if unchecked, the stress that results can affect a person mentally and physically. As noted, not all leaders work in the medical profession for physical healing, but all leaders can be used as part of God's plan for bringing absolute wholeness to the body of Christ or to members of an organization. The contribution of each of these elements to wholeness may not be equal. For example, a person's ailments may be more than 30% due to emotional issues, compared to 40% spiritual, and the remaining 30% due to physical and mental states. Understanding where we are in each of these states of wholeness is the beginning of self-healing, or healing with the assistance of a leader-servant.

An important aspect of a leader's ability to bring wholeness to others falls under the effectiveness of his or her ministry of relational *reconciliation and comfort.* Emotional sickness can be the result of hurt caused by a lack of forgiveness or conflicts between two or more people in a fellowship. This is sometimes seen in churches among believers, between husband and wife, and between relatives. However, we also see leaders who have problems forgiving their followers of offenses or lack the empathy to comfort those who are hurting. Such leaders lose credibility in trying to reconcile differences between followers.

Paul addressed this issue and reminded us that it is God "Who has reconciled us to Himself through Jesus Christ, and has given us the ministry of reconciliation" (2 Corinthians 5:18). The healing attribute of a leader-servant is a measure of his potential to soothe himself and others of hurts and disappointments, and allows him or her to recognize opportunities to help make whole followers with whom he comes in contact. His comfort allows him to comfort others in his ministry of reconciliation. Reconciliation must be the goal in the healing attribute, through the strength of comfort we receive from God. Paul wrote, "For the Father of mercies and God of all comfort, who comforts us in all our tribulation, that we may be able to comfort those who are in any trouble, with the comfort with which we ourselves are comforted by God" (2 Corinthians 1:2-4).

The Gospels shows that Jesus' leadership was motivated more by his sense of compassionate love of the people than by his obligation to the calling. Jesus demonstrated this through His willingness to die for the sins of the world and through His feeding of the multitude. When leaders are moved by a deep inner sense of love for the people they lead, they can go an extra mile beyond their obligation to bring wholeness to the people. Jesus and His disciples departed to a desert place for rest. The multitudes saw and ran on foot from all the cities, and arrived together to be with Him. The Bible says that Jesus "saw a great multitude and was moved with compassion for them, because they were like sheep not having a shepherd" (Mark 6:34, NJKV). The disciples had asked that the crowd be allowed to go "that they may go into the surrounding country and villages and buy themselves bread" (Mark 6:36, NKJV). It is easy to miss the action of this multitude running on foot to be with Jesus. It was an act of empathy for Jesus to walk through that experience in His heart. Moved by that awareness and his sense of love for them, Jesus saw beyond the disciples' sight, which this multitude needed to be fed before they should be let go.

We see this example also in the feeding of the four thousand. "Now Jesus called His disciples to Himself and said, "I have compassion on the multitude, because they have now continued with Me three days and have nothing to eat. And I do not want to send them away hungry, lest they faint on the way" (Matthew 9:32, NKJV). His understanding that they could faint along the way is demonstration of His walking in the suffering of this multitude.

The disciples' attitude is like some of us who, when we hear or see a need in someone, respond by dismissing our commitment with the phrase "I will pray for you", and often will not even remember to fulfill that promise of prayer.

The Principle of the Healing Care Attribute

We can surmise, based on the above discussions, that a leader's leadership-based healing-care attribute to bring wholeness to others can be characterized by his acts of *Self-Healing, Empathy, Reconciliation, and Comfort* of others and himself, leading us to a working definition:

> *The servant leadership healing-care attribute is the combined acts of providing comfort and empathy to make others whole emotionally and spiritually along with tending to the follower's physical and psychological well-being* (Wosu, 2014b).

Healing the wholeness of someone includes the act of filling gaps in the person's emotional, spiritual, physical, and mental wholeness, to the human extent possible, and recognizing that it is God Who ultimately brings lasting cures and wholeness. The primary outcome of the Healing-Care Attribute is wholeness and the well-being of another person. The Healing Care principle states that "comforting others in any trouble, with the comfort with which we are comforted by God, brings wholeness-healing" (Wosu, 2014c).

The outcome of this attribute can be expressed as a four-dimensional, linearly dependent cause and effect relationship on our wholeness, as:

SELF-HEALING + EMPATHY + RECONCILIATION + COMFORT = WHOLENESS HEALING CARE

Figure 6.1 shows inter-relationship between the characteristics of leadership Healing Care (Self-Healing, Empathy, Reconciliation, and Comfort) and the four states of well-being (spiritual/psychological, relational, emotional, and physical) of human wholeness. Wholeness is the result of dealing with the different elements of wellness based on the indicated acts of healing care. Being whole and complete inside produces the indicated wellness outside.

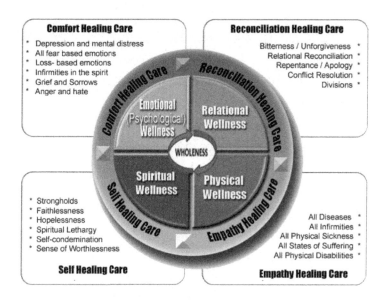

Figure 6.1: The Inter-relationship Model of Four States of Well-being of the Human Servant Leadership Healing-Care Attribute

Can a leader-servant heal or help his or her followers develop wholeness? The answer is an absolute yes. The essence of the healing-care attribute in servant leadership is to lead a process to help others become whole through ministrations in several forms, not necessarily providing the needed medical services. The prayer of a leader-servant, for example, directed to the healing-care of others, goes a long way in the complete healing process. Many have been totally healed of diseases otherwise declared incurable by the medical profession, through the fervent prayer of a leader-servant or anybody that faithfully believes, trusts, and depends on God's healing power. We have seen some medical doctors concede that "they cure, but it is God that heals." Strategies of developing or enriching the characteristics are discussed below.

Developing the Acts of Wholeness Self-Healing

Wholeness self-healing is the emotional and spiritual capacity of a leader to comfort him- or herself with the comfort he or she receives from God, and the manner in which he extends the same healing to others. Your state of non-material well-being could be due to such things as a lack of forgiveness, a need for reconciliation with someone, a state of hopelessness, infirmities in the spirit or diseases in the body, or struggles with works of the flesh. Whatever they might be, a leader must be healed of them. Your follower may also be going through the same low state of spiritual well-being. You must first heal yourself to be strong enough to heal others.

He must hold on to God's promises of protection from diseases by diligently walking with God and hearing from God. In developing the personal self-healing that enables him or her to heal others, a leader-servant needs to invite the presence of God, develop a sense of oneness with the followers, and hold a sense of self-worth, a sense of purpose, and self-efficacy in his own healing in relation to others' healing. Here are some examples of how we can develop in these five areas:

1. **Invite the presence of God into the healing process.** Inviting the presence of God into the healing process occurs through fervent prayers. The power of a leader-servant's prayer with his trusted inner circle over his situation or that of a hurting member can go very far. Healing miracles can be activated through such fervent prayers or sometimes fasting over the situations. Leaders are

commanded to do this as noted in James 5:14: "Is anyone among you sick? Let him call for the elders of the church, and let them pray over him, anointing him with oil in the name of the Lord." The power and effectiveness of such a ministry by a leader depends on his own wholeness and ability to put others' needs above his needs. Jesus' purpose in healing others was to cleanse the entire fellowship of their suffering and deliver them from pain, even at the cross when he forgave one of the criminals who was hung beside him (Luke 23:39-42). A leader must also invite those he trusts, or to whom he feels accountable, to pray for or with him.

2. **Develop a sense of oneness with your followers.** The body of Christ is one, and the health of the group is often measured by the spiritual health and vision of the leader. If a leader has a sense of meeting the healing-wholeness obligation to his followers, he must work on his own wholeness through comfort that comes from God. Leader-servants must recognize that their primary responsibility is to help make whole those with whom they come into contact as one healthy body of Christ. It is the hands of the leader which the Chief Healer will use to bring healing in some cases. Our capacity to walk through the valley of that physical or emotional situation is as powerful as the medication human doctors prescribe. It may even be the only medication needed. The leader must lead the followers to recognize that members of the organization are perfectly joined together in the same mind.

3. **Develop a sense of self-worth for your healing.** Part of healing wholeness for others is comforting them and assuring them of their self-worth to God. God loved us so much that Christ died for us, even in our worthless state. To be effective in communicating this message, the leader must display a strong inner self and sense of worth. In my life, I have had friends who acknowledged that they received significant emotional strength and comfort in that God can meet our everyday needs by their watching me display my

faith and self-worth in God. This demonstrates that your words of encouragement and comfort can go a long way toward uplifting someone else, when you live those words.

4. **Develop a sense of purpose for your healing.** A sense of purpose is a feeling that you are not only important to God, but that also your followers depend on you for their wholeness. It is a feeling that God created you for a purpose that only you, walking with Him, can fulfill. Hence, you must work on your own healing by self-regulating areas of your life that can take you away from the purpose of serving others. As a leader-servant, healing others is an important act of service in your ministry. This means that you must walk with God for your healing if you will meet the obligation of healing others.

5. **Develop a sense of self-efficacy.** Develop a sense of self-efficacy for your healing. How can a leader bring healing to others, unless he has a feeling that God can use Him as a vehicle for that purpose? Self-healing often depends on one's sense of self-security, self-leadership, and self-efficacy. A leader's values affect his self-efficacy, and his belief in his power and competence through faith, to produce the desired outcome of healing others. This has been true in my life. Every time I needed personal healing, a strong sense of self-efficacy, born out of full faith and past experiences with God, has positively affected not only the power I had to face those challenges competently, but it has also affected the choices I made in those situations.

Developing Wholeness-Healing Empathy

Wholeness-healing empathy is the act of responsiveness to walk with others through their own states of suffering. It means intentionally extending care-giving actions to assist in others physical and emotional health. Empathy healing-care is especially critical in all bodily sicknesses, infirmities, and all states of suffering requiring the leader to walk through the associated emotions with the hurting person. A leader must understand the intentional actions a person with compassion performs to aid another person who needs healing—from the loss of a loved one, the loss of a job, in health, any kind of hurt, etc. Empathy healing-care-giving actions could include the following:

Identify with the state of suffering of others

What did Jesus bear in Isaiah 53:4-5? He bore our anguishes, sorrows (pains), feebleness of mind, frailties, sicknesses, weaknesses, infirmities, diseases, and so on. Infirmities are any physical weakness in the body, soul, spirit, and ability; sicknesses, for example, are bodily diseases. We note that infirmities differ from diseases; one can have infirmities, but not diseases. For example, Paul had infirmities because of his suffering, but no indication of sickness and disease (2 Corinthians 11:24-30, 12:5-10; Galatians 4:13). As Jesus bore the grief, sorrow, sicknesses, and afflictions of humanity, we are assured by the Scriptures that "by His stripes we are healed" (Isaiah 53: 4-5). Thus, a leader-servant must bear the emotional and spiritual states of his or her followers by being intimately connected with their healing until they achieve wholeness. The ultimate leader-servant, Jesus, was stricken, wounded, bruised, chastised, and humiliated, as evidenced by the stripes on His body. Eventually, He died as a ransom for the wholeness and abundant life of His followers. As Peter said, "Who Himself bore our sins in His own body on the tree, that we, having died to sins, might live for righteousness—by whose stripes you were healed" (1 Peter 2:24, NKJV).

Connect your human emotions to bring healing

We are expected, as part of our responsibility to others, to physically and emotionally connect to bring healing to others whenever possible. How did Jesus go about healing people? Jesus physically touched the sick, in some cases in the areas where they were hurting, such as their ears, eyes, or hands. The sick and those who had fallen out of faith sought out and touched Jesus. "And as many as touched Him were made well" (Mark 6:56). Very often, leaders receive phone calls from a member of the fellowship or congregation for zealous support, especially during the loss of a loved one, marital difficulty, child-related issues (especially among single parents), loss of employment, and so on. Such phone calls are equitable to reaching out and touching the leader for support, and must be handled with all purposeful urgency, such as through visits for support, praying for emotional healing, lending open ears to listen to hurt, or offering needed encouragement.

Take intentional actions to bring wholeness

Jesus himself reminded us of this: "For I was hungry and you gave me something to eat, I was thirsty and you gave me something to drink, I was a stranger and you invited me in, I needed clothes and you clothed me, I was sick and you looked after me, I was in prison and you came to visit me" (Matthew 25:35-36, NIV). Jesus' statement was a surprise to the people. He made it clear that our service to each other, or to any one of those who Jesus loves, and has come to die for (and that is all of humanity) is a service to Him. He said, "…inasmuch as you did it to one of the least of these my brethren, you did it to me" (Matthew 25:40, NKJV). As leader-servants, we may not need to die for our followers, because Jesus already paid the price once and for all, but we must be willing to lay down our own pride and make all possible sacrifices for the wholeness of the followers. "Greater love has no one than this, than to lay down one's life for his friends" (John 15:13, NKJV). This was so important to the Lord, as He wanted to make sure that, deep down, Peter was committed to the healing-care of His lambs and sheep, as shown in His last few words before He ascended to Heaven. Three times, He asked Peter, "Do you love Me?" To Peter's three affirmative answers, Jesus responded, "feed My Lambs," "tend My sheep," and "feed My Sheep" (John 21:15-17, NKJV). Peter, in his answer to the first question, "Do you love Me more than these," responded, "Yes, Lord; You know that I love You," but omitted the reference to the real emphasis of "more than these" (John 21:15), putting the sincerity of his heart in question. Peter was aggrieved, perhaps, on the reflection of his denial of Christ; his faith and love were not in doubt as much as his conduct, courage, and resilience in challenging times. He needed full faith and courage for the responsibilities ahead. Leader-servants are only qualified to serve to feed the sheep and lambs of Christ if they love Christ the good Shepherd more than any earthly materials, rights, or objects. We must learn to develop deeper engagement in the process of walking in someone's experience through our own broadened experience and emulation God's empathy. Our actions must be deliberate to care for the followers—providing the needed spiritual and physical necessities whenever possible, and healing to touch the souls of the hurting and hungry world. Intentional actions that contribute to the wholeness of others include the following:

Gauge your actions and their impact on followers. The healing attribute calls for continuously gauging our actions and their impact on the people we serve. Leaders, when not careful, can cause impassioned sickness to their followers. This can come in the form of disrespecting your followers, verbal abuse, being demeaning, and being condescending in your relationship, participating in gossip, and servitude leadership actions, all of which can cause emotional damage. The best way to heal is to prevent or avoid behaviors that cause sickness in the first place.

Provide opportunities to release and transform negative emotions. Leaders, even if they are the offended, must provide opportunities for the hurting to release and transform negative emotion into a positive action by working with the person and relating to their feelings. This helps the person take responsibility for self-healing.

Be an empathetic reflective influencer. As fully discussed elsewhere, to be sensitive and guard against actions that do not contribute to wholeness, a leader must empathize with followers. The leader can do so by reflecting to understand the other person's experience and point of view by looking at issues from their perspective. They must also let go of preconceived ideas, have an open mind, empathize by reflecting on content, and feeling at a greater level to understand what may be deeper issues. The leader must understand the unspoken words by focusing on spiritual concerns (self-esteem, meaning, hopes, fears, etc.) to understand the issues, and listening to the emotions and feelings expressed: words in the spirit (emotions, hurts, joys, etc. hidden in words)

Look for affirmations. Emotional healing often requires simple affirmative words to build up a person, particularly because some issues may be due to low self-esteem. Use statements that will produce a positive outlook in the mind of the hurting. Various tools of beneficial self-talk can be used to transform negative thinking patterns into increased positive feelings. This is also a place a leader can connect spiritually with the hurting person in shared beliefs, faith, and prayer to enhance awareness of God's presence in the healing process.

Expend yourself and your energy on the things you can control. A leader can only pursue with 100% energy what he can attract and control. We can attract the best to us by first seeking God and doing what is most important to Him (Matthew 6:25-33). If you are uncertain what the follower needs, it is always a good strategy to ask. For example, some people are very private. One could ask, "What you are experiencing is like what I went through when I was doing similar things. Would you like me to share that experience with you?" In this way, you show authenticity in walking with the person through the experience.

Developing Wholeness-Healing Comfort

Wholeness-healing comfort means to aid someone who is "cast down" or in any kind of trouble, in order to bring wellness to that person or alleviate the excessive sorrow the person might be going through (2 Corinthians 2:7). The Bible says that we are comforted by God so that we may be able to encourage others in trouble (2 Corinthians 1:2-4). What does it really mean to comfort others? In what are we being enlivened so that we can strengthen others? We are expected to comfort others with the same comfort we receive from God. What, then, are the comforts we receive from God? How do we comfort others? These and similar reflective questions are worthy of the consideration of a leader who desires to be effective in the healing-care attribute.

The typical sorrow that needs comforting can often be attributed to one or more of these (2 Corinthians 7: 8-10):

- Leader-inflicted sorrow—sorrows resulting from mistakes, presumptuous sins, corrections, convictions, condemnations from truth of what the leader said in love, etc.;
- Godly, good sorrow that works repentance to salvation (broken spirit, repentance for sin, contrite spirit);
- Worldly-sorrow that works death (such as unrepentant sorrow, pain over a loss, grief, lack of pleasure, punishment, bondage, homelessness, bareness, betrayal, etc.).
- Other sorrows could be self-inflicted, such as bad sorrow, which are caused by bad choices, including leader-inflicted bad sorrow such as abuse (emotional and verbal) from a leader or a burden-sorrow caused by burdens of service or obligation (good and bad). This can be likened to the sorrow

Jesus felt in the Garden of Gethsemane, "My soul is overwhelmed with sorrow to the point of death" (Matthew 26: 38), or when His disciples fell asleep because they were "exhausted from sorrow" or by their grief (Luke 22:45).

The intended impact of comfort is to bring wholeness by removing the unhealthy bad sorrow (2 Corinthians 7:10) or helping someone deal with good sorrow that leads to the intended purpose in God. However, the primary purpose of the comfort may not always be to completely remove the trouble, such as those caused by sickness or accident, but to ease the sorrow caused by the trouble or to prepare the mind to deal with the sorrow. In the case of Jesus, we read that the angel came and strengthened Him to ease His sorrow (Luke 22:43), but did not remove the burden. In some ways, we can comfort others through the comfort we receive from God, which includes the following:

Comfort with human emotions and feelings

Comfort others with your own comfort. The sorrow a leader brings to his followers must be measured by its impact and how the sufferer is strengthened with actions that touch the ordinary human emotions and feelings. Is the sorrow a vindictive act birthed out of a desire for revenge to get even or hurt someone? Or is it a correction with an ungodly method? The impact of the godly sorrow will not lead to (godly) repentance if the benefit of the correction does not lead to regret. The benefit of godly sorrow includes things such as leading someone to repentance, based on God's will; working out obedience; a desire to make things right; cleansing from sin; and zeal to do the correct things; and so on. We can regret the pain of the godly sorrow we cause, but rejoice in the benefits those sorrows bring to the sufferer (2 Corinthians 7:3-10).

Comfort others by showing love

The most life-changing action we can take is to speak the corrective truth to others in love. Paul, in his letter to the Corinthian church, acknowledged that his words were strong, but did not regret because he spoke them in love. He rejoiced with them for the impact of his words, and affirmed that he had confidence in them in all things. That must have been encouraging to them, to hear this from a leader they respected. However, the most important lesson for leaders in this case was that Paul had the ability to follow through to assess the impact of his words, and to reassure his readers of his love and intentions. In so doing, Paul showed that he cared for them. He explained the reason for his letter, "That our care for you in the sight of God might appear to you…. Therefore, we have been comforted in your comfort" (2 Corinthians 7:15-16). As demonstrated by Paul's example here, it is exceedingly joyful and refreshing when a leader sees that his well-intentioned action has yielded the desired change.

Comfort others by empathy and comfort from God

Leaders are great comforters when they express and channel their feelings of emotions, empathy, and comfort as based from what they get from the Lord. David, for example, usually found comfort and empathy from the promises of God. He said, "Why are you cast down, O my inner self? Hope in God and wait expectantly for Him, for I shall yet praise Him, my Help and my God" (Psalm 42:5) and "You have turned my mourning into dancing for me…" (Psalm 30:11). He expressed feelings of depression and sorrow, and yet found comfort in the awareness that God was his chief empathizer. The Apostle Paul acknowledged possible feelings of fear, frustration, anxiety, and weakness. Nevertheless, he rested on the assurance that strength in Jesus is made perfect in his weaknesses. We see in these two leaders' expressions different kinds of feelings from sadness, fear, sorrow, and anxiety, on to desires for love. These examples also suggest ways to control these emotions, including hope in God, prayer and supplications, thanksgiving, walking by the spirit, and casting down sinful imaginings. People can experience what they express in others. You experience love in a relationship if you deposit more love actions into that space. An expression of love creates a culture of love. Having a clear sense of your emotions and feelings is critical in developing empathy to comfort others.

Comfort in obedience to the Father's will

Servant leadership is all about service to others, according to the purposes of God. At Cavalry Cross, Jesus voluntarily laid down His life. So, too, must a leader-servant give his whole life to heal the hurting world (Matthew 27:50). Jesus saw the complete work of salvation as more important than His life or will. He voluntarily released it all to the Father. Thus, a leader-servant must lead others through the process of reconciliation.

Comfort in order to care for the people

This is comfort you give to take care of people who depend on you. Jesus, in his own hurt, also recognized and acknowledged the hurt of his mother, her need to be comforted, and to have the protective covering of a son. At Calvary, He declared, "Woman beholds thy son. Son behold thy mother" (John 19:26-27, NKJV). He did not let his suffering blind him to the needs of those who depended on him. Likewise, you must let people around you know your hurt, but do not let them suffer because you are suffering (Philippians 2:3-8). What Paul is saying is to bring comfort to others: "Let the mind of self-emptying be in you, which was in Christ" (Philippians 2:5, NIV). Healing is one of the most abstract and the least understood attribute in this book, and yet it is in my estimation one of the most important. Why? Because it crosses over most of the other outward and outbound attributes— empathy, responsibility, accountability, etc.

Acts of shepherding for immediate need

In Matthew 14:13-20 and John 6:1-18, Jesus directly involved his disciples in feeding the five thousand people with two fishes, five loaves of bread, and the miracle of several baskets over. Jesus gave his disciples hands-on experience through direct participation and observation of the miracle. They gained first-hand experience in what it means to serve others in a ministry. The leader needs to be observant and understand the human conditions of people they serve, and be empathetic and compassionate. Leaders (Moses, Jeremiah, Isaiah, and David, etc.) are always inadequate for the task Jesus has set for them in leadership. Paul reminded them of this fact in 2 Corinthians 3:5: "Not that we are sufficient in ourselves to claim anything as coming from us, but our sufficiency is from God..."

Compassionate servants offer care for hurting sheep. As with Moses leading the Children of Israel, sheep often outnumber the desired number of caregivers. We need to pray for more shepherds, which is what Jesus tells his disciples to do in Matthew 9:37: "The harvest is plentiful, but the laborers are few"; more shepherds are needed for the lost sheep, as well as an increase in compassionate leaders who can offer more care as needed. The disciples learned the leadership act of shepherding the sheep who may often feel helpless, hopeless, scared, and desperately in need. In picking up the pieces of 12 baskets, Jesus wanted the disciples to demonstrate on a practical level that God's provision was more than sufficient to meet the needs. Jesus is always more than adequate in every task and challenge we face.

Humility is a part of authentic leadership. The leader-servant cleans up after others. Leaders pick up the messes of their followers as part of service in servant leadership. Jesus commanded his disciples to pick up after everyone. How easy and justified would it have been for these tired disciples to feel frustrated and remark, "My job of distributing the food is over," or "it's not my job to clean up." This is one great lesson in humility in servant leadership. They had to clean up the mess they did not make.

CHAPTER 7

WHOLENESS COMMUNICATION

Wholeness communication is an empathetic two-way process of exchanging the *content, feelings, and spiritual concerns* in a message, and in ways that bring wholeness or emotional well-being to the people engaged in the process. Wholeness communication in a marriage relationship, for example, requires compassionate understanding, mutual submission, and confidence-trust between husband and wife.

The communication process involves the exchange of information between two parties, or the transferring of information or messages from one point to another. Dictionary.com defined communication as "the imparting or interchange of thoughts, opinions, or information by speech, writing, or signs." 'Imparting' in this case, means communication as a process that involves the ability to talk, hear, listen, and understand the thoughts, opinions, or information exchanged by speech, writing, or signs to achieve a purpose. This talk may be verbal or non-verbal or both. Listening in such a communication process between two people or between a person and group of people requires *attention, concentration, and hearing* (with understanding), and involves *patience* and active *participation* of all of the people involved in the process. Communication breaks down when the intended message is misunderstood or when information is missing from what is being communicated.

Figure 7.1 shows that the key elements of wholeness communication are in the:

1. Content of the spoken word— which specifies the make-up of the message, and what, why, and how it is related to what the other person is saying. The content comes in the words spoken in the communication.

2. The feelings— which are revealed and exchanged from the unspoken or the expressed reasons and emotions behind the content; the feelings also come from the words within the spirit and communicate the emotions expressed in the content.

3. Spiritual concern— specifies the hopes, questions, or joys caused by the situation or oppressions outside of God. Spiritual concerns are embedded both in the content and feeling, and are the spiritual elements in the communication.

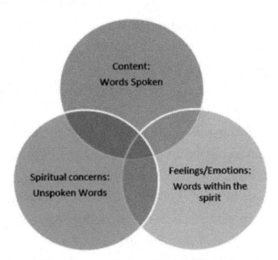

Figure 7.1. Interrelatedness of the three elements of empathetic communication

There could be some overlaps, as shown in Figure 6.1, in the interactions between these three but to ensure wholeness at the core, each participant in the communication process must work to foster an environment where these elements are understood.

Developing Listening-Patience

Listening-patience is an important catalyst that begins and drives the three characteristics (*attention, concentration,* and *hearing*) of listening communication. Patience is the ability to endure waiting, delay, or provocation without becoming annoyed or upset, or to persevere calmly when faced with difficulties. Listening-patience is the patience or patient attitude that produces effective listening. Without an exercising of patience between parties in listening, paying attention, hearing, and good processing to understand, real communication will not take place. A leader-servant strives to pay attention to what is said patiently, listening reflectively to best understand, and responds empathetically in order to be understood. Patience has been identified as an important character trait that directly impacts listening communication. Leadership challenges in dealing with the several human factors in the workplace can be traced to the leader's character trait of patience. A good natural example is one from Nelson Mandela. He recounted in his autobiography, *Long walk to Freedom,* that his "notions of leadership were profoundly influenced by observing the regent Reverend Matyolo and his court." He reflected on how this leader would patiently spend hours listening to both friends and foes in a gathering of national and local matters. In a typical gathering in his court in Great Place, the regent would open the discussions with greetings, and for the next several hours that followed, he just listened patiently as people spoke, often to vehemently criticize him. Mr. Mandela summarized this observation and its impact on him as follows (Mandela, 1994):

"But no matter the charges, the regent simply listened, not defending himself, showing no emotions at all….As a leader, I have always followed the principles I first saw demonstrated by the regent in the Great Place. I have always endeavored to listen to what each and every one has to say in a discussion before venturing my own opinion…. I always remember the regent's axiom: a leader, he said, is like a shepherd. He stays behind the flock, letting the most nimble go out ahead, whereupon the others follow, not realizing that all along they are being directed from behind."[43]

The scriptures makes it clear that God is patient, love is patient, and that you are to *"walk in a manner worthy of the calling to which you have been called, with all humility and gentleness, with patience, bearing with one another in love, eager to maintain the unity of the Spirit in the bond of peace"* (Ephesians 4:1-3). At the core of our ability to listen is humility, gentleness, bearing with each other, and a demonstration of love when speaking with or listening to each other. In general, patience denotes long-suffering and the capacity or calmness to endure a wait without complaint. Patience produces an effective listening ability to tolerate delay in one's turn to speak, or respond when challenged, as seen in the case of the regent in the above example. Here are a few practices to develop listening-patience:

Develop patient-humility

In all of its forms, patience is driven by humility to think of the other person as equal or as even better without prejudging. Patient-humility listening is one way of empathetic listening, as David expressed, "O Lord, you hear the desire of the afflicted; you will strengthen their heart; you will incline your ear" (Psalm 10:17-18, ESV). Humility allows us to concentrate, to listen, and to submit to one another out of reverence for Christ. Humility is the way we serve others and our reality, and therefore links us to oneness, equality, and divinity all at once. Other qualities of humility that allow us to be patient in communication include the following (Slamka, 2010):

- Humility assists our reception in empathy by helping us to see the other person's need to be served or heard.
- Humility gets us out of our personal mind, and out of our individual ego and our own perceptions, long enough to let us see, hear, and sense what others feel and suffer.
- Humility helps us to self-regulate the verbal and nonverbal behaviors in interpersonal relationships in service to others, allowing our self-reflection to be deeper and more accurate.
- Humility allows us to recognize others and see them as equals; it allows us to be open-minded, decrease our sense of pride, and serve others by listening.

Develop patient-emotional regulation

Regulating your emotion is a product of self-control and the ability to shift your perspective to that of the speaker, with a focus and open mind to want to understand. Having the correct perspective will reduce conflict and anger that otherwise results when people are unable to handle the differences in their perspectives. It also involves emotional intelligence that allows one to regulate his emotions in order to control urges for interrupting the speaker.

Develop a sense of maturity and respect

Impatience in communication always results in irritating both the listener and the speakers, resulting in breaking down the communication. A sense of mutual respect and regulation of emotions requires understanding the impact of losing your temper in listening engagement. When one person wants his way rather than the other person's, or wants to achieve superiority, or wants to protect his own views, they are more likely to be impatient. At the end, nobody wins because, at the height of anger and uncontrolled emotions, nobody is listening.

Patience produces healing through listening

Most conflicts between friends or married couples are known to be due to pride resulting in a breakdown in communication. Opportunities for the couples to just listen or be listened to will often produce some beginning resolution. The same is true in most care-giving ministries. The opportunity for a trusted friend to just patiently listen to your life issues could be as healing or therapeutic as a medication. Dr. Rachel Naomi Remen, MD, an author, teacher, and pioneer in integrative medicine, summarized it best (Remen, 2014):

> *"Listening is the oldest and perhaps the most powerful tool of healing. It is often through the quality of our listening and not the wisdom of our words that we are able to affect the most profound changes in the people around us. When we listen we offer sanctuary for the homeless parts within the other person...When you listen generously to people, they can hear the truth in themselves often for the first time."*

Patience in listening provides people a great sense of inner peace, strength, and emotional control that then produces effective communication and understanding.

Positive attitudes produce patience

Positive attitudes that produce patience are those which encourage respect, and demonstrate care and love for the speaker or listener. One such attitude is the ability to control or show no emotions, even when reviled in a communication. The notion that two wrongs cannot make a right is true in this case. The positive attitude of one person (in a two-person communication) remaining in control of his emotions creates a pathway for patience. A positive attitude of displaying affective signs so simple as a smile, reflective questions to the speaker, or frequent words of affirmation, can have profound effects on the practice of patience. Constructive attitudes that build trust and confidence create a sense of comfort and an exercise of patience between people who want to be in a communication process.

Developing Listening-Concentration

Listening-concentration is the attentive ability to concentrate actively toward listening patiently in order to understand what is being communicated or transmitted. Communication through active listening occurs at the point of an interception of understanding the words that are spoken, unspoken, and in the spirit. This requires attentive concentration. Words are interconnected to make meanings, and understanding their full meaning requires undivided attention. We will deal with each concept separately. First, let us explore the full process of concentrating, communicating, and understanding. Adler et al (2001), in their book, *Interplay: the process of interpersonal communicating,* showed that adults spend an average of 70% of their time engaged in some sort of communication; of this 70%, an average of 45% is spent listening, 30% speaking, 16% reading, and 9% writing. These same statistics suggest that most adults remember between 25 and 50% of what they hear in a typical conversation. Learning to concentrate means learning to pay attention to the words, with the mind focused on the meanings of what is being said or understanding non-verbal presence. The critical step to improving our attention is to resist the natural tendency to respond too quickly, rather than being quiet and walking along with the speaker in the process, with full attention. Concentrated listening can be characterized by the level of attention in the listening engagement, as discussed below:

Be an attentive-concentration listener

Attentive-concentration listening is the inner strength that allows a leader to concentrate in the listening process by giving respect and absolute attention to the speaker and what is being said or demonstrated. It requires an attitude of humility and recognizing the other person's values. The writer of Hebrews puts it this way: "We must pay the most careful attention, therefore, to what we have heard, so that we do not drift away" (Hebrews 2:1). Attentiveness allows the leader and follower to listen and hear each other. It is the care we show through attentiveness that speaks about our compassion and respect, more so even than the words.

Be humble in your listening engagement

Listening is the same as saying to yourself, as you listen to someone, "Your message means something to me because we are the same, and I feel interchangeable with you." The very nature of humility is to provide the open door for well-being. A humble leader does not usually feel the need to be above or below another person. "They do not engage in power struggles during interpersonal experiences and do not need to have the last word" (Slamka, 2010). Apostle Paul writes: "Do nothing from rivalry or conceit, but in humility count others more significant than you. Let each of you look not only to his own interests, but also to the interests of others" (Philippians 2:3-11, ESV). Humility listening is one way of empathetic listening, as David expressed it: "O Lord, you hear the desire of the afflicted; you will strengthen their heart; you will incline your ear" (Psalm 10:17-18, ESV). Humility allows us to concentrate, to listen, and to submit to one another out of reverence for Christ.

A high level of self-awareness is important if we are to be good communicators as leaders. A leader's self-awareness enables him to be an effective listener by paying close attention to what is most important and fostering a deep perception and sensitivity to other people's issues, as well as an excellent understanding of how to adjust one's behavior to relate positively to people.

Developing Listening-Hearing

The critical purpose of paying attention in communication is to hear the message being transmitted. Hearing-listening means patiently paying attention to hear the words with all of your ears, open mind, and attentiveness to understanding. It means paying close attention to the content of the words—that is, the message behind the words, lest we drift away from it. Hearing is the most critical of the three elements of listening because, without hearing the words, there will be no meaning drawn and, therefore, no understanding, thus no communication. Lack of attention to what is communicated will lead us to "drift away." In listening to God, a leader wants to hear God, and His Word; he or she will grow in faith and come to know the depth of the love responsibilities in service leadership.

Hearing the word in the communication is the beginning of our understanding not only the message conveyed in the words, but our empathetic response to the message. Hearing is maximized when a leader shows a reasonable level of patience and empathy; indeed, without empathy and intentional connection to a follower, it is hard for a leader to hear effectively what a follower is saying. Hearing-listening can be characterized by the following qualities:

- **Self-discipline** is what guides the leader's ability to hear what he is listening to. Effective listening requires self-discipline to control the tongue, appropriate responses, and emotions that often can impede communication.
- **Patience** controls the tendency to interrupt the speaker or prejudge what the person is trying to communicate. An

impatient attitude creates a channel to lose part of what is being said.

- **Initiative** must be taken to hear and include intentional actions such as keeping quiet, not interrupting, and avoiding distractions. These behaviors enable the leader to comprehend and to be understood.

Here are some hearing-listening tips to improve your self-discipline, patience, and initiative, as involved in listening communication:

Be focused and open-minded

Be focused and open-minded to hear the speaker. Open-mindedness means keeping a simple spirit, being humble, and giving attention to what is communicated while holding back your own judgment or opinion. It is being open to what someone else wants to say. We must be attentive to the words, and the exact meaning communicated in the words. The Scripture said: "And your ears shall hear a word behind you, saying, 'This is the way, walk in it when you turn to the right or when you turn to the left'" (Isaiah 30:21 ESV). In wholeness communication, you must resist the temptation to give your own interpretation of the meaning. Rather, the listener must emphatically come to an understanding of the meaning, with respect to the speaker. When meanings in the communication are not clear, we must reflectively seek clarification to understand. This means repeating the word or statements back to the speaker to ensure what you heard is what was communicated.

Be a sympathetic listener

The basic elements of sympathetic listening are showing concern and feeling for the speaker's experience. The listener or compassion-giver first believes the experience of the care receiver or speaker, and then enters into the experience by participating or walking along with the experience. The result is that the compassion caregiver believes and actually feels the experience at some level. It is this ability to believe in and feel part of another person's experience that makes empathy attributes an important tool for servant leadership. We can sympathize by reflecting, understanding, and showing a capacity to share in the feeling, and allowing ourselves to be used for healing. Actions to improve our sympathetic listening include avoiding the following "negative listening habits" as identified by Adele Lynn, a consultant and the author of *The Emotional Intelligence Activity Book* (Lynn, 2001):

- The Rebuttal: Listening long enough to formulate a rebuttal.
- The Advice Maker: Jumping in too quickly to give unsolicited advice.
- The Interrupter: Being more anxious to speak his word than to listen.
- The Logical Listener: Rarely asking about the underlying feelings or emotions attached to the message.
- The Happy Hooker: Using the speaker's words only as a way to express his own message.
- The Faker: Pretending to be listening.

Be patient and humble with love to hear

Be patient and humble with enough love to hear the speaker. Often, communication breaks down due to our impatient heart that forces us to interrupt each other; as James said: "Know this, my beloved brothers: let every person be quick to hear, slow to speak, slow to anger" (James 1:19, ESV). Exercising patience when we listen is necessary to implant the word in us. This occurs when we submit to each other in a communication setting and put the other person ahead of ourselves. To be patient, the listener needs to be humble and kind to the speaker. Our speaking must be with love and respect to each other, putting the other person first. Impatience in listening to and hearing each other usually impedes communication, as each person insists on his or her own way. This often results in the irritation of each other.

Showing empathy through love can yield the required gentleness, humility, patience, and kindness for effective listening and hearing. As the Apostle Paul said: "Love is patient and kind; love does not envy or boast; it is not arrogant or rude. It does not insist on its own way; it is not irritable or resentful" (1 Corinthians 13:4-5, ESV).

Be in control of your emotions to hear

Be enough in control of your emotions to hear the speaker. Negative emotions such as anger block our ability to hear what is being communicated because "the anger of man does not produce the righteousness of God. Forgiving one another is important, as we 'put away all filthiness and rampant wickedness'" (James 1:20, ESV). Controlling our emotions is the beginning of regulating our response to allow the word to be implanted in us in order to build better relationships. Self-regulating our emotions also means controlling our tongues. "If anyone thinks he is religious and does not bridle his tongue but deceives his heart; this person's religion is worthless" (James 1:26, ESV). Even when a follower is the aggressor, the leader has the responsibility to bring calmness because, as the Scripture said, "A gentle answer turns away wrath, but a harsh word stirs up anger" (Proverb 15.1, NIV).

Be a doer of the words you hear.

Doing what is heard in a listening communication is a practical way of transmitting your understanding of the message. James said it best: "For if anyone is a hearer of the word and not a doer, he is like a man who looks intently at his natural face in a mirror...and at once forgets what he was like" (James 1:23-25, ESV). This applies, in that acting practically with perseverance on what is heard is an effective way to demonstrate understanding, and a way for the hearer to be blessed as a result.

Be an affective communicator

An effective communicator reflects God's love in hearing, listening, and communicating with a loving attitude. Jesus reminded the Pharisees, "Out of the abundance of heart the mouth speaks" (Matthew 12:34, NKJV). A heart filled with unresolved issues with another is an unforgiving or ungodly heart, and will likely reflect these issues in the communication, either verbally or through facial expression, body language, or other non-verbal means. Hence, a leader must readily resolve issues with his followers; otherwise, these same issues could cause barriers in communication. Being an effective communicator means doing the following:

- *Speak the truth in love to the hearer.* "Rather, speaking the truth in love, we are to grow up in every way into him who is the head, into Christ" (Ephesians 4:15 ESV). Jesus said, "And you will know the truth, and the truth will set you free" (John 8:32 ESV). Table 6.1 (based on Philippians 4: 8-9) is a guide to speaking the truth in love by testing how affective our words are in communication. If the answer to any of these ten questions is no, then the words are not effective and should be avoided.

- *Do everything out of love to communicate affection.* "Let all that you do be done in love" (1 Corinthians 16:14, ESV). This means exercising all acts of godliness with brotherly affection and love (2 Peter 1:7).

- *Guide your tongue in speaking.* Being sensitive and withholding meaningless words, body language, and gestures that commune anger or hatred toward another eliminates barriers that can block communication. Words can be corrupting and defiling, and can easily reflect bad taste to the hearer. If a word cannot build up the hearer, as in Table 7.1, it is not worth using. The Apostle Paul said it best: "Whoever guards his mouth preserves his life; he who opens wide his lips comes to ruin" (1 Corinthians 13:1-13, ESV). "Let no corrupting talk come out of your mouths, but only such as is good for building up, as fits the occasion, that it may give grace to those who hear" (Ephesians 4:29, ESV).

Table 7.1: Tests of Affective Words in Communication.

	Tests of Affective Words	YES/NO
1	Are they true (correct)?	
2	Are they noble (honorable)?	
3	Are they just (fair)?	
4	Are they pure (godly)?	
5	Are they lovely (provoking love)?	
6	Are they kind (caring)?	
7	Are they of good report?	
8	Are they of good virtue?	
9	Are they wholesome?	
10	Are they uplifting?	

- **Demonstrate love more by actions and truth than words** (1 John 3:18 ESV). As the Apostle Paul said to Timothy: "Follow the pattern of the sound words that you have heard from me, in the faith and love that are in Christ Jesus" (2 Timothy 1:13, ESV). We as little children are not to love in empty word or talk, but in actions and in truth. This means true love patterned after that of Christ without presence and partiality requires us to be "kind to one another, tenderhearted, forgiving one another, as God in Christ forgave you" (Ephesians 4:32, ESV). Use words in action to affirm love to the hearer.

- *Share yourself with each other.* "Being affectionately desirous of you, we were ready to share with you not only the gospel of God but also our own selves, because you had become valuable to us": these were Apostle Paul's words to express how dear the brethren were to him (1 Thessalonians 2:8, ESV). Spending time with your followers is one great way to share yourself with them. Jesus communicated a lot through parables, but often found time to spend with his disciples to further explain things for them as a part of his mentoring, empowering, and revealing other inner and deeper meanings of His life and ministries. The Apostle Mark reported this fact: "In fact, in his public ministry he never taught without using parables; however, afterward, when he was alone with his disciples, he explained everything to them" (Mark 4:34, NLT). On other occasions, after returning from an assigned mission, "The apostles gathered around Jesus and reported to him all they had done and taught" (Mark 6:30, NIV). This type of sharing with followers communicated love and care, and offered Jesus an opportunity to get to know what had been accomplished, how the mission had gone, and any difficulties. It is more about showing care than measuring progress.

Developing Listening-Understanding

Listening-understanding means patiently paying attention to what is being spoken for full understanding of its meaning. The human brain is known to work significantly faster than the mouth, requiring the listener and speaker to self-regulate and control the thoughts and what the mouth says in order to understand. Understanding is Habit #5 in Stephen Covey's 7 *Habits of Highly Effective People* (Covey, 2004). Covey recommends that we seek first to understand, then to be understood. Listening, according to Covey, takes place on four levels: One can choose to ignore concentrating by making no effort to listen, or by pretending to be listening by giving the appearance that one is listening; or selective listening by hearing only the parts of the conversation that interest you. Alternatively, one can perform "attentive" listening, which means paying attention and focusing on what the speaker says relative to one's experiences, or "empathic" listening, by responding with both the heart and mind to understand the speaker's words, intent, and feelings. Listening is a way to show that you care for others. Leaders self-regulate their listening attitude to understand and be understood as an act of caring and building relationships with others.

A leader-servant's choice is always to be an emphatic listener. The two important attitudes in understanding listening as an element of effective listening and communication are empathy and reflection. Empathy is a critical element of full understanding of what is being communicated. Empathy is "an intuitive act in which we give complete attention to someone else's experience in a way that allows the other to realize that we both share and understand the essential quality of that experience" (Hudson-Smith et al, 2013). The empathy attribute enables the leader to really hear what others are saying. The second attitude is reflection. Reflection in listening is another way of empathizing to understand the other person's experience and point of view, by seeing issues from their perspective.

Developing Active Listening Skills

Developing an active listening skill begins with setting personal goals to actively hear messages. Such goals must include a commitment to hear what other people are saying fully by setting aside all other thoughts and behaviors and concentrating on the message. The three elements to be developed in communicating with followers include building skills for understanding: the words spoken (content), the words unspoken (nonverbal), and words in the spirit (emotions within the words):

Understand content of the spoken words

Paying attention to the key elements of active reflective listening will help ensure that you understand the words. This includes paying attention to word content (thoughts, beliefs, evaluations, etc.) to understand the issues. Giving your undivided attention and acknowledging the message being communicated improves your engagement in the process. The listener must reflect back the content to the speaker to ensure they both are on the same meaning. This is done by paraphrasing the key content of the message to show that you are interested, and clarifying the message for mutual understanding and correct interpretation. Table 7.2 shows an example of a leader's response to show understanding of the content of the words spoken.

Empathize by reflecting a person's point of view through looking at issues from their perspective, letting go of preconceived ideas, and having an open mind with the speaker.

Understand the unspoken words

How does an infant child communicate with a mother without words? The child will cry when he or she is hungry or needs some kind of attention. Imagine you are a mother listening to a little child or a leader-servant listening to a concerned follower. Table 7.3 demonstrates how one can get meaning from unspoken words.

Table 7.2. Understand the content of the words spoken

Examples of efforts to reflectively understand content include the following:	
Reflective Content	**Examples: Response by Leader-servant**
Thoughts	"So, you're thinking this would be a good time to change jobs."
Beliefs	"Am I right in saying that your beliefs and convictions are very different from your father's?"
Evaluations	"It seems to me that you really don't like what's going on at work."

Table 7.3 (Scenario 1) Leaders empathize by reflecting   a follower's point of view and feelings

Reflecting on speakers' content and associated feelings:	
Speaker	**Content and Feeling perceived**
Leader-servant (Framework):	"Your main issue was [state content], but you think it was [state perceived content] and you feel [state feelings]." End with a responsive assessment question.
Examples:	

Follower to leader-servant:	"I am really upset how he called me yesterday and, without getting my side of the story, he started judging me and telling me how wrong I was."
Leader-servant to follower:	"Your main issue was that he did not express your side of the story [content], but you think he was judging you [perceived content] and that made you angry [feelings]. Is that what you are saying? [Assessment].
Leader-servant to follower:	"I sense your issue was how he approached the issue [content], and you feel he was judging you [perceived content]. I am wondering if you were upset [feelings] because that was not the correct story. Am I correct or am I missing something?"

Research work by Albert Mehrabian of UCLA, in his book, *Silent Messages* (Meharabian, 1971), and his research papers on the subject of non-verbal communication, concluded that in communication, words account for 7% of the message, tone of voice accounts for 38%, and body language accounts for 55%. This means that the predominant form of communication is nonverbal—93% (38% + 55%)—rather than being in the literal meaning of the words (7%) (Meharabian, 2009). To understand this 93% non-verbal form of communication requires full attention and the patience to observe and understand all the non-verbal elements, such as gestures, voice intonation, body postures, proximity, facial expression, eye contact, voice volume, and many facets. These elements work together in communication to emphasize, empathize, complement, and regulate verbal messages, or sometimes give mixed signals. Non-verbal messages such as silent expressions of anger, joy, and sadness during communication can positively or negatively affect how the meaning of words heard is interpreted by the listener. Body posture which could suggest how and where you stand on an issue, for example, can also influence some form of meaning. A listener leaning closer toward a speaker could indicate high interest, while looking away from the speaker could mean rejection, impatience, or a lack of interest. Non-verbal communications such as physical touches are effective to the extent that the context is correctly understood. For example, in a funeral situation, a touch of skin will be well understood to mean non-verbal sympathy intended to express comfort. Similar touches in other situations could leave mixed signals and must be practiced with care.

Some non-verbal elements such as gestures— movements of hands to convey specific meanings—are usually influenced by the speaker's culture. My daughter, who was born and raised here in U.S.A., visited some West African countries. When she returned, we had some fun moments comparing culturally-based dispositions. One of her questions to me was, she wanted know why people in Africa speak too loud with great passion when they speak. The fact is that most people of West African nations usually speak with high intonations, and very aggressive hand movements; sometimes they are very passionate in their facial expressions and hand gestures. In other cultures such as in the United States, these same mannerisms are often misinterpreted as ill-mannered, arrogance, or yelling. Along the same lines, people in the United States may use their index fingers to point, while pointing with index fingers in many Asian cultures is considered rude. This means that 93% of communication being non-verbal presents a challenge of which a leader must be aware, and learn to overcome.

To be an effective listener requires that the leader develop his listening-communication attribute to meet these challenges. Here are examples of how you can hear and understand the unspoken words (showing a correct perception of unuttered words or feelings):

- Focus attention on the spiritual concerns (self-esteem, meaning, hopes, fears, etc.) to understand the issues; learn to reflect back the transcendent concerns.
- Look for the unspoken words: facial expressions, tone of voice, and body movement, gestures, eye-movements, etc., behind the words spoken to reveal what is not spoken.
- Discern the unuttered words and what lies behind the words spoken.
- Listen with your ears, eyes, and feelings open
- Listen to both the words and the ideas behind the words with the virtues of a mother's heart (Mark 10:45).
- Watch the speaker's body language and recognize the nonverbal communication.
- Listen to the tone and volume to help you understand the emphasis of what is being said and the emotions in what is not said.
- Check your perception to evaluate your assumptions. Example: say, "Let me make sure I have this straight. You said that you loved your wife, and she is very important to you. At the same time, you can't stand being with her. Is that what you are saying, or am I missing something?"

Understand the feelings expressed.

The feelings expressed are the emotions in words, body language, or gesture. To hear and understand the words hidden in the speaker's spirit (the emotions, the hurts, the joy, etc., hidden in the words), a leader-servant can follow these suggestions:

- Be empathetic and sensitive to the expressed feelings (Luke 14:26; Hebrews 4:15).

- Listen with neutral emotions, focusing on the speaker's tone of voice and emotions in the tone.
- Strive to understand the meaning of what is expressed.
- Be fully centered on healing the hurt.
- Reflect back the feelings as much as possible. Why would you laugh when someone is weeping in the spirit, or show apathy when the other person expects you to show interest?

Examples of how you can empathize by reflecting on content and feeling is demonstrated in Table 7.4.

Table 7.4 (Scenario 2) Empathizing by Reflecting on Content and Feeling

Leader-servant **reflects on content and feeling** at a deeper level in order to reach an understanding of what may be deeper issues.	
Speaker	Feeling and Content Reflections
Framework (leader–servant):	"What I am hearing is that [state content], and that is why you feel [state feelings]". Then, invite a response to confirm understanding.
Example:	
Follower to Leader-servant:	"We worked hard in planning the program [content]. I invited but received no feedback on the program from members. I am sad [feeling] that two days to the event the same members are criticizing and having serious issues with the program."

Leader-servant to follower:	"You are feeling discouraged [feeling] that members did not give feedback in time to the program design [content]. Is this what you are saying?"
Or:	
Leader-servant to follower:	"It seems that what happened was members were absent from a meeting you spent time to plan [content], which is why you feel sad [feeling]. Did I understand your feeling correctly?"

Table 7.5 shows examples of how the typical feelings—sadness, anger, joy—can be reflectively decoded

Table 6.5. Reflectively decoding typical feelings—sadness, anger, joy

Feelings	Leader-servant Reflections
	"You said what happened was [state content] and this is why you feel [state feelings]; is that it?"
Examples:	
Sad:	"You said you're feeling very sad about your mother's death; is that what you mean?"
Angry:	"You said what happened was... and you're really angry about it, is that it?"
Joy:	"It sounds as if you're really happy and pleased with how it turned out; am I correct?"

Be empathetic and sensitive to understand

Be empathic and sensitive to expressed feelings. Strive to understand the meaning of what is being expressed with a focus centered on comforting the emotions of the weaker person.

If the issue being discussed involves a broken relationship due to an action, focus on reconciliation rather than resolution. By being another person-centered and putting that individual above your needs, as read in Philippians 2:3-4), the resolution of the issue becomes less important than reconciliation. Be patient and do not interrupt or be quick to dismiss concerns (Hebrews 4:15). As we have learned earlier, feelings are expressed with several emotions—anger, sadness, joy, regret, etc. Each of these emotions is usually based on some history, or some incident or event in the life of the person expressing it. Suppose the speaker is relating to the sadness or sorrow from the loss of a loved one, feeling of regrets over something that happened, or feeling a hurt that was caused by the listener. Take, for example, an example where a particular spouse came back from work and was emotionally depressed because of what had happened at work. Or, consider that a speaker is joyful because of something good that happened in his or her life. Each of these communication situations may involve somebody's language that might give out some positive or negative clues as to what the speaker is feeling, or body language from the speaker showing clues of how he or she is responding to the feeling. For example, leaning forward may mean more interest in what the speaker is saying, as high tones of voice may mean anger. Facial expression may also be very revealing of acceptance or a disagreement of respect. We can be sensitive to expressed feelings through the following responses:

- Do not interrupt in the middle of communication when a sensitive feeling is being expressed unless there is a valid reason; just as in reflective listening, desire to understand some clarification of missing facts. If the speaker is taking too long, and you do not have much time, then you as the listener must politely ask for continuance at another time, rather than display any act of impatience that will show insensitivity.

- Do not be presumptuous, like adding information to complete a statement or trying to fix the problem, as most men do without getting the complete details. It may be that the speaker just wants you to listen; be considerate and understanding, whether you agree or not.

- Do not attempt to fix the person or the problem, at least not at the immediate moment, unless the speaker expressly asks for your suggestion for a solution. Even in those cases, you must judge whether the person is ready for a hard truth, should that be warranted. You must focus on bringing healing and not making the speaker's feelings worse, especially if you sense the speaker is too inclined to his or her opinion. Wait for the appropriate time of calmness and then revisit the situation; even so, you must not ignore the issue if you desire to bring wholeness to the hurting person. Unresolved conflict will generate more conflicts or cause the original conflict to escalate or extend to other areas of life.

Be empathetic to the expressed feeling

To empathetically respond to the expressed feeling is the key to compassionate communication that yields impassioned healing. It starts with the listener walking along in the emotional feelings of the speaker. Wisdom of God is needed, and you have to pray that "you may be filled with the knowledge of His will in all wisdom and spiritual understanding; that you may walk worthy of the Lord, fully pleasing Him, being fruitful in every good work and increasing in the knowledge of God" (Colossians 1:9-10). Your focus is to be filled with the wisdom of what the other person is expressing in words and feelings, so that your response will yield positive healing. A measure of appropriate response is in "being fruitful in every good work and increasing in the knowledge of God." For example:

- Be filled with knowledge of the will of God in the situation. This then will allow you the spiritual understanding, which is the understanding of the mind and deep emotional feelings of the speaker.

- Be gentle and respectful in responding to the speaker, without being judgmental, after you have clarified and have a full understanding of the situation. You must empathically reflect on the speaker's feelings to make sure you have your interpretations correct. A gentle response to the expressed sentiment is an act of compassion that could make the speaker feel safer and empathized.

- Validate and walk with the person in the feeling. Instead of saying "I know how you feel," you can say, "I can understand how this would hurt your feelings." Whether you agree on not, it is a first point of healing to validate the speaker's experience or feelings. Statements like "it is not a big deal," "why is this a problem?", "I do not feel the same way about this," "I am not sure what your real issue is," etc., can be misinterpreted as insensitivity.

Show that you care about the expressed feeling.

Another effective strategy for reflective listening and response to expressed feeling is to show that you care about what is being expressed by looking directly at the speaker as he/she speaks to you. Even when the speaker pauses, it may not be time for you to speak. As leaders, we must show restraint and set a good example. It is not the person who speaks the most words that show effectiveness, but the person that uses a few words of wisdom and knowledge to influence the desired change in others, as we read in the Proverbs. "The one who has knowledge uses words with restraint, and whoever has understanding is even-tempered" (Proverbs 17:27, NIV). Respond to the speaker only when necessary, and with respect and gentleness, asserting your opinions respectfully and without prejudging.

Elements that Hinder Listening-Communication

As I conclude this section, it is important to reflect on three key elements that can hinder a leader's or follower's ability to listen:

Subjectivity in an opinion: Watchman Nee in his book, *The Character of God's Workman*, defined subjectivity as "an insistence upon one's own option while refusing to accept the opinions of others" (Nee, 1988). Communication or the ability to listen in order to understand can be hindered by subjectivity. Subjectivity also refers to the notion of partiality in which a listener takes sides with the opinion that aligns only with his or her own opinion. Obviously, this is contrary to our model of servant leadership. The focus should be for the leader to listen first and understand the follower's point of view, and then by example lead the follower to understand him.

Prejudice and blind spots: Hearing and understanding messages are also generally hindered by prejudice. Prejudging wrongly or rightly before hearing the whole story is a kind of blind spot, an unconscious attitude or assumption. Prejudice is generally caused by an attitude, opinion, or feeling formed without adequate prior knowledge, thought, or reason. However, at the heart of prejudice is a stereotype— a generalization of characteristics that is applied to all members of a cultural group. We must strip away stereotypes because they block our ability to think positively about other people. We must learn to listen and probe for differences in people's assumptions while suspending our own judgment to understand shades of meaning more effectively. Listening can also be done by building authentic and significant relationships with people you regard as distinct, which enhances personal empowerment. We must hone our inner ability to accept, move toward, or embrace different ideas and perspectives. We must learn to explore, identify, and value group differences by listening actively, openly, and respectfully to others, and framing every communication as a joint opportunity to build a better relationship.

Inclination on an issue: Inclination refers to completely holding onto one's own ideas and emotions on a matter that there is no room for considering another's ideas. Like subjectivity, inclination is not an attitude of a leader-servant and can hinder his or her ability to be an empathetic listener. The same is true for followers. Through perceptive, nonjudgmental observation, and empathic listening, a leader must intently listen to the interests and concerns of others before expressing his needs and wants.

CHAPTER 8

WHOLENESS COMPASSION IN MARRIAGE

Compassion can be a call to unity or wholeness beyond the differences expected in a marriage, and it is necessary in building a successful marriage. Husband and wife are called to be one in each other and in God. They are called to be complete or make one another whole in God's creative plan. Without such unity, they may not be resilient in meeting God's purpose together and in the family. If not strong in God, they cannot be "perfect" in unity, and if not complete in unity, then they cannot hope for an impeccable marriage. In this context, a "perfect" marriage is not one where perfection rules the relationship, but a covenant other-centered relationship in which each person selflessly chooses to overlook a multitude of imperfections in the other. The marital bond of perfection is through a love for each other (Colossians 3:14). If you want to have a great marriage, you must be ready to overlook the imperfections and serve each other.

The unity above can be found only through the love in Christ that enables us to "put on tender mercies, kindness, humility, meekness, longsuffering; bearing with one another" (Colossians 3:12-13, NKJV). Apostle Paul also implored you (husband and wife) as Christians to "walk worthy of the calling with which you were called, with all lowliness and gentleness, with longsuffering, bearing with one another in love, endeavoring to keep the unity of the Spirit in the bond of peace" (Ephesians 4:1-3, NKJV).

The Purpose of the Unity

The secret of the purpose of the perfect unity is found very clearly in these scriptures above. Husband and wife are called not only to one hope, Lord, and Father as Christians, but toward one united covenant which promises to build up the family of God through love-based compassion that starts with one another.

Unity can be found when both accept and celebrate it as a gift from God. The unity is a divine command that requires shared commitment, hard work, and submission. The love the husband and wife share is a mutual covenant commitment to each other's will and best interests, regardless of the cost.

The unity in marriage that is born of such love is needed to break down the barrier that serve as impediments for fulfilled marriage.

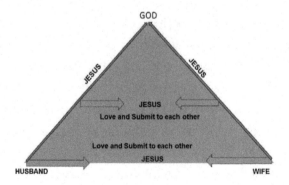

Figure 8.1. Husband and wife draw to each other as they intentionally draw toward Christ-likeness

As shown in Figure 8.1, it is love that drives one to move toward the other through Christ-like acts of tenderness, mercy, kindness, humility, meekness, and longsuffering, preparing them for bearing with one another, and giving forgiveness shared between husband and wife, and extending the same to all members of the family.

We can also see the purpose of the unity in the plan of their roles— "I will make him a helper comparable to him" (Genesis 2:18, NKJV); He created woman to be a cognate helper, to share a oneness in God's purpose. She was created for him and to be in unity with him for that purpose (1 Corinthians 11:9).

Of course, in case you were wondering, without that unity, there will not be procreation in God's purpose for the marriage; the companionship God wants for them and to which every marriage partner seeks will not be realized in a wholesome way. Without the sense of unity, the strength in the differences becomes a deficit; sex becomes what you endure to do, and not what you enjoy for greater intimacy; respect to your husband becomes an act of servitude and not that of servanthood; love for your wife becomes accidental rather than intentional, and the marriage relationship becomes sacrificing (manageable) rather than satisfying (fulfilling).

Sustaining and Strengthening Unity

The wholeness that builds a successful marriage happens when spouses make intentional efforts to unify the differences in their marriage. Some of the actions we can take include the following:

Develop trust in the relationship

Oneness between people who are different—male and female— is born of mutual trust in each other. Most often, individuals trust each other because they first loved each other, and because of that affection, the trust can easily be taken for granted until a crisis surfaces. A couple can achieve closeness only through the trust that their emotions will not be hurt or an assurance that a spouse feels secured in the love and protection of the other's sentiment. No marriage can be satisfying without a good measure of trust. The oneness called for in this Scripture, "For this reason a man will leave his father and mother and be united to his wife, and they will become one flesh" (Genesis 2:24), can only happen with trust.

Good relational connections or relationships that empower sustainable growth in a conjugal relationship are based on true trust on several different levels. Genuine trust produces confidence and a readiness to freely and wholly commit to the relationship. The confidence that a spouse (trustee) has in the other is a direct result or measure of the confidence of the trustee on the trusted. The above definition means that the trust attribute is a mutually interdependent husband-wife interaction. That is, trust can be formed when a husband leads by first extending trust to his spouse. True spousal trust produces assured confidence and readiness in one partner to join and to be one as based on the shared relational connections with the other.

This principle means that trust is developed, earned, or given when the quality of one spouse's confidence in the other's relational connection inspires assuredness and willingness to be one. Here are some ways we can build trust:

Making trust a marital priority: If a marriage is to be sustained, trust between the spouses must be a priority worth working on. Infidelity is one great betrayal of trust and a major killer of marriages because it is one that is unpredictable in the beginning of marriages. Other betrayals of trust include lying to your spouse, keeping secrets, not being transparent, displaying dishonest behavior, etc.

Confess and forgive the past failures: Paul wrote: "But one thing I do: Forgetting what is behind and straining toward what is ahead, I press on toward the goal to win the prize for which God has called me heavenward in Christ Jesus" (Philippians 2:13a-14). Confessing and forgiving each other is a powerful wholeness-healing attitude. It also means being transparent to each other. Do not wait until you are caught before you confess. The readiness to forgive and reconcile is diluted when you confess and apologize because you were caught. To be one, each must be completely, wholly, and willing to let the other know everything—past and present, especially those items that could easily be found out. I do recognize the risk here, as people handle information very differently. So, be prudent! I have grown to believe in full disclosure as much as possible; you cannot hide anything for too long. Sooner or later, he or she will find out, and when that happens, trust-growth is affected. You better be sure that what you are hiding is worth more than your family—spouse, children, and even reputation. The more humble and willing you are to expose your vulnerabilities, the more you know each other, the better we know, and the further we love and trust.

Develop Trust-Character

Trust-character is any quality that builds one's spouse's ability to trust the other or earn the trust of the other. Such character qualities include integrity, truthfulness, motivation, and consistency. The level of trust one spouse earns from the other is built on acts of integrity constantly displayed. In this context, integrity can be seen as the quality of his inner character consistently applied in how he behaves externally toward his chosen other. Trust-character is learned or can be trained through the following actions:

Develop a sound value system that builds trust. The value includes his diligence, faith, virtue, knowledge, self-control, perseverance, kindness, and love. A leader is secure in his abilities based on these values and sound moral principles. Such a strong sense of security earns him trust from others.

Build relational security. This means erecting good fences to protect unity, intentionally choosing to be faithful, and not keeping secrets or hiding unresolved sexual feelings, but revealing all to your spouse and not to outsiders. The couples must set limits and not permit external ungodly relationships. There is also a need to build an accountability network. In building a defense that lasts, you must never think you are invulnerable, but always look for any crack in the fence that needs fixing!

Extend positive behavior toward each other. Not only must you build fences; you must always act in beneficial ways to protect your fences. This can be done by flagging behaviors to warn of vulnerability; a husband must love and affirm the beauty of his spouse, and avoid any action that will reduce her self-esteem.

Develop positive character traits to build people's trust. The leader's ability to build trust is measured by a good sense of character, which is composed of beliefs, values, skills, and traits.[29] Spouses must clearly communicate the overall expectations of each other, and commit to working on those expectations. They need to help each other understand the plan as it relates to the family, and the marriage with no hidden agenda based on the covenant vow that they share. They must help each other understand how they can be engaged and contribute to achieving key family objectives.

Commit to honesty, integrity, and sound judgments. Honesty, integrity, and sound judgments function together to externally display the trust and credibility of a leader. It matters very little how strong a leader is if truthfulness integrity, and sound judgment are missing; in fact, these qualities define what makes us the "salt" described by Jesus: "If the salt has lost its flavor, how shall it be seasoned? It is neither fit for the land nor for the dunghill, but men throw it out" (Luke 14: 35, NKJV). This is because the salt functions for not only taste, but purification and healing. Honesty, trust, and integrity are the bonding glue that cements the leadership attribute of a spouse.

Create value from your differences to build trust. Valuing the unique contribution each spouse's difference makes in the relationship can build trust. People work best when they feel valued. A wife, for example, when included by her husband in the management of finances in the home, because she is more gifted in that, will feel more valued and empowered. When people feel valued, included, and empowered, they can trust and engage with others to build relationships in which they work interdependently and synergistically. Valuing the diversity of people, and their perspective, increases the ability to build trust and productivity. Here are some ways to achieve this goal:

- *Explore and identify the value in a group's differences.* Listen actively, openly, and respectfully to others. Show that you understand the key challenges your followers are facing.
- *Manage marital differences as a joint trust-building opportunity.* Be open to other people's ideas and perspective by fostering a respectful environment in which ideas flourish, and where the structure has the flexibility to accommodate new ideas and provide regular opportunities for collective action.
- *Develop a family-wide culture that supports free-flowing ideas.* This encourages collective efforts within the family and recognizes the need for ongoing reflection and renewal. Make intentional efforts for everybody to collaborate around a common goal, and show that you value others' contributions through an effective reward system.

Build the quality of trust-competence

In addition to character, competence is a fundamental dimension of trust. According to John C. Maxwell, competence is a leader's "ability to say it, plan it, and do it in a way that others will recognize as demonstrating that the leader knows his business, and knows that they want to follow" (Maxwell, 2007). Trust-competence is the leader's ability to base his action on moral principles and good judgment, and to complete a task that will make people trust him.

What has trust-competence got to do with compassion wholeness in marriage? A lot! Trust competencies are those qualities, such as behaviors, skills, knowledge, capabilities, and *emotional intelligence* that influence a person's confidence (or the confidence of others) to complete a duty properly. The key to trust-competence is this important term called "emotional intelligence." Mayer et al. (2001) defined emotional intelligence as "The ability to perceive emotion, integrate emotion to facilitate thought, understand emotions and to regulate emotions to promote personal growth." Emotional intelligence manifests itself in certain adaptive behaviors related to perceiving sentiments using emotions, understanding emotions, and managing emotions. According to research, emotional intelligence explains why—even in an organization or corporation with people of equal intellectual capacity, training, or experience—you find some people who excel while others of the equivalent caliber do not, and why people react differently and better to exposure of the same event (Mayer et al, 2001). Can you imagine what happens when a spouse feels that the other is not competent in adapting appropriate impassioned intelligence to know how to regulate anger?

A case in point: Earlier in my marriage, I had a serious problem with anger. At that time, our daily family altar and devotion started at 7 P.M. In this instance I'm thinking of, my wife had gone to the store and was running late. Of course, there was no cell phone to call to say that she would be late. She thought that I was going to be angry, so in her rush to get home, she nearly had an accident. When she returned, she was surprised that, out of compassion and understanding in response to her readiness of an "I am sorry", that I was not mad.

Nevertheless, she had almost lost her life for a lack of confidence in my ability to regulate my emotion.

Trust-competence is built over time, and can be measured by your performance results and track record as relative to your set of competencies. The life of Moses and Joshua serve as typical examples. Moses did not even believe in himself, and found it hard to agree with God that he could be competent enough for God's agenda for the deliverance of Israel from Egypt. Yet, God provided him with all that he needed to be a strong leader. Moses then mentored and prepared Joshua for leadership, but God built the competency skills of Joshua, beginning with trusting him enough to usher the military campaigns from the wilderness into Canaan, to leading the nation of Israel as a transformed leader (Joshua 11:16-23; Numbers 13:16). Jesus also worked on selecting the disciples He could trust. Here are five competency skills or actions to build trust, based from Jesus' teaching (Luke 14:27-35):

Build an attitude of commitment and trust. Husband and wife must commit to what really matters. For a husband to build trust for a spouse to follow, he must let his wife understand what matters most to him in the family, and demonstrate his commitment to that purpose in relation to the wholeness of the family. The purpose must be family-centered and not him-centered. A wife, on the other hand, must respond by showing that she trusts the husband in her following; she must show her willingness to sacrifice and commit to the husband and his plan. Jesus demonstrated both commitment and trust: His work of salvation with the expressed love for humanity was important enough to Jesus and the Father who sent Him that He gave His life for it. Here in this teaching, He says, "And whoever does not bear his cross and come after Me cannot be My disciple" (Luke 14:27, NKJV). The willingness to leave behind all else to follow Jesus is not only a measure of our commitment, but also of a trust attitude which says, "I will sacrifice all to follow you because you matter enough for me to trust all to you." Losing your life in Jesus is to save it for eternity. That is the attitude the Lord was expecting from them, and all of us who aspire to be leader-servants.

Be thoughtful, intelligent, and prudent in your decision. In your decisions, it is important to have the trust-competency skill to know the *what* to, *how* to, *when* to, *ability* to, and *where* to, start to do a project, or any act in a marital relationship; it is the hallmark of the farsightedness of a smart visionary leader. Spouses must be prudent and thoughtful about their abilities. Jesus wanted to trust only those who would commit to joining with Him fully in the ministry as disciples; however, they had to first measure, understand, and be able to bear the cost to follow him emotionally and physically. This is what is expected in a marital relationship. Retreating from a purpose due to thoughtless hasty initiation is a display of incompetency, and an easy way to lose the trust of your spouse.

Display the Quality of Trust-Credibility

Credibility is the quality of being believable. You cannot earn or receive trust without credibility. Building credibility starts at the personal level. The four elements of credibility, according to Steve Covey, are integrity, intent, capability, and results. It is an expression of who we are as people. You can display your quality of Trust-Credibility through the following actions:

Set goals and communicate results to build credibility. People develop confidence and trust in a leader based on measuring what the leader has accomplished or will achieve; what a leader has accomplished is measured as relative to a set of goals and expectations. Like the State of the Union speech for a president, a leader must unmistakably define the levels of accountability in relation to goals and expectations, and is then anticipated to be evaluated on how well he has met the goals. The expectation must be communicated clearly to all members of the organization. Starting with the leader and on down to the lowest person in the organization, a leader holds himself and every direct reporter responsible for consistently meeting established and understood expectations. Credibility comes when people see and believe you have accomplished what you said you would execute.

Increase trust-confidence by associating with credible people. A leader's assuredness to keep his enemies near and his friends closer is self-confidence. A wife who sees a husband associating himself with people of questionable character will begin to challenge the believability of her husband's true character. That could begin to damage her trust in him.

Be an inside-out spouse to display credibility externally. Jesus Christ, in addressing the crowd and His disciples on the subject of credibility, says, "For you are like whitewashed tombs, which indeed appear beautiful outwardly, but inside are full of dead men's bones and all uncleanness. Even so, you also outwardly appear righteous to men, but inside you are full of hypocrisy and lawlessness" (Matthew 23:23-30, NKJV). Hypocrisy is the direct opposite of credibility. The Lord calls leader-servants to be inside-out leaders and to reflect credibility. We measure ourselves "Unto the measure of the status of the fullness of Christ" (Ephesians 4:13). The Apostle Paul emphasized that what is most important is a change from the inside-out leaders to also be inside-out Christians. "…but he is a Jew who is one inwardly; and circumcision is that of the heart, in the Spirit, not in the letter; whose praise is not from men but from God" (Romans 2:28-29, NKJV).

Wholeness Communications between Spouses

Communication is the pathway to a successful marriage and to sustain and strengthen your wholeness. It requires you to spend enough energy on your communication. In the previous chapter, we defined wholeness communication as an empathetic communication that involves the two-way exchange of content, feelings, and spiritual concerns in ways that bring forth wholeness or emotional well-being of people through the communication process. It was also noted that, in the context of a marriage relationship, that wholeness communication requires compassionate understanding, mutual submission, and confidence-trust between husband and wife. As Apostle Paul advised, "Do not let any unwholesome talk come out of your mouths, but only what is helpful for building others up according to their needs, that it may benefit those who listen" (Ephesians 4:29). The expression "for building others according to their needs" is to say that our talks or communications require compassion and wholesomeness. Thus, effective wholeness communication provides a pathway for sustaining and strengthening wholesomeness (healthiness) in marriage.

Listening has been identified as one of the critical characteristics of communication. In fact, communication ceases when listening fails. The Scripture says, in James 1:19: "My dear brothers take note of this: Everyone should be quick to listen, slow to speak and slow to become angry." This scripture clearly puts our efforts to listen as a far higher priority than our readiness to talk. As the common saying goes, "God gave you one mouth and two ears. You ought to devote twice as much time to listening as you do to talk."

Males and females differ in many ways, and those distinctions can sometimes create conflicts; however, wholeness communication looks at these differences in marriage in a diverse manner. God may have given the wife 50,000 words per day and the husband only 25,000, but compassionate wholeness communication bridges the gap between the differences. She wants him to listen to her problem, but he wants to fix the problem; she wants to know what he's thinking, but he wants to keep certain things to himself. When she wants to be cuddled and loved, he wants to just have sex. The solution to these differences involves compromise. A man has a clear responsibility to "cheer up his wife whom he has taken" (Deuteronomy 24:5). He must press himself to open his heart and share his deeper feelings with his wife. For that to happen, couples must reserve quality time for meaningful conversations and relational connections. Deprivation of either function can be devastating in sustaining the unity in the marriage.

Factors Affecting Wholeness Communication

Lack of healthy commutation has been known to be one of the top killers of marriages, and yet the least of the items to which the couple pays attention. Some difficulties in marital relationships are caused by innate differences between the sexes, and the inabilities of the spouses to deal with those differences. The factors in Table 8.1 are common culprits that prevent effective communication.

Table 8.1: Factors affecting wholeness communication

1	Message not clear enough or not received because it was not heard clearly
2	Message was not understood by receiver.
3	Conflicting messages leading to wrong perceptions of the intended meaning.
4	Distractions—divided attention and preoccupation (noise, children, music) for both sender or/and receiver.
5	Lack of interest on the part of the receiver—no interests in the sender's message; conflicting interests.
6	Cultural differences (accents, gestures, body language) between the parties—sender and receiver.
7	Subjectivity in opinion–an insistence upon one's own option while refusing to accept the opinions of others

8	Inclination on an issue; holding one's own ideas and emotions on a matter so completely that there is no room for considering another.
9	Mixed and conflicting non-verbal signals; gestures, postures, etc.
10	Prejudice and blind spots—prejudging wrongly or rightly before hearing the whole story an attitude, opinion, or feeling formed without adequate prior knowledge, thought, or reason.
11	Emotional regulation—the inability to control emotions (anger, resentments).
12	Lack of empathy—lacking the humility and compassion for mutual respect and understanding.

Roles of Spouses in Communication to Build Oneness

Here are some key critical elements in communication between the spouses, all of which must be worked on in order to sustain and strengthen a couple's oneness:

Husband's role in wholeness compassion

A husband understanding his conjugal role is an important factor that affects how he shows compassion to bring wholeness to his marriage. Given the above factors in Table 8.1, what roles must couples play in establishing healthy communication in marriages? What acts of compassionate oneness must a husband play to lead to oneness? Here are a few examples:

A husband must love and meet his wife's needs. Meeting a wife's physical, emotional, and spiritual needs is the conjugal fulfillment of the oneness in the relationship. This means that a husband must be subject to Christ and to His Lordship (Ephesians 5: 25-28, 1 Corinthians 11:3). Here some ways he can fulfill this role:

1. The first and ultimate role of a husband is to see that he particularly loves his own wife as himself (Ephesians 5:33, NKJV). Because he is not wired naturally to love, he must be particular, through careful effort and attention, to see that he submits to Christ's Lordship, and is humble and compassionate enough to lead his wife as a servant, putting her needs above his rights. The husband must recognize the need to be willing to listen and emulate the love of God.

2. The Husband is the head of the wife, but must recognize that God is the infinite head of Christ; the head of man is Christ, and the head of a woman is man (Ephesians 5:24). Christ and the Father are wholly united as one entity and in love; He expects us to also be united to each other, and enamored, as He and the Father are. Hence, the head of the wife is meant to be as loving as Christ as in being the head of the Church. Being the head also means submitting to plan of God, carrying the burden of the wife.

3. A husband is the image of the glory of God, but woman is the glory of man (1 Corinthians 11:7). Being an image of the glory of God means representing the love and beauty of God, and in all actions toward his wife. A husband must build his wife as the pride of his own image and have an honorable picture of his wife as a crown through respect for her feelings, desires, and opinions.

4. The husband must give himself to his wife, to the extent even unto death; he could forgo sleep, his comfort, for her, and must provide all sustenance—shelter and security—for her (Ephesians 5:25).

5. A husband must make his wife glorious by contributing to her outward appearance, nurturing, complimenting her, and encouraging her (Ephesians 5:27-29).

6.   A husband must think of her unity, being positive always, even in negative situations, and correcting her in love to purify and build up her character; he must declare his wife true, pure, lovely, and holy (Philippians 4:8-9).

7.   A husband must nurture the wife. God demonstrates protection and nurturing "as a hen gathers her chick under her wings" (Matthew 23: 37); he must contribute to her growth through such acts as providing home Bible study to increase knowledge and strength.

8.   A wife should frequently use questions in Table 8.2 to explore how she is effectively playing the role of a wife in the perspective of the husband.

Table 8.2. Formative questions a wife should frequently ask her husband to improve her role in building wholeness in the marriage

	Questions a wife need to ask a husband…	Reference
1	What could I do to make you feel more respected as my husband?	Ephesian 5:33
2	What submissive attributes would you like me to develop?	1 Peter 3:2-5 Ephesians 5:20
3	What could I do to be in unity with you regardless of our differences?	1 Peter 3:8-9 Galatian 3:28, Col 3.11)
4	What could I do to be more patient with you regardless of situation?	Philippians 2:3-4
5	What could I do to make you feel more honored than me?	Ephesians 5.22 Philippians 2:3-4
6	What could I do to make you feel that you are my head?	Ephesian 5:23
7	How could I be more obedient to you?	1 Peter 3:6
8	How could I be subject to you in everything?	Ephesians 5:22-24

| 9 | How could I be more comparable as a helper to you? | Genesis 2:18 |
| 10 | How could I make you more complete as a man? | Genesis 2:21-23 |

Wife's role in compassionate oneness

A wife understanding her marital role is another important factor that brings wholeness in a marriage. A wife meeting a husband's need in a loving way and fulfilling her role as a helper, comparable to him in the conjugal relationship, leads to balance, completeness, and oneness. Here are ways she can play that role, based on Ephesians 5:22-33:

Wife must respect her Husband. The first ultimate role is for a wife, in particular, to "see that she respects her husband" (Ephesians 5:33, NKJV); this means she is to make every effort toward respecting her husband. The wife must submit to her husband as unto Christ (Ephesians 5:22). Obedient in everything in the Word of God, she must behave as befitting before the Lord. This means relinquishing to her husband's will, as he yields his to the Lord. Because she is not naturally wired to submit, she must see to it, to make all effort to be a good listener to him, respecting and forsaking all acts of stubbornness.

Wife must recognize the headship of her husband (v.23). This means following his leading, honoring him, especially in the presence of the children, and yielding to his authority. Of course, husbands must know the difference between leadership and degrading control. God calls husbands to leadership and not to humiliating lordship.

Wife must be subject to her Husband (v.24). She must be willing to be under his leadership, looking up to him as the head and stronger vessel, yielding to his instructions, and trusting God for him. The wife should feel reverence for her husband. (v.33); she must not attempt to ignore her husband in any way. Submission is born of love, and a wife cannot submit to a husband she cannot respect.

Wife must take care of her womanhood. This is to build her husband's manhood and fatherhood. She is called on and given the unique responsibility of helping him fulfill God's call. For example:

1. Only the woman can carry his child, and the wife must commit to that responsibility, having a career or not;

2. A woman's physical appearance is very important to the man; she must help in reinforcing his desire to nurture and make her glorious for God and him;

3. As the couple grows older, she should not neglect her body, even as the true temple of God, that includes always presenting our bodies beautifully, as much as possible;

4. She must commit to make herself attractive sexually in their sacred marriage relationship;

5. Her body is to her husband as his is to her; she must make every possible effort not to reject her husband sexually, unless they both agree on abstinence for a period or for medical reason;

6. Her womanhood is the glue in the home and the pathway to a heart that centers on her while focusing on God; and

7. Her womanhood also provides the balanced perspective in parenting in the home.

The wife is a comparable helper for her husband. The Bible states the role of the wife very clearly. God said, "It is not good that man should be alone; I will make him a helper comparable to him" (Genesis 2:18, NKJV). God created her to be a comparable helper; that is, to share oneness and like-mindedness in the God's purpose, and for Eve (the wife) to assist Adam (the husband) fulfill the calling God has given him as the leader. When a wife provides these things for her husband, including sexual intimacy, which he cannot do for himself, he is more empowered to do those things as a husband, and he will develop a better perspective and appreciation of her as God's gift to him. He will develop the Christlikeness and purity in him. The wife should use questions in Table 8.3 to assess how her husband is effectively grading her playing the role of the wife, from the perspective of the husband.

Table 8.3. Formative questions a husband should frequently ask his wife to improve his role in building wholeness in the marriage	
Question a husband need to ask a wife	Scriptural Reference
1 What could I do to be more compassionate toward you?	1 Peter 3:8-9;
2 What could I do to make you feel more loved?	1 Cor.13:4-8
3 What could I do to make you feel more honored and glorious?	Eph. 5:27; 1 Peter 3:7; Phil. 2:2-3
4 How could we live and relate with more understanding and be closer to each other?	1 Peter 3:5-7; Ephesians 5:21
5 In what ways am I not Christ-like in our relationship?	1 Peter 2:21-23
6 What could I do to make you feel more secure in our relationship?	SOS: 2:16, 7:10; Heb 13:4
7 What attribute would you like to be reflected in our relationship?	Gal. 5:22; 1 Tim 6:11
8 How can I better communicate with you and empathize with your feelings?	1 Cor. 13:4-8
9 What mutual goal would you like to see us accomplish?	Gen. 2:18
10 In what ways have I not been fulfilling my role as a husband in our marriage?	1 Peter 3:3-7; Eph. 5:25-33
11 What could I do to nurture you to be the best you can be in God and our relationship?	Eph. 5:29

Spend energy on making communication healthy

Communication in marriage has been shown by research to be a key factor for a healthy marital relationship. A couple must spend energy on making their communication strong. This means making effort to understand the content of the words spoken, and feelings and spiritual concerns as expressed in the spoken and unspoken words so that each party in the communication feels understood or listened to by the other. It means being very tactful in how you say words to your spouse. It means being authentic enough to use wholesome words toward your spouse. I have always wondered why we are more likely to be tactful in the office and the public, but too quick to be loose with our words to our spouses; we could easily control our anger with others, but easily be provoked to anger with the slightest incitement with our spouses. God commanded husbands to nurture and build their wives up, and that charity that is extended to others outside must begin at home—with our spouses.

Sexual Communication between Spouses

Understanding that sexual relationship is part of the total package in a relationship is too broad a topic to be covered in this book; only some highlights will be shared with respect to wholeness compassion. However, as a way of confession and full disclosure, I am a strong believer that sex in marriage, according to the Word of God, has a very important function in the sanctity and wholeness of the marriage. Instead of a husband and wife shying away from conjugal roles in that respect, they need to discover what pleases one another and what they enjoy, and should be able to share freely with each other. All couples are uniquely different and no standard fits all. Nevertheless, learning what constitutes a good experience from your spouse, and realizing that a series of steps exists between the first physical touch and the most passionate embrace are some of the frequent recommendations.

It is critically essential in any healthy marriage for spouses to work consistently in improving their communication skills, by understanding the weak areas in their communication. Table 8.4 below is a 10-point communication check to assess communication between spouses. Agreeing on what those steps should be in your marriage is the beginning of achieving wholeness in the marriage and a wholesome sexual encounter.

Table 8.4. 10-Point Communication Check in Marriage:
Understanding the Health of your Communication

On a scale of 0 (Absolutely No) to 10 (Absolutely Yes), indicate for both you (Me) and your spouse (Him/Her) the level (0-10) to which you or him/her measure Yes or No in these questions. Insert a number for both you (Me) and Him / Her			
Item	Communication Check	Me	Him /Her
Ex	Controlling anger is a common attitude of—	7	9
1	In resolving our conflicts, an objective look at contribution to the conflict is taken by——		
2	Rules in our home for sustaining lasting peace are understood by ——		
3	Thinking before speaking or acting is an attitude of——		
4	Attacking the problem, not the person, is a common action of——		
5	Avoiding generalizations is a strength for——		
6	Listening carefully to understand us better is a quality in——		
7	Using positive words to help family members build confidence is common in——		

8	I know all the larger and significant financial involvements by——		
9	I know situations that make love-making the best experience for ——		
10	I understand and am willing to deal with factors that may hinder sexual satisfaction for——		
	Total Scores		
	Average Score		
Average Score (Him+ Her)/2: >90 Healthy Communications, 80<Score<90 Good but not best; work on area of score < 90 70<Score <80, Need more work; , work on area of score < 90 60<Score < 70, Fair, Need help, work on all key areas Score < 60 Definitely Need help; work on all areas			

Ways to improve sexual communication

One problem some spouses experience in sexual communication is the discomfort in discussing or sharing their sexual likes and dislikes. To some, especially older women, some for cultural backgrounds, the word "sex" is a taboo, with so much restrictions in touching and fore play that those actions are forbidden. Some go to the extent of calling their spouses perverts because they express different sexual desires and wrongly use the scriptures to make sex almost unholy. The result is that to the opposite person, marriage becomes an enduring, punishing servitude rather than an enjoyable covenant union. Below are some ways to improve sexual communication between spouses that aspire for enjoyable covenant union:

Celebrate your sexual differences

Celebrate your sexual differences to build your wholeness. Your differences were created in you for a unique and holy purpose.

Celebrate your differences as a way of building your wholeness in obedience to God's command for the following reasons:

It is God's purpose in your unity. God's purpose was clear in the Scriptures, as the Bible said, "In the image of God He created him; male and female he created them" (Genesis 1:27, NKJV). God's image is reflected in the male and female, and the way they must interrelate as one is the way the Trinity interrelates. That unity is so important to Jesus that He prays to God for all believers, especially husband and wife. He said, "And the glory which You gave Me I have given them, that they may be one just as We are one: I in them, and You in Me; that they may be made perfect in one" (John 17: 20-23, NJKV). God reveals Himself in the value He places on the intimate loving relationship. God created sexuality to be celebrated, and the husband and wife need to understand their gender differences by comprehending the distinctive relational qualities of the person of God.

It is a command to complete your wholeness in one flesh. He created the wife as a helper comparable to him (Genesis 2:18) and to make the man complete. The primary role of the wife is to make him totally perfect. The mating relationship is for their enjoyment of that oneness; making love and creating the one-flesh union is a mysterious and dynamic process as part of the command to "be joined to his wife, and the two shall become one flesh" (Ephesians 5:31). We are to celebrate it, and not be ashamed of this process! After all, at the beginning, "they were both naked, the man and his wife, and were not ashamed" (Genesis 2:25, NKJV).

In God, male and females are different in their creative makeups, but equal in responsibility to God and each other "as there is neither male nor female; for you are all one in Christ Jesus" (Galatians 3:28) and "Christ is all and in all" (Colossians 3:11).

It is a spiritual and emotional union. Sexual union has both a spiritual and an emotional dimension to it. Your body is the "temple of the Holy Spirit, who is in you" and, because you are not of your own but God's, you must yield to God in all things to keep your purity before Him (1 Corinthians 6: 13, 16, 19). The union between husband and wife in any form is a communion that is molded after Christ's relationship with the Church (Ephesians 5:32), and can be celebrated for giving joy, excitement, trust, commitment, nurturing, and mutual fulfillment in playful companionship.

It is a celebration of your ever flowing 'well of water'. Although most of us are uneasy about the subject of sex, the Bible portrays marital love-making as an erotic celebration (From Eros=Sexual Love) of passion, attraction, fusion, and bonding involving fantasy, imagery anticipation, playfulness, emotion, etc. We read expressive feelings like "Let him kiss me with the kisses of his mouth—for your love is better than wine" (SOS 1:2) and others (SOS 2:16, 4:5, 13, 15-16, 8; 12). King David, in writing about the immoral woman outside of marriage, in advising his son from his personal experience, likened conjugal love-making with your wife to "drinking water from your own cistern, and running water from your own well" (Proverbs 5:17). Husbands are to be only for their wives, and not for any other, which he clearly referred to as "strangers with you." Husbands are to bless their wives and rejoice with them forever. The Bible declares, "As a loving deer and a graceful doe, Let her breasts satisfy you at all times And always be enraptured with her love" (Proverbs 5: 15-19). This means that a marital sex life is like a stream of flowing water with an ever-changing quality with which to rejoice, satisfy, and celebrate.

In celebrating your sexuality, we can also see, through the Scriptures, three possible keys to enjoying sex in marriage:

1. *The Right Attitude towards Sex.* How you see sex influences how much you will enjoy it. The right attitude for sex between spouses can be defined as any behavior, tendency, affective signal, endearment, or action, etc., that excites positive emotion or desire to want to make love. The act of love-making is so driven by sentiments that a small negative

attitude could affect the emotional response and desire for sex. On the principle of marriage and the associated attitude of the husband and wife in marriage, Apostle Paul writes:

> "Let the husband render to his wife the affection due to her, and likewise, also the wife to her husband. The wife does not have authority over her own body, but the husband does. And likewise, the husband does not have authority over his own body, but the wife does. Do not deprive one another except with consent for a time, that you may give yourselves to fasting and prayer; and come together again so that Satan does not tempt you because of your lack of self-control" (1 Corinthians 7:3-5, NJKV).

This scripture clearly describes key elements of the right attitude the spouses should work on:

First, both husband and wife should submit to selflessly rendering to each other and celebrating what is already theirs. Putting your spouse's needs ahead of yours to nurture him/her is a selfless act that allows you to focus on and celebrating your sexual feelings within a godly balance.

Second, each spouse has authority over the other's body as an expression of their oneness. The authority of one over the other's body must be nurtured and freely allowed, and not rejected or resisted. However, that requires understanding of each other and a sensitivity to what makes each more fulfilled. All actions must be mutually enjoyable, or it is not wholesome. That is why the act of love-making ceases to be love-making when it is forced by one on the other or when a spouse has to beg for what God has already commanded to be freely given, and received, from each other.

Third, each spouse is not to deprive the other of sexual intimacy, except for in specific and agreed upon situations for fasting and prayer, and for an agreed upon period. The Apostle Paul makes it clear here that they must agree for the period of spiritual waiting. The attitude of one waking up to announce, "I am going into fasting," for some 3 or 7 days, even 100 days of fasting without both agreeing and preparing each other for such a period of absence from marital sex, could be a devil's pathway to destroy the oneness. It is contrary to the command in the Scriptures. Very often, the announcement is not given to be agreed to, but to inform the other, whether he/she likes it or not. God is first in our lives, but this same God makes it clear that our home is our first responsibility because it is the devil's first place to steal, kill, and destroy in his plan to stop the work of God.

Fourth, spouses must come together again after the period of waiting so that Satan does not tempt them because of the lack of self-control. The plan to take out some time for fasting and prayer must include a defined period or length of time, depending on how long each person can go in the waiting. For several reasons, including health reasons, what is acceptable for one couple may not be good for another. So, each couple should work toward understanding their limitations. Apostle Paul recognizes the devices of Satan and warns that a couple must plan toward coming together so as not to give Satan any open door due to a lack of self-control. The period must be mutually and voluntarily agreed to, and one should not attempt to force the waiting on the other. There is wholeness when both willingly agree to the waiting. However, in some cases, it is better for a spouse led toward fasting to go into it alone, rather than force the other to join unwillingly.

Fifth, couples must submit freely and selflessly. A critical dimension of shared love between spouses is the ability to submit unreservedly and selflessly to each other, in all things as fitting in the Lord. This, "as fitting in the Lord," applies to actions that are in alignment to God's ways and expressively communicated or implied in the Scriptures. Any attempt to make up, or create rules or reasons not to submit to each other in the areas of conjugal sex, is not what God intended in a marital relationship, and obviously will not bring any glory to Him or wholeness in the marriage.

And finally, sex should not be a reward or weapon, but should be honorable and delightful. God is glorified when couples do what He purposed in His creation of them. This requires fleeing all forms of sexual immorality, which is clearly stated as sin against one's own body. And since your body is not your personal property, but God's, and is "the temple of the Holy Spirit *who is* in you," a sin against the body defiles the wholeness and unity God intended for the body (1 Corinthians 6:18-20). The consequences are that it weakens your ability to glorify God in your body and in your spirit, both as individuals and as couples. The consequence of such defilement is very severe in God's own plan (1 Corinthians 3:17, NKJV). The body of a husband is just for his spouse and not for any stranger, and he is only to bless and rejoice with his wife, with his body, in all issues of sexual relationship (Proverbs 5:17-18).

Sex is most pleasurable when our attitudes are the same as God intended them to be, with body, soul, and spirit. Spouses, especially husbands, should never criticize their mate's physical body in such a way as to put her down. Each partner should take care of his or her body with positive and affective encouragement from the other. Negative criticism creates an atmosphere that is not conducive for love-making. Statements like, "You are too fat"; "when will you reduce this weight," etc., are positive emotion killers for sexual desires and must be avoided.

We read several examples of the right attitude in the Songs of Solomon (SOS). A husband makes his wife eager to make love through his compliments and his honor to her. He intentionally and specifically praises her loveliness and beautiful parts— her attractive eyes, her hair like the flock of goat; her washed and complete teeth like a flock of sheep, her temple like a piece of pomegranate, and together: "Beautiful as Tirzah, Lovely as Jerusalem, Awesome as *an army* with banners!"

(SOS 6: 4-7). These are powerful affective words carefully extended to nurture and build up. Can you imagine the impact of what such words could have on your wife for an evening of romantic atmosphere?

2. The Conducive Atmosphere: Marital sexual enjoyment needs a romantic conducive atmosphere, usually referred to as a romantic atmosphere. A sensual atmosphere is defined by the right environment, opportunity, privacy, loving signal, etc., which together contributes to positive emotional response and excitation toward wanting to make love. We have often heard the statement that a "Man is a microwave while a woman is a crockpot." This means that a man must understand that he must prepare and marinate his wife's emotions to allow her to be 'well done" before attempting the next step. Of course, we all know that a crockpot cooks food slowly, and such food usually tastes better than what is cooked quickly in a microwave oven. The husband can help in this area by meditating on what his wife needs for her womanhood (1 Peter 3:7) and the wife must learn how to accept her purposeful role to fulfill her husband's manhood. Each must look out not only for his or her own interests, but first for the interests of the other (Philippians 2:4).

A romantic atmosphere is more important to her than to him. The bride in the Songs of Solomon (SOS 2:4-7) expressed to the Daughters of Jerusalem her cherished atmosphere of love: "He brought me to the banqueting house, And his banner over me was love… His left hand is under my head, And his right hand embraces me."

Love language is an important catalyst to excite a romantic atmosphere. Do you know your love language and that of your spouse? If not, you need to find out! Gary Chapman, in his book, *The Five Love Languages* (Chapman, 2015) described the different love languages in a conjugal relationship as: Words of Affirmation, Acts of Service, Physical Touch, Quality Time, and Gifts. He argues that **you can** figure out your primary language by finding out in your upbringing what made you feel the most loved as a child (that is how you probably want to be treated now), understanding your basic instincts when want to show someone you care (that is what you probably want), and finding out what others in the past failed to do that hurt you most (you do not want those to be repeated). Those findings will point you to your mostly likely love language. Smalley and Trent (1991) in their book, *The Language of Love* also showed how emotional words can improve communication, understanding, and intimacy in conjugal relationships.

We also see, from Biblical examples, that affectionate touching in special places is important in conjugal language in a relationship.

David, in warning his son to keep his love to the wife of his youth, recognized this fact. He said, "As a loving deer and a graceful doe, Let her breasts satisfy you at all times; And always be enraptured with her love" (Proverb 5:19). Gentle touches go a long way to excite the emotions of the two people who love each other. The bride in SOS, in response to her excitement, equally recognized that her breasts could be the center of his word. She said, "I am a wall, And my breasts like towers; Then I became in his eyes as one who found peace (SOS: 8:10). In this context, we must be careful because the same element that is great to you as a love language may be less desirable to her. It may be held by other areas, other than words of affirmation or touching. For example, my wife's love language is my spending quality time with her while my language is physical touch. The rushed physical touch, unless at her own timing, is a serious turn-off for her. Even when she is ready, there are only a few places allowed! However, I have to understand her well because, when she wants to spend time bonding, my hand wants to be busy; her quality time can become uneasy for me and not fulfilling, but I choose to have the patience to wait. Thus, in such a fashion, a husband must understand his wife's primary love language and make a maximum use of it, or avoid those areas that kill your spouse's love language. It is highly recommended, and encouraged by Chapman (2015) and Smalley and Trent (1991), that spouses need to selflessly and intentionally work on accommodating each other's differences and love language for positive emotional and sexual fulfillment.

Another aspect of a romantic atmosphere is the fact that most men are visual, and get turned on by sight of the nakedness of their wife. Fieldham (2004) in *For Women Only*, showed the following statistics:

- 98% of married men are visual; the survey agrees that they struggle with recollection of images of other women.
- 83% of these men say appearance is important, and they want to see their wife make an effort to take care of herself.
- 74% of married men need more respect; men would feel unloved and then inadequate when disrespected.
- 97% of married men surveyed need more sex. To the wife, according to Shaunti and Jeff Fieldham (2006) in *For Men Only*, "your sexual desire of your husband profoundly affects his sense of well-being and confidence in every part of his life" (Fieldham & Fieldham, 2006)

Beyond research, the Scripture supports the findings above and shows the power of the visual image of a beautiful spouse to a husband. The Songs of Solomon (SOS) reads, "You have ravished my heart, My sister, my spouse; You have ravished my heart. With one look of your eyes" (SOS 4:9, NKJV). These statements show the power of the sight of a beautiful spouse to a husband—it goes to the heart and soul of his manhood. It is not surprising then that they were created to complete each other.

Similarly, the sense of his smell of her could also be a center of his attraction and desire: "How much better than wine is your love, and the scent of your perfumes... than all spices! And the fragrance of your garments is like the fragrance of Lebanon" (SOS 4:10-11, NKJV). While the sight and smell will create a romantically conducive atmosphere, the husband's readiness to notice and complement his spouse adds to her sense of emotional security. The endearments and compliments communicate love and extend the affection that itself yields positive emotions and desires for love-making.

As it has been generally said, most women need to feel safe to make love, while most men need to make love to be secure. The wives need more privacy and some monetary and emotional security. Men have the tendency to think that security means financial security, and so they work long hours in order to provide for the family. In that situation, the wife will end up not seeing the husband come home, in time, as a husband not caring enough. In their book, *For Men Only*, Shaunti and Jeff Fieldham (2006) revealed that, to most women, "emotional security" is much more important than financial security. According to these authors, women, in fact, see emotional security "as a sense that the husband will always be there for them; and closeness to them means her husband is her best friend." (Fieldham, 2004). Be considerate of these facts if you have to work many long hours; a consistent call to your spouse by phone call, Skype, text messages, or email could help to assure her of your closeness. There needs to be balance, consideration, and understanding of what really fulfills her oneness. Overall, for most women, affection is the ultimate atmosphere, and sex is the event to celebrate that atmosphere.

3. The Right Adjustment and Regulation. The attitude and atmosphere could be great, but unless the couple can make the right adjustments in themselves and to each other, sexual intimacy will not be fulfilled. Adjusting to each other means that they should not hold their bodies from each other for any reason, unless they agree for a spiritual or medical reason. It means regulating your emotions and attitude to balance that of your spouse, especially in those times she is not in the mood, or those times he is highly in the mood. Effective sexual adjustments require your understanding of the real factors that hinder your sexual satisfaction, and your understanding that a sexual relationship is part of the total relationship. To summarize this, I will posit that:

Mutually understanding sexualities + communicating feelings + understanding and accommodating differences

= Sexual Satisfaction

Mutuality here means walking along with each other, where each spouse focuses on satisfying the other. Adjusting to each other will also require the spouses' mutual determination to make their home a haven. A home is the place where family members can feel safe, accepted, and grow in the Lord. Since all are different, though one entity, for a home to be a haven, husband and wife must work together to adjust to each other's dispositions; they must self-regulate their emotions to create a climate of peace in the home. This is accomplished by learning to resolve differences quickly and privately, looking for opportunities to express appreciation and love to each family member, and establishing peaceable rules: the Do's and Don'ts. Some rules I have used with my spouse in the past have included the following: we must not go to bed angry; we must let each other know when we are offended; we must not wait to be reminded to apologize for offenses; we must not refer to past forgiven or resolved offenses; we must not keep a "big offense" unresolved; and we must not vacate the marriage bed, unless in cases where a spouse had to travel or had medical reason to sleep separately, etc.

Celebrate the strengths in your differences.

There is God's purpose in the differences He created in the sexes, and those differences are designed to bring the sexes closer and more intimately connected with each other; there is the need to focus on building strength out of these differences, to improve all aspects of marital communication. Here are some ways:

Create a sense of unity in practice and actions. There is a unity that manifests when couples see their differences as strengths; this creates an amazing intergenerational strength, healthy functionality among their children, broadened vision, and a singleness of purpose for the family. God saw strength as the people came together as one, and with that strength, they could accomplish more than they could have without unity. "And the LORD said, "Indeed the people are one, and they all have one language, and this is what they begin to do; now nothing that they propose to do will be withheld from them" (Genesis 11:6). Because this unity was for the wrong reason to disobey God, He scattered and disunited them.

A sense of unity can also be seen in the life of the early apostles. The Scripture says that "the multitude of those who believed were of one heart and one soul; neither did anyone say that any of the things he possessed was his own, but they had all things in common" (Acts 4:32, NJKV). The gospel describes the unity of attitude and goal in the early Christians, and that unity is reflected and expressed in their group worship activities. The disciples were "all" with "one accord", continuing steadfastly in prayer and worship (Acts 1:14); they all had unity of purpose and attitude as demonstrated by the people being together for worship (Acts 2:1, 46). When challenges arose, such as in times of persecution, the church met (Acts 4: 23) and raised their voice to God "with one accord", demonstrating unity and strength (Acts 4:24). These people were all like-minded and desired to be in cooperation to accomplish a purpose that was most important to them—serving God by defending and spreading the gospel message. Those who did not share in that attitude of oneness, such as Ananias and Sapphira, were disciplined (Acts 5:11, 12). This attitude of the early Christians is what is needed in Christian homes today—the need to see the importance of the wholeness of the family; husband and wife must be so concerned about the unity that holds the family system as a whole, in that they see the absolute need to be together as God intended it to be.

When there is unity, the isolation of any element of the family is reduced, and the acts of compassion increase as each person sees him or her in the other. The attitude becomes that of 'if you hurt, I also hurt." Thus, the reduction in isolation builds confidence and happiness.

Create room for satisfaction in your marital intimacy. Satisfied matrimonial intimacy builds personal strengths in each other's life issues. Show me a husband or wife that leaves his or her home in the morning with a fulfilled sense of marital intimacy, and I will show you a husband or wife with a sense of wholeness, well-being, and a positive attitude at work. For the man, he thinks better and is more patient with people. He cannot wait to return home happy and ready for his wife. The same is true for the wife. She finds complete fulfillment to know that her husband is satisfied. She is more emotionally ready for the days, whether at home or at work. This stability in both individuals is additionally sustained with a better understanding and knowledge of each other. An enhanced understanding also allows them to listen patiently to each other; plus, they grow together in wisdom, even with different perspectives that will further strengthen the relationship.

The husband's manhood must build up his wife's. In the same sense that his manhood builds his wife, a wife's womanhood energizes her husband. His strengthened manhood, and sense of service to the family to lead her, gains a good perspective and a deep appreciation of her as God's gift, especially in those things he cannot do for himself, like love-making, bearing children, and yes, perhaps even good cooking. His understanding of his manhood in God's purpose helps him to better develop the Christ-likeness in him and understand her womanhood as the appropriate glue and pathway to the wholeness in the home. It also enables him to work towards a balanced perspective in parenting. The ability to communicate with understanding and sensitivity can be maximized by allowing room to everyone to express their true feelings; they are free to say what they truly think and feel, not what they think the leader or others want to hear. It also allows them to be authentic, where the actions they exhibit toward each other are in congruence with their genuine values of each other and their inner feelings.

Be positive and kind. Husband and wife must be positive and kind toward each other by learning to express their positive affective feelings without casting blame. They must always acknowledge, validate, or empathize with each other's feelings. To be positive and kind, there is the absolute need to avoid generalizations. Comments that are too broad can create barriers. When you speak or offer advice, be specific to the details of the moment and the circumstances, without accusation of any kind, especially when you know the truth. Unnecessary accusation and generalizations create an unhealthy defensive attitude.

Other ways to improve communication between the sexes include:

- Patience, understanding, and a willingness to share (feelings, preferences, and responses)
- Frequent monitoring and acknowledgement of progress
- Willingness to teach or learn from each other
- Willingness to adopt to changes in the life cycle
- Understanding the real factors that hinder your sexual satisfaction

I will conclude this section with some caution and say with high degree of confidence and experience that a meaningful sex life in marriage is a command in God's eyes worth sacrificing for to obey; it is an assured pathway for healthy faithful marriage and lack of it can also be vice for its destruction. Any violation in God's command for meaningful sex life can take your marriage farther away from you and God than you are able to make up for, and can open devil's door wider than you want to open. So, spouses must be careful, as your attitude toward sex may as well be the weapon for the destruction of the marriage, sometimes even the family unity.

CHAPTER 9

MARITAL CONFLICT RESOLUTIONS

Conflict can be defined as an intense disagreement between two or more people, usually caused by differences in views or perspectives. It is a battle or fight for one's opinion to be accepted instead of another person's view; it is disagreeing to agree on a view or perspective. Do you have any major unresolved conflicts in your marriage right now? How many of those are due to your fault? How many are due to the natural differences between you and your spouse? What are you going to do about them? In this chapter, we will explore ways we can resolve those conflicts in the context of wholeness and unity in marriage.

Major Sources of Disunity and Conflicts

But where do conflicts really come from? The Scripture said, "What causes fights and quarrels among you? Don't they come from your desires that battle within you? You want something but don't get it. You kill and covet, but you cannot have what you want....... You quarrel and fight" (James 4:1-4, NIV). Conflicts come from the different desires that battle in your heart; they are the direct results of disagreements due to differences and self-centeredness.

Table 9.1 lists some common sources of conflicts that cause disunity, and sometimes break up marriages

Table 9.1. Sources of Conflict and Killers of oneness in the marital Relationships		
Ranking	Major Sources of Conflicts	Moderate or Major source
1	Anger/Unresolved Conflict	58%
2	Misplaced Priorities	44%
3	Romance/Intimacy/Sex	43%
4	Communication Style	43
5	Criticism/Unmet expectation	33%
6	Finances/Debt	33%
7	Unrealistic Expectations	32%
8	Busyness/Stress from Job	31%
9	Submissiveness	28%
10	Love & Care	28%
11	Children/Parenting Issues	23%
12	Self-centeredness/Controlling	23%
13	In-laws/Extended Family	18%
14	Health Issues	17%
15	Initiative/Boredom	14%
16	Pettiness/Complaining	13%
17	Customs & Traditions	9%
18	Physical/Verbal Abuse	9%
19	Infidelity/Emotional Affairs	6%

The starting point of any resolution is to identify the real cause of the specific conflict. This requires all parties to commit to finding the solution, and may entail some counseling and consultation with experts. However, from experience I can say, no expert can help unless the couples are serious about not only finding and agreeing on the problem or conflict but total commitment to solving or resolving it. Often times, they will appear to have listened to good counsel, only to go back to the old views. An unscientific survey of 67 Christians, of married men and women attending one of my family enrichment seminars on conflict resolution, reveals some interesting results. There were few spouses who attended without their other half. Participants were given a comprehensive pre-assessment questionnaire of 19 items, and were asked to rank them based only on their direct experiences and response, as having none, little, moderate, or major relevance to what had contributed as a source of conflict in their marriages. Respondents who selected none, and minor contribution, make up the difference of 100%. Though infidelity has been shown to be the outstanding source of divorce in American marriages, couples in this survey ranked infidelity the least when considered as a moderate or major source of conflict. This is probably because these couples were all in their first marriages and were asked to rank these items based only on their experiences; they may have had little or no experience in the areas of infidelity and emotional affairs in their marriages.

Managing Major Sources of Conflicts

Managing the identified conflicts caused by the differences requires intentional other-centered actions for possible solutions. From Paul's exhortation in Colossians 3:12-19, NIV:

"As God's chosen people, holy and dearly loved, clothe yourselves with compassion, kindness, humility, gentleness and patience. [13]Bear with each other and forgive one another if any of you has a grievance against

someone. Forgive as the LORD forgave you. ¹⁴And over all these virtues put on love, which binds them all together in perfect unity. ¹⁵Let the peace of Christ rule in your hearts, since as members of one body you were called to peace. And be thankful. ¹⁶Let the message of Christ dwell among you richly as you teach and admonish one another with all wisdom through psalms, hymns, and songs from the Spirit, singing to God with gratitude in your hearts. ¹⁷And whatever you do, whether in word or deed, do it all in the name of the LORD Jesus, giving thanks to God the Father through him. ¹⁸Wives, submit yourselves to your husbands, as is fitting in the LORD. ¹⁹Husbands, love your wives and do not be harsh with them."

The following key actions can be identified as strategies to guide achieving any resolution:

Focus more on your behavioral changes. Our behavioral changes start with a focus on putting bowels of mercies, kindness, and humbleness of mind, meekness, and longsuffering patience (v.12), all positive attitudes to others. Each spouse must concentrate on personal behavior changes and allow their spouse to do the same. After you have made the behavioral changes mutually agreed upon, evaluate their effects on your relationship (Ephesians 4:31). Get the log out of your own eye first (Matthew 7:5); that is, examine, acknowledge, and work on your behavior that may be contributing to the conflict. Overlook minor offenses and talk over "big" offenses.

Sources of Conflict

Figure 9.1 Source of Conflict Ranked in Order of Contribution to Discontent

Forbear with and forgive one another (v.13). If any man has a quarrel against any, we must manifest patience to tolerate each other's differences. This patience makes it easier to surrender our rights to be able to forgive. We are to forbear and forgive any offense resulting from a quarrel as an act of love to God. Apostle Paul writes, "Get rid of all bitterness, rage and anger, brawling and slander, along with every form of malice. Be kind and compassionate to one another, forgiving each other, just as in Christ, God forgave you" (Ephesians 4:31-32). Forgiving one another is an important act of compassion that frees you to begin more wholesome methods of resolving conflict.

Focus on the perfect love of God above all things. Submit to nurturing each other above all things as bonds of perfection (v.14). Perfect love bears all things and counts no wrong of the other (1 Corinthians 13:4-8). Work together to build each other's strengths in the areas of weakness in order to build stability (Ephesians 5:21-31).

Focus on achieving peace together as one body. Let the peace of God rule in your hearts, to which also you are called in one body (v, 15). Each couple must earnestly pursue peace and root out all bitterness as a positive non-choice or option of decision (Hebrews 12:14-15). A 'no-choice' option is the only option agreed to and acted on by the couples in any situation. Consider a case where, the couple wants the husband to come home from work before children can go to bed. The couple can, for instance, institute rules upon mutual consent, to the extent that these rules absolutely cannot be broken, such as that the husband must come home from work before the children will go to bed. Control your feelings to create a climate of peace between you (Proverb 25:24).

Focus on understanding God's purpose in your relationship. Let the word of Christ dwell in you richly in all wisdom (v.16a); this calls for each couple to seek God in order to be filled with the knowledge of wisdom of God's will in their relationship (Colossians 1:9-11).

Correct each other firmly but with love and gentleness. Paul said to admonish one another in psalms and hymns and spiritual songs, singing with grace in your hearts to the Lord (v.16b), and to do all things by the name of the Lord Jesus, giving thanks to God and the Father by him (v. 17).

Focus on submitting and making your husband feel respected. A wife is commanded to submit unto her own husband (v.18a). A wife yielding to her husband is a reflection of love and respect. Studies have shown that 74% of men need esteem and would prefer being respected to being loved. Both spouses need to work together to build emotional stability out of mutual love and submission (Acts 4: 31-34).

Focus on loving and making your wife feel cherished. As for the wives, husbands are commanded to love their wives, and be not bitter against them (v.18b). This means that they must seek and pursue genuine reconciliation (Matthew 5:23-24).

Managing Conflicts due to Financial Issues

When the conflict involves finances, the beginning step is for each spouse to identify his or her own relationship with money in relation to the value in the marital relationship. What money means to you, or your love for money, can easily influence how you handle the money-reflected conflict. Your love for money or your work to make money must never take priority over your relationships in the family. Honoring each other's needs can help you respectfully negotiate your financial decisions.

Learn from each other and be involved jointly in managing your finances as one. The important rule is to understand that whatever you have in the form of money belongs to God, and you are only a steward, and must account for what you do or did not do. In managing the funds, learn to list your priorities together, and identify and agree to what is most valuable to the family as one. That means that you must identify the top priorities you share and what this means to your budget. It also requires you to be transparent on all issues of finance. Believe me, sooner or later, any secret will be found out.

Managing your finances to avoid conflicts also involves learning to negotiate your wants as relative to your needs, bearing in mind that when resources are limited, your needs must take precedence over your wants. On the issues of finance, some wives have a greater tendency to prioritize wants than husband do. Remember that different perspectives can strengthen your relationship toward the use of money. You must openly discuss challenges and desires, but be willing to compromise to agree. Be truthful and keep problems private (Proverbs - 12:22). The Lord detests lying lips, but he delights in men who are truthful. So put away all falsehood and "tell your neighbor the truth" because we belong to each other (Ephesians - 4:25, 29).

Managing Conflicts due to the Differences

Husband and wife are created to be different, and yet commanded to be one. Due to those differences, disagreements and conflicts are expected to be a part of the process of marriage, or any relationships between two people. Instead of a couple choosing to coexist with unresolved conflicts (choosing to endure and live with the conflicts), run away from the issue causing the conflict, or simply use power and control to force the other person into unwilling submission, God expects a wholesome marriage that ensures stability of the family, and demands couples to continue working on through these phases to resolve their conflicts.

A Case Study of Managing Conflict

In my Marriage Enrichment Seminar referred to earlier, and the 67 married men and women who attended, mostly in couples, a session was included on how to correct our attitudes in order to successfully manage the identified conflict. The starting point of managing conflicts due to the differences between the sexes is to understand what bothers a spouse about their other. Table 8.2 shows the result of survey of 67 Christian couples to assess their likely methods for resolving conflicts. In addition to identifying major conflicts in the marriages, each participant in the survey (Table 9.2) was asked the following three key questions, designed based on the article, " 'Fighting Fair' in Marriage" by Herbert G. Lingren (2013), Extension Family Life Specialist.

Question #1: Identify the most likely tactics to get what you want when resolving conflicts.

Figure 9.2 shows that the least probable tactics these couples use when resolving conflicts are irrational tactics (71%), as compared to impassioned withdrawal (67%), followed by each spouse quitting on cooperation with the other completely (42%). More women (35%) than men (32%) identified emotional withdrawal as a likely tactic, either from them or from the husbands.

Question #2: If you or your spouse withdraw and create emotional distance from each other, which of these best describes your most likely tactics in living with the other?

- Not talking to each other
- Walking out in anger and slamming the door; "when you come to your senses we will talk"
- Giving in, but still with anger inside
- Withholding love and affection, and other positive strokes from each other
- None

On question 2, Figure 9.3 confirms the most likely reactions for most couples (66%) when attempts to resolve the conflict fails, in that they withdraw and create emotional distance from each other, allowing for them to not to talk to each other. It is interesting that men and women have equal (33%) reaction on this item. However, the men (25%) are more likely than women (18%) to withhold themselves and withdraw emotionally. Because she by her nature is a more emotional than her husband, the wife will likely get more hurt from the husband withdrawing himself.

Table 9.2. Assessing likely Tactics for Conflict Resolution
Each was asked to answer Yes/NO to these Questions.

	Assessment Questions	YES/NO
Tactics to get what one wants		
Irrational tactics	Do you or your spouse use extreme or_irrational tactics to gain your point?	
Store up grudges	Do you or your spouse store up grudges and use them to get revenge at a later time?	
Quit cooperating	Do you or your spouse quit cooperating if you do not get what you want?	
'Right Now' expectation	Do you or your spouse continuously exhibit a 'Right Now Expectation' to do things the "right way"?	
Emotional withdrawal	When attempts to resolve conflict appear to have failed, do you or your spouse create emotional withdrawal and distance from each other?	

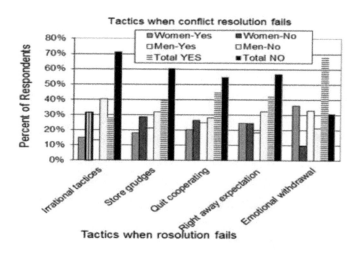

Figure 9.2: The Most likely Tactics Used to Get What You Want when Resolving Conflicts.

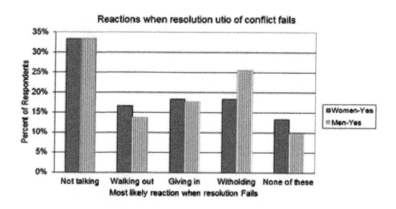

Figure 9.3: The Most Likely Tactics Used in Living with Another During Periods when Resolution Fails

Question #3: Lastly, the respondents were asked to identify their most likely constructive method of resolving their disagreements. Questions were:

a. Identify conflict & what you want with respect and understanding
b. Treat the disagreement as a choice point for growth, rather than an opportunity for a power struggle
c. Get the log out of your own eye first
d. Overlook minor offenses and talk about big offenses
e. Cooperatively negotiate & commit to seek and pursue reconciliation
f. None of the above
g. All the above

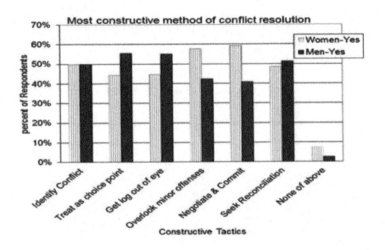

Figure 9.4: Most Likely Constructive Method of Resolving their Disagreements.

In response to question 3, Figure 9.4 shows that the most likely tactic for men (69% of men) and women (40% of women) is to negotiate and commit to behavior change, seconded by treating the conflict as an action or choice they must take.

Model of Resolving Conflicts in Marriage

There are several methods of resolving conflicts. I will discuss key highlights on the strategies as given in question 3 above, and others that I have seen work in the past: identify conflict, treat it as a choice point, get the log out of your own eye first, overlook minor offenses, cooperatively negotiate, and commit to pursuing reconciliation.

Get the log out of your own eye first.

A log is a type of blind spot that impedes correct evaluation of a situation (Matthew 7:5). There are two kinds of "logs":

1.   Critical, negative, or overly sensitive attitude that leads to unnecessary conflict. You get rid of this log by spending some time meditating on the good of your spouse and adopting the kind of attitude that avoids conflict (Philippians 4:8-9).

2.   Hurtful words and actions are the second log. This type of log is removed by taking an objective look at yourself, facing up to your contribution to a conflict, identifying ways that you have wronged the other, and admitting your misdeeds honestly and thoroughly.

Identify and define the specific Conflict.

There may be so many possible causes of a particular conflict, but one or two may be the main issue, themselves leading to others. The issue needs to be identified as the primary cause of the conflict. Your goal is to find out, together, what the major issue is. It may be too presumptuous to guess why the other is upset. You must define the specific reason, and with both of you involved in the process. This means that couples must work together to identify the actual issue, and why and how this issue is causing a conflict. Oftentimes, understanding the real issue creates an opportunity to comprehend each other. This is because what one person may see as a serious problem might not be so major for the other, and that in itself causes conflict. Each person must be ready to own up to the behaviors the other person sees as contributing to the conflict. Until both of you identify that you have a problem and are willing to accept responsibility or contribution to it, you are not prepared for a solution or resolution.

Earlier in my marriage, my wife and I noticed that sometimes we would be saying the same thing, but arguing or disagreeing because one person had a way of exaggerating the situation, such that the main point was missed. Alternatively, she would be speaking, but I was not paying full attention. We turned those moments into opportunities to learn how to listen patiently and focus on the real issue. Here is a model that worked for us:

Make resolution a choice point (an action or choice to take)

A choice point is when the couples intentionally select to use the conflict as an opportunity to understand each other better. Work upon satisfied intimacy to build your strengths and reduce negative emotions. Some of the strategies to achieve this goal include developing a better understanding of each other to increase your knowledge for each other, developing cross emotional, physiological and physical understanding to increase tolerance of each other's differences, and evaluating the outcome of your action to make changes if necessary (Gen. 11: 1:9; Act 4: 31-34).

Work together as one to build each other's strength. Both are commanded to submit to each and live with each other with understanding. Husbands must take note of (Ephesians 5:21-31), that is, building their spiritual, emotional, and physical strength by good character toward their wives. A husband's love must be action more than words. A husband who increases emotional security in the relationship builds his wife's assurance of his care and love.

Concentrating on your own behavioral changes will inspire your spouse to do the same.

Overlook minor offenses

An offense should be overlooked if you can answer "no" to all of the following questions:

1. Is the offense earnestly dishonoring God?
2. Has it negatively impacted the relationship?
3. Is it hurting other people? And,
4. Is it seriously hurting the offender or victim?

If you answer "yes" to any of the above questions, an offense is too serious to overlook. Actions to take include:

*   Go and talk with the "offender" privately and lovingly about the situation (see Matthew. 18:15);
*   In that situation, plan your words carefully; be specific and to the point. Assume the best about your mate until you have facts to prove otherwise (Proverb 11:27);
*   Each should readily admit each person's contribution to a conflict and clearly apologize (see Proverb 19:11);
*   Listen carefully to each other. "He who answers a matter before he hears it, It is folly and shame to him" (Prov. 18:13, NJKV);
*   Speak only to build the other up. Test what you say (see Table 3.1) and how you say it: is it immoral, debasing, edifying, and graceful? Paul said it best: "Let no corrupt communication proceed out of your mouth, but that which is good to the use of edifying, that it may minister grace unto the hearers" (Ephesians 4:29);
*   Ask for feedback; do not dominate the discussion. Recognize your limits (only God can change people) (see Romans 12:18; 2 Timothy 2:24-26).

The Seven Stages of Conflict Resolution

There are seven possible stages of identifying and resolving conflict—Problem, Feeling, Need and Desires, Solution, Reconciliation, Commitment, and Implementation Stages. Consider a couple working through a conflict.

1. **Problem Identification Stage.** Identify the primary issues or problems causing the conflict:

    - **Wife:** "I do not know why you are always angry with me for the slightest provocation... Do you really love me?"

    - **Husband:** "I love you but sometimes I just feel angry about the way you ignore my request of sharing yourself with me."

What is the main problem here? The problem appears to be that the wife is ignoring her conjugal duties or role as a wife, or that the husband's attitude does not reflect the love he professes. If correct, that is, if they have agreed on the problem, then move to the next phase – The Feeling Stage.

2. **Feeling Identification Stage.** Identify your feelings about the problem or issue (Ephesians 4:26-32):

    - **Wife:** "I feel you do not love me because of your anger and the way you talk to me. I also feel frustrated because you come to bed late after you have treated me badly all day, and then you want to touch me for romance."

    - **Husband:** "I appreciate all your great qualities, and am sorry for coming to you late, but I feel annoyed and irritated when you show a negative attitude toward our romance and intimacy, including even touching you."

What are the feelings expressed here? Both are angry and frustrated; the husband's anger is the result of the wife's attitude toward intimacy, and the wife's feeling of being unloved is caused by the husband's inflamed response to the wife's attitude. The major conflict is a negative attitude toward sex/romance and intimacy. If there is agreement on the issue, move to the next state.

3. The Need and Desire Stage. In this stage, identify what needs and desires are needed in order to feel resolved in the issue (See James 4:1-4); they are what must be resolved in this segment:

- **Wife:** "What I need and desire is for you to work on your emotions, stop being angry with me, and show me love."
- **Husband:** "What I need is for you to be considerate of your romantic role, have some positive attitude toward a consistent need for better intimacy, and show that you care."

What is the primary need here to be met? Both define their needs in one primary need: the husband needs a positive attitude from her toward sex and romance, and the wife needs a positive emotional response from him to feel loved, and that will increase her desire to reciprocate to his needs. Basically, attitude adjustment is what is most needed. They both need understanding and humility to submit to each other's needs and desires. Go to the next phase, The Solution Phase:

4. Solution Identification Stage: Now that the issue and needs are identified, begin the process of identifying possible solutions.

- **Wife:** "Yes, we need attitude adjustment. Let's start and plan on going to bed early before 10 P.M. instead of your coming when I am already tired or asleep."

- **Husband:** "I agree, we can do better on our attitudes; I suggest that a plan for 11 P.M. instead of 12 P.M. will work better.

Is this conflict resolved? Almost, but not quite! A promising solution, out of other possibilities, is to attend to the primary problem when it has been identified. A lasting solution is one in which both must commit to the agreed actions which both parties will put into effect individually, and together, as a resolution. A solution calls for both to understand and share positive behavior toward their intimacy and romance.

A problem revealed is a problem half-solved; the required behavioral change becomes clear to both when problems caused by the behaviors are revealed; changes are needed in both since both share contributions to the conflict. Many possible alternative solutions may need to be identified. The idea of one person saying, "You are the major contributor," "you have the problem, not me," or "I really do not know what to do," will appear as a rejection of resolution and will lead to worsened situations in the conflict. It is even worsened when one person goes to the extent of justifying inaction with a wrong application of the Scriptures. At the end of this phase, find a mutually acceptable solution out of the identified alternative solutions, and be willing to make the needed compromises to decide on the best way forward, with the specific implementation plans toward the desired behavioral change for both individuals.

In compromising, each must expect to lose something in order for both to gain something so that each person's need is met. In some cases, as noted by Herbert G. Lingren, it is possible for a spouse to be willing, as a gift of love, to end the disagreement by agreeing to the other person's choice. This has been referred as *deference*. [36] Two types of deference are a creative loving gift freely offered, or a destructive surrender demanded by coercion.

5.   Reconciliation Stage. Seek and pursue genuine settlement; reconciliation brings healing to the conflict.

Compromise in the solution stage is the beginning of reconciliation that yields commitment to permanent resolution. To pursue genuine reconciliation, you must forgive totally in order to open the way for authentic reconciliation; you must remember that forgiveness is a spiritual process that you cannot fully accomplish on your own without God; you must Bear with each other and forgive whatever grievances you may have against one another.

- Wife: "Honey, I am sorry for being inconsiderate. I do care about your need as my husband. Let us work it out."
- Husband: "Thank you, Honey; I am also sorry for being too selfish and angry with you. I hate it when I do that. We need to begin to work it out."

"You must forgive as the Lord forgave you" (Col. 3:12-14; see also 1 Cor. 13:5; Psalm 103:12; Isa. 43:25). As a pathway to reconciliation, you must commit to not think about this incident, not bring this incident up and use it against the other, not talk to others about the incident, and not allow this incident to stand between you or hinder your personal relationship.

6.   Commitment Stage. The most critical element in their work to resolving this conflict is the opportunity to explore their feelings honestly about the issue. Clear understanding of the source of the conflict, and respect of the other person's perspective and feelings, result in quick resolution. Willingness to make a mutually agreeable compromise is very important to a resolution. Nevertheless, until a commitment is made and agreed to by both parties, resolution will not be achieved. We state a rule here:

Agreement plus commitment to specific actions toward a solution yields lasting resolution, that is,

Agreement + Commitment + Actions = Resolution.

- **Wife:** "I agree for us to spend better quality time. However, 12 midnight is late. Let us agree to 11 P.M. as the latest time. I also agree to improve in my attitude to make you feel more accepted and respected."
- **Husband:** "I agree to 11 P.M. and will work on concluding my work by that time. I also agree to learn to control my anger and act in ways that will make you feel more loved.'

With the heart of reconciliation, these actions make more sense, and commitments to them will now fall on healthy forgiven hearts. The commitment shared in an atmosphere of love and oneness leads to mutual ownership of the implantation plan.

7. **Implementation Stage:** In implementing the plan to achieve the desired behavior changes, couples need to remind themselves of their individual commitment to a covenant, and not contractual marriage, as in Table 9.3. This means that each spouse must focus on working on his or her behavior changes and allow each other to change without force. The "If you do not change, I will not change" attitude is not allowed. After you have made the behavior changes to which you have mutually agreed, evaluate their effect on your relationship, using the formative questions in Table 9.2 and Table 9.3. Each spouse should frequently ask the other to improve their roles in building wholeness in the marriage. These questions could also serve as a quantitative tool toward continuously assessing the effectiveness of the implementation plan. Couples must also be open to adjust the plan if the assessments show that they are not where they are supposed to be.

Table 9.3. Comparison Between Covenant and Contractual Marriages

	COVENANT	CONTRACT
1	Divine unconditional binding promise to man (Hebrew. 8: 7-13)	Enforceable mutual agreement between parties
2	Divinely and spiritually (Galatians 3:15-17) made by the Holy Spirit (Hebrews 10:15-16)	Legally enforced by earthly agents
3	Ratified by the blood of Christ (Matthew. 26:28, Hebrews 9:-12-14, 20) and based on law of grace (Romans 6:14-15) and not works (Law of works) (Romans 3:26-31)	Agreement follows an offer and acceptance: If *you do this,* I will do *that* under these *conditions (works)*
4	Valued Free Gift based on grace; no exchange of other's giving or reward expected	Agreement calls for an exchange of something of value: If *you give me* that, *I will give you* this
5	Upheld with complete mercy through faith (Heb 8:12; Rom 4:1-8)	Made to change based on natural program
6	A mystery and gift designed by God to be discovered and enjoyed	Understood and performance-based

Create a climate of peace in your home

Creating a climate for peace will require you to understand the 4 peaceable 'P's: **Peaceable Perspective.** The good in others must be our perspective. Our focus should be working with an open mind and a beneficial attitude, to find the good things in people and base our relationship on those things.

Our positive attitude can be a pathway for the peace we seek. Paul said: "whatsoever things are true, things that are honest, things that are just;

whatsoever things are pure, and lovely… think about these things" (Phil 4:8).

Peaceable Process. Creating a long-lasting peaceable relationship is a process of submitting and understanding one another in all things (Ephesians 5:21). It is a process that may start roughly at the beginning, but we must keep submitting and respecting each other as a way to break down those attitudes the devil can use to cause conflicts.

Peaceable Problems. How can a problem be peaceable? By seeing the inevitable problem in relationship as an indispensable growth opportunity, the conflict presents choice opportunities for growth and understanding, and the victories in those problems bring Glory to God. Thus, to sustain the peace in that "difficult situation," according to Romans 12:18, our love must be more than an act of our will. It is based on God's covenant and command to love (1 Corinthians 13:4-8).

Peaceable: Pardon. To sustain the peace means that we must commit to being kind… Forgiving and forbearing one another (Ephesians 4:32, Col 3:13).

CHAPTER 10

PARENTAL INWARD COMPASSION

In the previous chapter, we looked at wholeness compassion primarily through dealing with the husband and wife within a family. In this chapter, we want to look at parental inward compassion for the wholeness of the children. Specifically, we will deal with compassion extended to children who are often at another disposition as opposed to their parents. These children sometimes make jokes of the ways in which their parents handle issues. I once watched my children demonstrate how I struggled with my deep language accent in order to communicate in a different culture. They perceived my passionate persuasions as "yelling." How do I relate to them at any point of brokenness to bring wholeness to them?

Compassion in the nuclear family is an important subject that may be too complex and comprehensive to be covered in this book. This is not a chapter on parenting, nor do I attempt to teach the reader how to raise children. Based on my experience of raising four children, now adults, my goal is to share some highlights with specific reference to compassion. Rather than spending your energies on your own needs and comfort, what sacrifices can you make to meet the needs of your family first, rather than your needs alone? How do you build pathways for strong forgiveness and reconciliation ministries within the family? The answers to these questions come from our compassion, driven by our inner strength.

Developing inner strength for compassion that yields personal wholeness to your children and others is accomplished through cultivating the caring empathy discussed earlier. Exploring the how to cultivate compassionate empathy is developing our capacity to be aware of another's feeling and state of suffering, and choosing purposefully to walk with them in that state of experience.

The family is our first institution, our primary organization, and in fact, our principal fellowship. The parents are leaders, with the father at the head, and Christ the head of the man and at the center, connecting all. Godly parenting is about leadership, and good leadership influences and impacts our children only when we are in closer relationships with God and the home (family). When we lead well at home with love and compassion, we model integrity, respect, and credibility outside the home. Inward compassion will occur in the family when there is an intentional act to walk through difficulty with a member of the fellowship personally, or the nuclear family, and extend a helping hand to bring wholeness, affection, care, etc. to others. It takes special generous acts of expending yourself for others, and without expectation of reward, for the primary purpose of bringing self-healing to you. It starts from extending the strength of your own emotional intelligence and wholeness to others by giving the same healing and experience to others.

In this chapter, deliberate effort will be made to cover a range of relevant parenting issues, bearing in mind the cultural peculiarities, intergenerational gaps, and the needs of our children as Christians and individuals. Our primary responsibility in whatever we do in parenting is bringing wholeness to the family through unconditional love of our children as demonstrated by our acts of compassion. It is not about the parents, the parents' egos, or parental rights. It is about them—the children in God's purposeful will. In that respect, we are accountable to God in how we invest and nurture growth in our children as our primary entrustments to be kept whole and unbroken. This chapter presents practical tools to aid parents in the process of fulfilling their God-given assignments as parents.

Parents are the children's role models and the greatest influence in their lives; they are always acting in the presence of their children. What are some of the major parental issues for today's children, on and up to their adulthood before they leave home? —what can we do to entice our children to imitate us more? Parents must be better than what they wish their children to be—parents must desire their children to do better than they have done. What are some of the most effective Biblical commands and examples for fathers and parental duties? How do we apply these principles and what are some areas of difficulty? Children are not merely creatures of imitation, but creatures of intellect. Consider the Scripture below:

> *"And these words which I command you shall be in your heart, and you must diligently teach them to your children—when you walk— when you lie down—and when you rise up. You shall bind them as a sign on your hand, and they shall be as front-lets between your eyes. You shall write them on the doorposts of your house and on your gates…" (Deuteronomy 6:4-9).*

What does this Scripture say about parenting in order to model integrity? What are some practical ways to teach our children, and what could be our possible challenges in that regard?

Good Parenting by Modeling Godly Principles

We are our children's role models and the greatest influence in their lives. Here are some key strategic actions as to how we can influence desired changes in their lives:

Be what you desire your child to be

We are always acting in the presence of our children—so let us do it in such a righteous and yet authentic way that they are enticed to imitate us more by examples than by rules. A good example is very inspiring and serves as memory peg for the simple rule or behavior you desire in the child. David, in advising his son in Proverbs 23:26, said this: "My son, give me thine heart, and let thine eyes observe my ways." And in Proverbs 17:6, he said, "Children's children are the crown of old men; and the glory of children are their fathers." In this first place, he was intentionally inviting his son to learn from him. Second, he communicated that learning from him would bring glory to God, as he brings glory to God as the Father. Well, the challenge here is to make sure that what you do indeed brings glory God. The action of allowing your children to observe and learn from you also passes to your children's children. Children learn behavior from their parents. Children watch their parents and repeat what their parents say and do, good and bad.

Godly parents can show the good example of following actions which have proven to be effective:

- You want your children to be honorable and completely truthful, punctual and thorough, so you must let them hear or see you extol these virtues.
- You want your children to choose their friends carefully, so then you must not be careless or be the yoke with unfruitful friends and works.

- You know the evil impact of modern entertainment— gambling, drunkenness, pornography, prostitution—waiting to entice our children, so you must not allow these vices into the house for an easy opening to their hearts.
- You must become, today and now, whatever good quality you want to see as a part of the positive habits of your children.
- Show them the love of Jesus. Teach them to pray to their Heavenly Father in the mighty name of Jesus.
- Demonstrate God's love by telling them your testimony and how Jesus saved you from your sins. Tell them about what God has done for you. If their names were based on a testimony of some event in your life, tell them. Honestly.
- Plant Bible verses in their hearts every day of their lives, and in an interactive fun way without making it pushy. Allow the Scriptures to speak into them.
- Lead them in a consistent and serious family devotion, especially when they are young (less than 10 years old), and continue until they leave home.

Follow biblical principles as a father

A father must instruct them (Proverbs 1:8; 22:6) by both words and examples. Children need to be taught the differences between rights and wrongs, and will need to see it demonstrated by their father or parents. Take decisions thoughtfully and carefully in front of them, and use them as teaching moments to explain why you came to such resolutions as you did. Talk to them about choices you made in the past and why they did (or didn't) work out. Just as you want to ask how Jesus would handle this situation, evaluate all of your own decisions by thinking: "What would I want my child to do in this situation?" and "What negative impact will this decision have on them?" Some decisions, such as schools they go, neighborhoods you live and expose them to, interference in their choice of spouse or careers, how you model your marital lives in front of them, etc., that may impact their lives should be handled with absolute consideration of the potential impacts. It may be the beginning of a generational curse or blessing beyond you. Other suggestions include:

- Teach your children that making mistakes or failing is part of life, but they must learn from their mistakes and try to avoid making the same mistakes repeatedly. Show them examples from your own life experience.

- Instill Biblical values. Instead of constantly hearing the world's point of view (on creation, abortion, etc.), take sides through God's word and teach them God's point of view. For example, Paul writing to Timothy said in 2 Timothy 3:15: "And that from a child thou hast known the holy scriptures, which are able to make thee wise unto salvation through faith, which is in Christ Jesus.""

- Make them see and feel the compassion of the love of Jesus from you, extending to them and their mother. Live out how you want them to live for the glory of God. Live a life that is pleasing to the Lord. Love the Lord. Your love for Jesus will put a desire in your child to do the same. Set a good example.

- Let them see you pray and hear you share the testimonies of God's goodness, as in this example with David: Psalm 66:16: "Come and hear, all you who fear God, and I will tell what he has done for my soul." When they seek your counsel, set the example and pray with them that the Lord will show you what to do.

- Teach your children how to pray effectively, and when to pray. Children need to be taught the Word of God that will cancel and overcome the counterfeit worldly principles. A child who sees his parents' reliance upon God will most likely follow in the same footsteps.

A Father must guide, command, encourage, and warn them. A father's first duty is to give his children affection and warmth – you must readily tell your child "I love you; I'm proud of you." This is the example Paul was referring to when he wrote in Thessalonians 2:11: "As ye know how we exhorted and comforted and charged every one of you, as a father doth his children." Other methods include:

- Fathers are to nurture them with good food, valid words, and notable fun. Make time to be with them. A father shows support and love through actions as well as through words.
- Spend time with and take responsibility for your children. If you don't establish an intimacy with your children when they're young, it will be difficult to catch up when they're older.
- Instruct and guide them until they understand Proverbs 4:1: "Hear, ye children, the instruction of a father, and attend to know understanding."
- Bring correction to them whenever necessary. The Scripture said, in Proverbs 22:15: "Foolishness is bound in the heart of a child; but the rod of correction shall drive it far from him." David never deviated in this, as we see constantly in his life. He advised, "Correct thy son, and he shall give the rest; yea, he shall give delight unto thy soul" (Proverbs 29:17), and in Proverb 6:20, he said, "My son, keep thy father's commandment, and forsake not the law of thy mother."

Fathers must restrain them from doing immoral things (1 Samuel 3:12-13). We read about the sad case of Eli, who could not lead his son in the right way of the Lord. God told Samuel: "In that day I will perform against Eli all that I have spoken concerning his house, from beginning to end. For I have told him that I will judge his house forever for the iniquity which he knows, because his sons made themselves vile, and he did not restrain them..." Here is a guide of what we can learn from this case:

- When they are misbehaving, they must be corrected and/or disciplined. Correction, discipline, and understanding do go together.
- You must reform a child with some explanation in love; tell them why they are receiving correction and/or discipline for a specific misdeed.
- "Because I said so" is not the way to correct your child or explain a punishment. Explain why their action is displeasing to you by showing why and how it is displeasing to God.
- Parents, who neglect correction and restraint of children when they purposefully disobey godly rules, await correction and rebuke from God.

Fathers must discipline with the rod of correction (Deuteronomy 21:18; Proverbs 23:13-14; 29:17. A stubborn and rebellious son who will not obey the voice of his father or the voice of his mother must be chastened (corrected) first, and then punished if he does not heed. Specific punishment that will not amount to physical abuse can deliver him from greater evil, and give the parents rest and delight (See Hebrew 12:9-11). The punishment is only effective when delivered in a culture of love for the child. Proverbs 19:18 says: "Chasten thy son while there is hope, and let not thy soul spare for his crying."

Fathers must be considerate of their needs and requests (Matthew 7:10). This includes knowing how to give good gifts to your children or members of your family. Efforts should be made to honor their request that is fitting to their needs, and not their wants. Let meeting their wants be fashioned as a form of reward for good behavior.

Fathers must not provoke their children, but instead bring them up in God's way (Ephesians 6:4). Show affection. Being affectionate with your child shows them that you love them. It also teaches them to show affection to others.

Fathers must provide (financially and emotionally) for their needs (Timothy 5:8). "If anyone does not provide for his relatives, and especially for his immediate family, he has denied the faith and is worse than an unbeliever" (Timothy 5:8, NIV). Other examples based on similar principles include:

- Show that providing for your family, by not being lazy or neglecting gainful employment or business, is a command from God.
- Protect your family and set the family above all else in conversation, decisions you make, and even your career pursuit.
- Demonstrate that you are the leader and the prophet of the home by providing the needed spiritual nourishment for growth.
- Provide them with the proper estimation of the world and its culture by modeling excellence and differentiating that which the gospel requires from that which flows from a selfish and worldly heart.
- Cultivate in them higher and nobler principles than the love of earthly things; they must not be shielded from the world—but instead taught how vain and empty a thing it is outside of God.
- In your reaction to worldly gains (wealth) and losses (of investments), let your children understand that to bear fruit unto eternal life is gain; show that there are more elevated and enduring joys than the base and passing pleasures of time and money.
- Let children be taught to honor God in whatever they do.

Make your home a God-centered dwelling place. This means nurturing a home that prepares and matures your children for life outside of home. While we ought not to be completely separated from the world, every family ought to be a little world within itself. A home is the heart of God with the shadow of God to abide in—we dwell in it and abide under its protection as it is the "secret place of the most high" (Ps 91:1-3). Ways a father can make the home God-centered include the following actions:

- Deal with problems and conflicts while they are still small. Do not reward a child who is throwing a temper tantrum.
- Every day at home is a training session they will use for the rest of their lives.
- No matter where they are, their entertainment should never bring reproach upon a well-governed and godly family.
- Parents may need to deny themselves some comforts through a few sacrifices (those favorite TV programs)
- Most psychologists agree that a child's behavior is primarily the product' is the product of the environment to which he is exposed—at home, in school, in media; so also is a violent prone person.

Be a Model of Industrious Habits. Industrious habits have such a happy influence on the intellectual and moral character of children. However, we must balance our diligent habits with time out to relax with family. As God told the Prophet Jeremiah, "Do you seek great things for yourself? Do not seek them!" (Jeremiah 45:5); teach them to find contentment and satisfaction in the work God has given them through the following actions:

- Do not let them see a father disrespect his wife in the presence of the children.
- Mutually do things heartily as unto God and not men (Colossians 3:23).
- Let them know that you care and are always there for them, and that they are valued.

- Encourage them to meet their full potential, but know that they are unique.
- Ensure that your home is managed in the proper way.

Be an authentic model to follow

Be an example of uprightness. In all circumstances, live out a pattern of life worthy of emulation: "Teaching us that, denying ungodliness and worldly lusts, we should live soberly, righteously, and godly, in this present world" (Titus 2:12) and "have no fellowship with the unfruitful works of darkness, but rather reprove them" (Ephesians 5:11).

- When you are displeased with a certain program on TV, explain why the program is wrong.
- Teach your child to cling to the good and abhor the bad. Teach them the things that displease the Lord and why they should want to do things pleasing in God's sight.
- Discuss at dinner how their day went at school. Listen to their stories more than you attempt to fix their problems. Observe their feelings and body language; show you care and be attentive to their problems and struggles.

Model humility by being humble. Respecting your children's mother, for example, is a direct and effective way to model humility, and yet the easiest goal to take for granted. It also negatively impacts the children to see a father disrespect his wife in the presence of the children. Mutual respect between parents models understanding and humility; this translates to great respect of the fathers from the daughters, who look up to the father as the model husband (Romans 12:16; 1 Peter 5:5-6). Consider following these actions: Humble yourself under the hand of God and in all things and persons.

- Admit when you make a mistake. Tell them how you should have done things better or explain why it was a mistake.
- Let your children evaluate your choice of people with whom you associate.
- Let them see you help your spouse with joy and through showing an appropriate positive and loving attitude, thereby instilling in them the attitudes of servanthood.

Model responsibility and accountability by being responsible. The LORD told Jeremiah, "Before I formed you in the womb, I knew you; before you were born, I sanctified you; I ordained you a prophet to the nations" (Jeremiah 1:5). The generation of our children needs to be guided to discover what their real purpose is in life, and the perfect will of God for their lives. Some are lost and look for opportunities for 'permissive will', chasing things they want rather than what they need, because they have the opportunities. Recently, I have seen students, especially male students, lost in a world with very conflicting messages. Some are questioning their gender as they see homosexuality become acceptable; some see Islam as a better pathway because the message conforms more to what is happening in their worlds. These are some of the challenges in today's culture where children continue to have an independent attitude, and they lack the ability to take on responsibilities. There is a need for parents to be more compassionate in understanding the struggles of their children in order to instill a stronger sense of responsibility in the children. Here are some tips:

- Give them tasks or chores to do around the house.
- Teach them how you found your "sanctified" purpose to get to where you are today.

- Teach and guide them to use your talents well (profitably) and to the Glory of God.
- Teach them accountability by standing as answerable to your own actions.
- Include them in major decision-making such as buying a house, changing jobs, etc.
- Include them in the process so that they will better understand how things work in the real world.

Model obedience of the law. Being subject to authority must be a model in the family in order to cultivate the habit of subordination and respect for the law. It is dangerous to always seek the easy way out or to take short cuts that may not be allowed by the law. At one time, I was taking inner roads to make a journey briefer, because of the traffic. I followed an alley road, and sometimes drove through some unsafe crossings with my son in the front seat with me. I found out later that he too would drive following the exact same path I had shown him, regardless of when there was any traffic hold-up, and once even while I was in the car. His justification was that I had done it, so it must be acceptable for him to follow. I regretted showing him that shortcut. How could I correct the bad behavior I had modeled for him to emulate?

Model faith and perseverance by leading from Paul's principle of Philippians 4:13: "I can do all things through Christ, who strengthens me." We must lead them by good examples, through encouraging them in all that they do. We need to expect and encourage their best more than their perfection, supporting them, complimenting them, and praising them when they do well. Children do not forget that you did not show up to events that were most important to them. You must make every effort to show up at their concerts, games, and other events. Don't criticize them if they miss the basket, or if they strike out.

Model Integrity, credibility, and self-reliance by being truthful and dependable (Proverbs 20:7): "The just man walketh in his integrity: his children are blessed after him." This requires us to always be honest and sincere. Teach and model integrity to your children by you walking in integrity, as the example. You must be a person of your word and a promise keeper. Here are other examples:

- Avoid a lying tongue because it throws a barrier in the way of holiness and heaven. Children must be taught the immense importance of always speaking the truth.
- You're every false statement, art of concealment, every exaggeration, and every broken promise will only harden the heart of your child.
- Be honest to your children and freely share your wilderness experience – failures and successes – in a culture away from your own parents

Model principled leadership. Authentic biblically-based principles have proven to be effective through the years. I have to emphasize that there are also several principles that appear appropriate, such as different treatment of women in some cultures, gender-based value system, or the different understanding of what marriage is, but are rather contrary to sound biblical teaching. A father is accountable for good teaching to the children. If you are not sure, it is better to ask someone who is trusted in the Word rather than take on any teaching that may end up destroying the child for life. The best way to guard the children of this generation is to better prepare them for life through good and authentic hands-on-teaching and the practice of godly principles such as faith, forgiveness, diligence, hard work, truthfulness, belief in God's promises, and wisdom from the Word. Other methods of moving forward with teaching include:

PARENTAL INWARD COMPASSION

- Help them to become mature, growing into fine adults, letting them see you live on good biblical instruction.
- Help them to think of the welfare of others and acts of generosity. Show them that "it is more blessed to give, than to receive."
- Honor God in their presence with each of your increases in wealth because everything we have really belongs to God.
- Seek out only the things that are in line with God's word and his righteousness, and let those take precedence in every plan and arrangement for human life!

Model good manners and social skills. Your own exceptional manners are integral offerings to make in the lives of your children. The apostle Paul set an excellent example for Timothy and Titus, those he considered his children in the Lord. To Titus, Paul wrote, "That they may teach the young women to be sober, to love their husbands, to love their children" (Titus 2:40). To show children why manners are important, make an effort to include them in conversations and monitor their social skills through their interacting at home. The effective way to teach them is through hands-on and direct observation of the positive things you do.

Our cultural uniqueness often has the tendency to make us passionate and irrational, and too quick to prejudge our children. Parents should control their emotion and never yell at their children for telling them the truth or revealing their own perspectives in things. What is necessary is your understanding. You do not want to run the risk of discouraging them from telling you the truth in the future by yelling and screaming at them. Following Paul's instruction, "Fathers, do not provoke your children, lest they become discouraged" (Colossians 3:21, NKJV).

Be a model of temperance. This you can do by showing that you can control your temper; showing them temperance in thought, word, or deed in the way you treat others is an act of understanding and compassion. A child's mind is the door to his heart, and God has appointed parents to be the immediate guardians of their children's hearts, happiness, virtue, and hopes. Parents must be careful how they sow 'seeds of intemperance' in infancy, and nurture them in childhood.

Be a model of a good teacher. "And these words which I command you shall be in your heart, and you must diligently teach them to your children—when you walk—when you lie down—and when you rise up. You shall bind them as a sign on your hand, and they shall be as frontlets between your eyes. You shall write them on the doorposts of your house and on your gates." (Deuteronomy 6:4-9) There are three elements to be noted in these Scriptures:

1. **Instill the Word of God in their hearts.** Parents are commanded to place the word of God in the hearts of the children first. This means that parents must demonstrate that they live by those words and so become examples to their children. If you cannot show obedience to the words, you lose credibility to expect the children to submit them.

2. **Be consistent in living out the Word.** The second element of this instruction in God's word is that living by the words should be steadfast and frequent. "You must diligently teach them to your children—when you walk—when you lie down—and when you rise up."

3. **Systemically apply the Word.** And the third element is that the act of the Word of God must be systemic; that is, the word needs to be felt and used everywhere in the house, in the works of your hands and in how you see and evaluate things. "You shall bind them as a sign on your hand, and they shall be as frontlets between your eyes' word." The following lessons can be learned, as to how you teach them to the children:

- Conversation with your children must be personal, and broken down interactively in simple terms around specific biblical principles. The child's heart must be guarded, and his choices guided to discover the truth, to help inform and enlighten his understanding for God's promises and be prepared for outside influence. As the Scripture commanded, we are to "train up a child in the way he should go, And when he is old he will not depart from it" (Proverb 22:6, NJKV).

- The instruction needs to be selected to teach the moral truth, to his empty corrupt mind before he or she becomes a slave to the more attractive worldly passions from the outside: "and that from childhood, you have known the Holy Scriptures, which is able to make you wise for salvation through faith, which is in Christ Jesus... All Scripture ...is profitable for doctrine...that the man of God may be complete, thoroughly equipped for every good work" (2 Timothy 3:15-17).

- Parents have responsibility, power, and authority from God to be the first to shape the character and destiny of their children; that responsibility cannot be delegated to anybody or even teachers; the Christian education must begin at home.

- A rebellious child needs to be restrained with all the compassion, kindness, and discretion with firmness of a godly parent. Demonstrate to your child by being a living example, in that you are his or her best friend. "And you, fathers, do not provoke your children to wrath, but bring them up in the training and admonition of the Lord" (Ephesians 6:4, NJKV).

- You must not compromise on any godly principle, but must gain the rebellious child with love and compassion for his wholeness, more than your right or ego is to be respected.
- Words are critically powerful in communicating love and shaping the self-image of family members. This is done most effectively by listening to each other in training the children.
- You must use positive words to build confidence-love and acceptance. Parents, you must let your children be who they were created to be, and avoid labeling them.

Dealing with Intergenerational Realities

Assuming that you are a Christian family with high moral standards, you have led your family through sound biblical teaching and have modeled all that we have discussed above. Everything seems to be going well, following these guidelines. Suddenly, one of the following realities sets in:

1. Your daughter informs you that she is pregnant.
2. Your daughter becomes pregnant by a boy who, for whatever reason, you would not want to be your son-in –law.
3. Your son or daughter informs you that he or she has chosen a lifestyle in which you do not believe or of which you do not approve because it is biblically immoral.
4. You find some drugs in your son's or daughter's room.
5. You discover pornographic images in your son's room.
6. Your child attempts to commit suicide for whatever reason.
7. Your child has become so rebellious that he or she is no longer listening to you, and in most cases like this, has become more negative and confrontational toward you and/or your spouse.

8. Your 8th year old lying about whereabouts (an eight year old might say he's going to do homework with a friend and instead end up at an arcade, for example),
9. Young ones disrespecting a teacher, neglecting to pass on expected documents/report cards/forms from one party to another, or even stealing, or simply cursing.

This is just a short list of intergenerational or millennium realities that parents face or could expect today. How do you handle any of these? How do you show compassion to this generation in a way they will understand, or a way in which you can model and pass on the desired legacy? Answers to each of the above will require a different method. Let us focus on some key rational strategies:

Rationally deal with the cultural conflict

Leave your culture out of the issue unless your action is mingled with compassion. This is more in families in which the children are born and expose to cultures, example USA, different from their parents. I personally hold very strongly to my cultural values and up-bringing because they have proven to yield positive results in most of my life issues. However, often times, our emotional or practical responses to some of the issues parents deal with, including any of the realities above, depend on our cultural values even beyond our Christian moral values; rational actions with compassion for wholeness in the situation loses it meaning. Basing your response on your belief that your culture forbids what the child did or did not do is as ineffective as it could be, born out of a lack of compassion and a need for further understanding of the culture to which the children are exposed. By association, your culture is the culture to which you think you belong. Most children born of African parents in America, for example, are more likely to gravitate toward American culture than African culture because they are more a product of the American environment. Also, children have a tendency to move toward what pleases them most rather than what is permitted by parental culture. Even in Africa, the children are adapting to American or foreign culture more than to African culture. Why? With the media, TV, YouTube, social networking, Facebook, etc., the world has become too small for these children. For economic reasons and millennial adaptations, the American culture is more in Africa than the African culture is in Africa. In the media, for example, there are more American or culturally foreign inspired programs among movies, music, language, behavior, etc. than programs holding African culture. These children are in what I will refer as *cultural conflicts*. What they learn from home and what is passed down by parents is different from what media or their school system teaches them might be acceptable. While it is acceptable to correct a child with a "rod" in African context, it can end up with a parent being in jail as an abuser in American culture. The children know that, and in fact, are encouraged to report such corrections they perceive to be physical abuse to authorities. Since their minds are more attracted to what they want that pleases their eyes than what they need for life, they are more likely to take the 'good' they think their culture gives to them rather than what parents think is best for them.

As I have stated earlier, holding to our cultural values very tightly is important, especially if we must pass on a legacy of our cultural values to the generation of our children and children's children. However, there is an imperative need to be balanced in the approach as parents, to not be so embedded in the traditional or cultural values of fatherhood with, no compassion to the children's struggles between two cultures. This is also true in every ethnic nationality or group that holds strongly to their roots and identify.

The Bible holds the value that a father is the head and parents must be obeyed. In addition to these basic principles, some cultures add that a child must not question a father, and that the father is always right because he can see much more than the child can see, tradition must be followed, etc. These are important considerations, but we cannot lose track of the fact that parents out of a lack of compassion can cross the line of discouraging their children from even accepting the cultural legacy they want to pass on. When the legacy to pass on becomes cultural legalism, the children will withdraw to a culture outside their fathers', one which will allow them freedom to be who they want to be. Children often hear the tone of voice more than actual affective compassionate words. If the person a child wants to introduce to a parent as a potential life partner is from that culture, tribe, or family which the parents do not approve of or do not want, the child will hear the high-toned voice suggesting the phrases, "you cannot marry that person because he or she is from a different culture," or worse, "do not bring that person to the house."

On the other side, what if you arranged a girl and your son rejected her for the opposite reason? Or what will happen if children do read their parents reactions as indicating rejection of the person they bring? I can say from experience that it often yields unintended negative result if not handled carefully. The fundamental and unchanging truth is that our cultures come from God and the word of God. How can a parent reject a potential son or daughter in law because of the culture or the child's family's last name, even though in some cases, the person is a professing Christian? A case in point: When my son brought his first choice to the house, my reaction was outright rejection for the reason stated above. The second choice was also rejected because we judged that she had no manners and simply could not get along. On my son's third choice, he decided that whether we liked her or not, she was his choice. Compared to these three choices, we wished today we had left him with his first choice... The first girl was most compatible to our family values, though she was from a different culture. I will ever regret the fact that I rejected her from being his wife, simply because she was from a culture. I stereotypically presumed she would not be compatible to our culture. Now I know, in a hard way, that being from the same culture does not make a boy or girl automatically compatible as a son-in-law or daughter-in law.

Our ways of thinking are very different from our children's generation, and we must be careful that we see their future beyond cultural lines. The present generation cares less about culture, but more about their compatibility with each other, irrespective of where each comes from. Most do not even speak the language of their fathers! Thus, whatever the issues are, dealing with them to sustain wholeness in the family must be more about the child than the ego, culture, and pride of the parents.

Parents can be so strict on children who want to behave, culturally-speaking, that they are unwilling to be friend, or in some cases even interact with, children from a separate culture. In a country like America, that generally leads to the child being ostracized or ridiculed, or, at the very least, incredibly lonely on a social level.

Rationally deal with your rights

Leave your rights out of it; they know they have rights, too. A typical parent, especially fathers, feel disrespected when confronted with any of these realities we've listed above. The father's natural disposition is: "I have the right to be respected and obeyed because I am your father". Of course, that right is ordained by God, Fathers are held accountable, and the children are blessed forever when they obey. Yes, fathers do have those rights, but care must be exercised not to lord those rights over children without compassion. Otherwise, the child is more likely to do everything to resist a father's correction, rather than obey. The correction appears to a child as an absolute bullying when applied due to a child's mistake rather than to his or her disobedience. The worst thing a parent can do is to make a child respond to threats and leave the home in anger. The consequences are too costly to pay. The devil is right outside that door to fill that depraved mind with the wrong ideas, wrong shelter, and wrong advice. Many children have come back worse than when they left in anger over a smaller disagreement; some have even followed wrong habits and ended up in jail. No matter the rebellion of a child, the shelter of a parent with compassion and love will eventually break that child down from immoral behavior, with time and patience. The key responsibility is to keep communicating with love, and the right path to follow, even when they do not or are not willing to follow immediately. The loving compassionate voice of a father to a rebellious child can pierce deeper than a sword of correction. That voice is as correcting through the power of the Holy Spirit of God.

Rationally avoid threats

Leave the threat out, as they do not always work. Although threats can be used as a tool for correction or submission to desired behavior, some parental threats of punishment to their children are often born out of ego and pride, and the feeling that they are the children and their father is in charge. A father's ego has often done more damage to their children, especially their male children, than their few acts of compassion have yielded growth. Why? This is because angry moments and threats are so frequent that the few moments of compassion are not remembered. It should be the reverse! Could any father reading this text really say that your threats have always worked? They may have worked when they were in elementary and middle school, at which point you acted as policeman. In high school or college, being that policeman could be a turn-off and an unnecessary act of aggression; they feel that they are grown and, in reality, some are even much taller and bigger than you. So a different method is needed; you need to be a counselor and mentor! You must learn to lead them as a servant this time—relinquish the display of your rights. A lot of times, when you are angry and yelling with a sense of condemnation, love cannot be felt. The mistake has been made. In some cases, the child is brokenhearted for what he or she has done. Parents must leave their ego out of it, as the children have very fragile egos, too.

Rationally reject the sense of failure

Think about the case of you as a minister, the head of a known family ministry in the church, and your family is known to be of moral reputation, etc., and you have just found out that your unmarried daughter has become pregnant. What could be your response?

Of course, your first natural response is anger and disappointment. For a typical father, pride and ego may take over. Your cultural values come into play. The first thought that comes to your mind is why this should happen to your family. You look at the child and ask, "What will people now say about us?", "You are not supposed to behave like this!" "What in the world came over you?", and "Why did you do this to us?" Often, these questions will all be directed to the child at the same time, and with no display of compassion and unconditional love toward hearing and understanding the child. Yes, the child disappointed the parents, and often disappointed herself, too. A child brought up from such a family will feel ashamed. Yet, the deed has been done and the wholeness the parents seek must be more about that child than them; it must not be about the world out there or your reputation as parents. As much as we want to condemn the act, your first response must not be to condemn, but to love. You must be assured in your spirit that you have not failed in your duties as parents. Unless, of course, you did! But even in that case, you must not let your self-condemnations of your mistakes impede your responsibility toward that child in his or her own mistakes. Rather, channel every negative past toward positive teaching moments for the present.

Consider the following examples to illustrate the above points:

A case of a mistake: My wife and I were on vacation in Canada when the phone rang. She was speaking to someone, and I heard my wife express some emotions and shock: "When did this happen?" she asked. Someone was crying and she was trying to console her. Then I heard her say, "I do not know how your father is going to take this." At that moment, I was coming out of the bathroom. I saw the facial expression on my wife, who is usually quiet-natured, especially with her daughters, who are too perfect in her eyes, but she was calm and not condemning. After she hung up, I asked, "What is the matter? Who was that?" She said, "Sit down first to hear this." I said, "Tell me; is someone pregnant?" She looked at me and said, "Yes." I am the opposite of my wife. My immediate response was, "I cannot believe this; why would she be so stupid to do a thing like this?" I sat down and began to think through what my next action should be. On a second thought, I realized the deed was done. We knew we had trained these children well as the Lord would allow us. My best reaction was, "well, there is nothing we can do but love and support our daughter. She has been a great daughter all these years."

Our daughter, who was 27 years old at the time, already knew and had expressed by herself that she had disappointed herself, her friends, the community of brethren, her siblings, God, and her parents. That was enough for us! We learned from this experience that, in your action to address the children's mistakes, you must do so without condemnation. There was no need for the "you disappointed us" or those other remarks. She was broken and needed emotional healing and reassurance that we still loved her unconditionally. Our daughter and the young man were already planning their official engagement when this happened. She expected us to be rational, forgiving, and understanding, in that she knew that she had made a mistake in breaking her promise, and injured her pride in failing to remain pure until marriage. It was not the time to repeat the lecture of her upbringing or question where we had failed.

In a moment of such brokenness, you must mind the words and tone of your voice. What she needed was healing words such as: 'we love you', 'we will do all we can to walk along this path with you', 'we also are not perfect and have been comforted by God', 'God loves us, even though He hates our sins'. The use of "us" and "our" in this context is to be non-condemning, and to communicate that you are compassionately empathizing and walking through the experience with your child. Healing begins when the child actually feels that you are walking with her in the suffering.

A case of an uneasy choice: Assume that your son or daughter informs you that he or she has chosen a lifestyle in which you do not believe or feel disapproving of because it is biblically immoral or culturally unacceptable. Many parents are today faced with these realities. It is an area that needs the greatest sense of compassion. A father is like a watchman ordered by God to keep watch over his children, and if he fails in that responsibility, God will hold him accountable. God told Ezekiel, "I have made you a watchman for the house of Israel; therefore hear a word from My mouth, and give them warning from Me" (Ezekiel 3:16, NKJV). It clear that God holds the fathers as prophets and stewards of God's laws, to warn their children. The consequences are severe, not only for the children, but also for their fathers. God said, "When a righteous *man* turns from his righteousness and commits iniquity… he shall die; because you did not give him warning, he shall die in his sin…but his blood I will require at your hand" (Ezekiel 3:17-21, NKJV). A child that has been well-behaved and cultured in the family, but takes the pathway of disobedience and sin later in life, is like a righteous child that turns from righteousness into iniquity, according to the Scripture above. So, what do we do?

Our first responsibility in the above example is to turn to God, pointing that child in the right direction as God would hold us accountable if we did not, as He also did with Eli. Eli's sons sinned against God, but he honored them more than he honored God. God not only killed his two sons, but he cursed Eli and his household, and his generation to come forever. God said to Eli, "Why do you kick at My sacrifice and My offering which I have commanded *in My* dwelling place, and honor your sons more than Me... for those who honor Me I will honor…I will cut off your arm and the arm of your father's house... And there shall not be an old man in your house forever" (1 Samuel 12: 29-32, NKJV).

You must tell that child how much you love him or her unconditionally. However, no matter the depth of that love, the word of God cannot be compromised on any issue. You have no right to condemn that child. In your spirit, let God do the judging of the sins, not you. You owe it to that child; in a loving way, make sure he or she knows and understands the consequences and your stand on any issue based on sound biblical reasoning, without passing any judgment. The atmosphere of compassion and regulating the emotions involved in the issue are the keys to positive results.

In dealing with any such issue, the husband and wife must work together as one voice to communicate the warning or the consequences of the actions from the biblical principles more than cultural norms. This is because the child is likely to see the biblical principles as absolute, but cultural norms as relative to what the child considers to be his or her own culture. The millennial generation may be embedded in cultural conflicts, or even blinded to the same, and often resists being forced into their parents' stricter culture.

A case of parental rights: One case in point. My only son, who at this point was in college, had his room right in front of our master bedroom. But my son has a way of keeping his room so untidy that it looked like a room that has been scattered apart by a strong wind. And that was driving me crazy. It did not matter how much I threatened: he would not clean his room. In fact, he found a way of ignoring me. One time, he designed a sign that read, "Keep off. This is my room". That even angered me the more. I said to him, "Son, this is your room because I said so." This very encounter between my only son and I negatively impacted my relationship with him. My son at this time had no friend who lived close by, and he never went out or returned home late. He had every good disposition of which a father should be proud. But instead of spending time with him, bonding with him as the only other man in the house, I was busy complaining about his room. Instead of coming in and asking him, "Son, how did your day go?" my reaction would be: "You still have not cleaned this room." He felt no compassion, empty of anybody to share his life with as a growing black male child. Rather, he had the fear that I was going to yell at him about my room. And so most of time, he avoided me and resisted emotion toward me. He became so stubborn about this that he intentionally refused to change. It took another father who had gone through a similar experience to bring total healing to me and my son. My friend visited the house and advised me concerning my son's issue. "It is his room, not yours; you must leave him alone or you will lose him completely; which is more important?" my friend asked me as he got to get a peek into his room. Till today, I still regret all the years I lost. My son stayed home until he got married, with no more incidences about his room. I let him be himself, though I promised him that I would share pictures of his room (which I kept) with his children. Now he is married and has a son, and sends me the pictures of how his son scatters things everywhere he is in the house. I am sure, at the back of my son's mind, he may be saying, "Daddy, this is what I did to you, and your grandson is doing the same to us!" He never told me or expressed any bad feelings on the situation about his room. It happened to be the only encounter and rebellious act he ever had, until he left home at 26 years of age. I know some damage was done in the relationship, and opportunities for growth may have been missed. Instead of bringing wholeness to my son and my relationship with him though intentional acts of compassion, I chose to focus on my right to be obeyed. My action provoked a child that never had had a rebellious disposition or intense rebellion, just to resist me.

Dealing with Strongholds against God's will

A common mistake that some parents make in dealing with struggles the children face in growing up at home is through handling the issues only in the flesh or as the world deals with such issues. In the conflicting cultures to which the children are exposed, there are special strongholds for the children that turn them away from pure godliness into worldliness, setting parents at war with their children or society. Paul wrote:

> *"For the weapons of our warfare are not carnal but mighty in God for pulling down strongholds, casting down arguments and every high thing that exalts itself against the knowledge of God, bringing every thought into captivity to the obedience of Christ, and being ready to punish all disobedience when your obedience is fulfilled"* (2 Corinthians 10:4-6. NKJV).

Strongholds are those tendencies and patterns that one chooses knowingly and unknowingly, and which hold the person in bondage against God's purposeful will. They have roots in our thought patterns that lead to other strongholds such as wrong desires, habits, and associations to help reinforce the stronghold. How do we demolish or cast down these strongholds in the lives of our children, in this evil culture or in our lives? Here are some breakthrough points:

Channel their thoughts to the perfect will of God

Dealing with generational realities begins with guiding and helping the children discover God's perfect will for them. Rick Warrant's book, *Purpose Driven Life,* is a place to start as a part of family devotion. If you must at least reduce the chances of those realities being real, you must start early, around the late middle school to early high school years. It starts getting too late, around the point of 10th grade or when the child is 15 years of age and over.

Paul also provides us another pathway to channeling their thoughts toward God's perfect will. Paul writes, "I beseech you therefore, brethren be not conformed to this world; but be ye transformed by the renewing of your mind, so that ye may prove what is that good, and acceptable, and perfect, will of God" (Romans 12:1-3). The key question to prove a purpose is, whether it is good, acceptable, and perfect. It is not enough to be good; it must be more than good and acceptable; it must be of eternal value to God in His perfect plan for you.

As illustrated in Figure 10.1, God declared all His purpose and creation to be good. For example, He created Adam and gave him dominion over all the good things He had created. However, a certain fruit out of many good ones in the garden was not acceptable by God for Adam to eat. God said, "You are free to eat from any tree in the garden; but you must not eat from the tree of the knowledge of good and evil, for when you eat from it, you will certainly die" (Genesis 2:16-17, NIV). This Scripture clearly illustrates my point: only what is acceptable by God, what brings honor to Him, glory to Him, and eternal value to His plan for you and others— this is what God permits you to partake. In this example with Adam, what was acceptable to God was life sustaining and perfect. God's will was for the goodness of His creation to continue, undefiled by evil. Adam and Eve, by eating the fruit God had instructed them not to touch, inevitably added evil to

His good creation. God allowed them free choice, but gave them clear instruction of how and why to choose. They failed to conform their minds to God's and their choice of eating the fruit in this case was because it was desirable and good in their eyes, which was not the perfect will of God for them; the good that God wanted to continue on earth died, not only in them, but in others after them, when they chose to disobey.

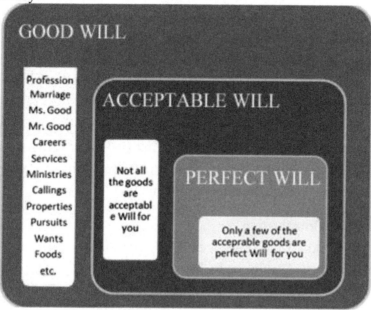

Figure 10.1: The Perfect Will of God Nested with the Good and Acceptable Will

Thus, as shown in the figure, only a fraction of those good things that God freely allows for you are acceptable. Within that acceptable list, there are things that God has destined to be perfect for you — flawless, life and joy sustaining, and fitting to His plan for you. If it is to choose a career or business, all professions and trades may be good, and some are acceptable within your gifting, but only a few of such professions are perfect. If it is to choose a spouse for marriage, all men and women out there are good in God's creation, while simply some few are acceptable for you, and only one is the perfect choice in God's will for you; in the context of God's calling to service or to a ministry, many paths are possible, but only a few are the perfect will of God, etc.

Cast down Prideful dispositions.

How can a parent transform the mind of a child or teaching the child a better ways of life? In general, pride is the first stronghold of the enemy to pull us down. Our pride and thoughts are not meant to make us think of ourselves more highly than we ought to think. We are not to conform to the actions of the world. Our minds are to be renewed daily and brought in check to the purposeful Will of God as a way of changing our insides to bear the fruit of transforming our outward conduct and integrity, credibility, and motives. Parents can as an act of compassion instill the value of humility and mentor the child with new information to begin the mind transformation.

Cast down imagination.

Children are always exploring and imagining things with current advert of multi-media. We must cast down all imaginings that are not aligned to God's word. As parents, we all can attest to the fact that the imaginations of youth run wild during their teenage years, and begin to mature just before they enter adulthood. They try many things to find out who they are, what they like, who to model their lives after, and the vices that will fulfill their exploratory minds. The advent of the computer, the Internet, and social media has reinforced these issues.

Imagination and fantasizing can be as simple as entertaining negative thoughts, which could mean dwelling on the negative past or trying to figure it out for ourselves. Imagination can also be playing out our thoughts. Our imaginations must be cleaned, captured, or transformed to align with the Word of God (2 Corinthians 10:5-6) because our thoughts are the first to be triggered in the chain reaction that defiles our insides. We must begin by rejecting these thoughts and bringing their accompanying prideful imaginations under our control. Our thoughts stir up our emotions; our emotions then influence our desires, and our desires are what produce our actions. Furthermore, our actions, good or bad, create our habits and attitudes, and our habits and attitudes develop our characters, again for good or bad. Taking every bad thought captive will prevent that chain reaction before it even begins. Anything that exalts itself has a tendency to stir up pride and defile our humility to serve. Thus, we must reject pride in all of its forms, for "God resists the proud, but gives grace unto the humble" (James 4:10).

Cast down and demolish all external sources

External sources of strongholds include:

- Bad associations and demonic linkages
- Covenants, pledges, secret oaths
- Wrong senses of freedom
- Music, video/computer games, media outlets that compromise good judgement and values
- Pornography and sexual addictions
- Drugs and substance abuse
- Books and magazines that compromise good judgement and values
- All Occult practices
- All forms of demonic worship and symbols
- Bitterness against parents
- Rebellious tendencies

Casting down and demolishing all sources or roots of stronghold are keys to final breakthrough. As a college administrator often faced with the responsibilities of dealing with these tendencies, I find that the independence of youths (away from the parents' watch) on college campuses, and with friends of similar feathers, allows some individuals to advance their vices. Unknown to their parents, they will pierce their ears, tattoo some part of their bodies, change their hairstyles, or pledge to some group, to accentuate these vices. However, there are also some who will reduce their vices as they see their grades plummet down and, at this time, the reality of graduating and getting jobs will set in. All of a sudden, at the end of sophomore year, they will suddenly grow up, especially male students, to face their studies.

To bring closure to this chapter, we must note that the acts of inward compassion extended to children provide a pathway for dealing with generational realities in this conflicting cultures. The heart of compassion, driven by the inner strength of parents, provide answers to the questions we posed at the beginning and can yield wholeness to the family, often broken down by the challenges of the present cultures. We must work on cultivating the caring empathy discussed earlier by making effort to walk along with the children in their different needs without judgmental attitudes. The family, as our first institution, demands our primary responsibility in whatever we do in parenting and mentoring the children to bring wholeness to the family through unconditional love of our children as demonstrated by our acts of compassion.

CHAPTER 11

WHOLENESS RECONCILIATION

The wholeness-reconciliation attitude is the specific action taken to resolve conflicts to bring healing to a broken relationship between two or more people. Has somebody ever lied against you, betrayed your trust, cheated you, cheated on you, enslaved you, abused you, stolen from you, or physically or emotionally hurt you? Have you done any of these things to others, lacked forgiveness, or had a grudge against someone? We are commanded to forgive those that hurt us. The hurt can come in different forms and occurs when someone or something causes a detriment or damage to your health or feelings. In general, when we hurt, it makes us physically, mentally, spiritually, or emotionally sick. When Jesus was flogged, humiliated, and nailed to the cross, and "was bruised for our iniquities…" (Isaiah 53:5, NKJV), he was hurt. Even so, he said, "Father forgive them, they do not know what they do…" (Luke 23:34). He refused to have that hurt affect them. His emotions toward others, even those that revile us should be like in the case of Jesus.

Pastor Lance Lecocq of the Monroeville Assembly of God defined reconciliation as a situation "when enemies become friends." Additionally, wholeness-reconciliation is an act of unifying or healing a relationship that was once broken, or developing mutual respect between enemies in order to make them once again whole, emotionally and relationally. Reconciliation occurs between family members, friends, organizations, and even businesses, not just enemies, because conflicts are expected to arise in the best of relationships, including marriages between two Christians.

As an act of compassion leadership, reconciliation provides healing time, the opportunity to make amends in relationships, a time of forgiveness, acceptance, understanding, and the whole healing of hurts. Humans are not wired to remain in a state of anger and hurtful feelings too long without serious health consequences. To be mentally healthy, humans must control their feelings and not allow hurts from conflicting experiences to rule their lives negatively. Research shows that sustained emotional instability from things such as anger can increase blood pressure, cause headaches, and cause anxiety that may cause physical health problems such as ulcers or heart disease. Often, it is the person that needs to forgive—the offender—and not the offended, that ends up hurting themselves the most, and thus blocking the blessings of God from their lives. The following principles can help the leader-servant bring wholeness to others through reconciliation:

Total Forgiveness Drives Reconciliation

As simple as forgiveness and states of unforgiveness may seem, there are several studies on the subject, and with often conflicting definitions. Unforgiveness involves holding back or keeping a record of emotional feelings (bearing grudges, bitterness, resentments, anger, malice, hurts, or any form of injustice or unpaid debt) caused by someone else. Worthington (2005, 2006), who has studied the subject extensively, broadly defined forgiveness as a "process of decreasing inter-related negative resentment-based emotions, motivations, and cognition." According to Worthington and others (2007), "most researchers who studied transgressions by strangers or people in non-continuing relationships defined full (true) forgiveness as simply reducing unforgiveness, and researchers who studied continuing relationships defined full (true) forgiveness as decreasing and eventually eliminating unforgiveness by replacing the negative with positive and eventually building to a net positive forgiveness experience. These two sets of studies imply that forgiving people in a non-continuing relationship is different from forgiving loved ones. Worthington (2006) and his group concluded that forgiveness is of two types: a decision to control one's behaviors (i.e. decisional forgiveness) and a multifaceted emotional forgiveness that involves changed cognition, emotion, and motivation. A combination of decisional forgiveness and emotional forgiveness is possible within my framework of a leader as servant leadership, although the two may have different pathways to true forgiveness.

Stating it simply, holding back those emotional feelings resulting from what another person or source (employer, government, or organization) did to you, without releasing them, is unforgiveness, but when you release that person or comfort the source of the guilty party who caused those feelings, it is forgiveness; it is canceling and letting those feelings or the record of them go. Unforgiveness could be of three sources or types: unforgiveness of the self (self-condemnation), of others, and feelings of unforgiveness from God for the negative or sinful thing that one has done which offended or hurt others or God. Forgiveness in each of these types may take different processes with distinctive effects, but the sum of true forgiveness in all of these senses (self, others, feeling forgiven by God) is what I will refer to as *total forgiveness*. It was an act of total forgiveness when Christ declared sinful humanity not guilty before God, or by His act of love canceled the debt of death humanity owed to God. The Scripture says that love "Does not dishonor others, it is not self-seeking; it is not easily angered, it keeps no record of wrongs" (2 Corinthians 13:5, NIV). You have forgiven as an act of love when you keep no record of the wrongs done to you. In the context of the servant leadership model, I posit that true forgiveness is a submissive obedient act of love whereby an offended party *chooses to transform his emotional perceptions using the inside-out motivation not to count an offender's hurtful actions, offense, or debt in his feelings or relationship toward the offender*; this must be done in a way that glorifies God. True forgiveness must include not only others, but the forgiver must also forgive self, and feel forgiven by God. God demands that we forgive each other (see Matthew 18:21-34; 1 Corinthians 13:4-7). It is difficult, if not impossible, to serve someone who has hurt you in the past if you have not let go of that pain as of yet.

Despite the Lord's command that we should forgive so that we will be forgiven, why is forgiveness so difficult, even for the best of Christian leaders? Lack of forgiveness is the major cause of divorce among Christian marriages. It is critical for a leader-servant to be ready to forgive in order to be a part of another's healing. Think of it this way: take forgiveness as an action whereby you count your hurt as if it didn't happen (because Jesus has paid for it). Alternatively, take it as an action for which you refuse to remain a victim, or better yet, you choose to forgive in order to reap the full blessings of God's gift. By thinking of forgiveness in these terms, it will become as direct as obeying a commandment so important to our loving God that He made it the *only* condition by which He would forgive your trespasses. "And when ye stand praying, forgive, if ye ought against any: that your Father also which is in heaven may forgive you your trespasses. But if ye do not forgive, neither will your Father which is in heaven forgive your trespasses." (Mark 11:25-26, KJV)

So, which is important: To forgive another or not to be forgiven by God? Truly, not to forgive is really a foolish shortsightedness that can affect one's health. Forgiveness opens the door for reconciliation. True forgiveness means that we might maintain our disapproval of what a person did or did not do, but relinquish the right for restitution from the offender and completely let go of the incident and all associated resentments. Forgiveness with reconciliation is really for our benefit because it is channeled through that which God blessed within us, and through the way in which we relate with God and rebuild broken relationships.

Forgiveness is not an act of excusing someone for an offense, but more for the benefit of the forgiver's blessing, as it is a condition for answered prayer and forgiveness from God who has the real power to judge. Forgiveness is not an act of reconciliation that requires two people to agree, or forgetting the action, but true forgiveness occurs when we choose not to remember the action. Forgiveness is not approval, meaning you can forgive an action without approving it, as Jesus showed in John 8:11: "Go and sin no more." Forgiveness is not pardoning or releasing someone from the consequence of an action; you cannot impose consequences or shield someone from God's dealing or the Law; forgiveness is not denying what was done; to truly forgive, you must acknowledge what was done; forgiveness is not forgetting the action. True forgiveness is different from reducing unforgiveness. According to Worthington et al. (2007) and Worthington (2001), some common unforgiveness-reducing alternatives include these:

1. Seeing justice done (including civil justice, criminal justice, restorative justice),
2. Letting go and moving on,
3. Excusing an offense,
4. Justifying an offense,
5. Condoning an offense,
6. Forbearing,

7. Turning the issue over to God because one does not believe oneself capable of judging, or

8. Turning the issue over to God in hopes of divine retribution.

However, I will state that true forgiveness can result from any of these states of un-forgiveness, reducing alternatives when it emanates from an inside-out submissive and obedient act of love that transforms the emotional perception of offended, and motivates him or her not to count the offense in feelings and in relationship toward the offender; such an alternative will glorify God.

Acts of forgiving others who have hurt you

The acts of forgiving others who have hurt you start from understanding what forgiveness is, and when and why to forgive. We are called to forgive instantly, as a Christ-like fruit! And why should you forgive him? You do not require the offended to apologize for the offense before you forgive. It is not a choice, but a commandment from God to be obeyed as stated before; it is more to the benefit of the offended than the offender. But most importantly, lack of forgiveness is one simple pathway to Hell!

The most critical question is: how do we forgive? Forgiveness is directly related to wholeness, and yet some people remain in their hurts, often because of pride or self-centeredness. Remember, forgiveness is the condition under which we are forgiven and blessed by God. Yet, there are situations where the leader, the Shepherd of God, is not on talking terms with followers. Because of accumulated hurts, the followers do not want to be hurt any further, and do not want to relate to the leader. Some will actually leave the fellowship, church, or respective organization.

The health of an organization and its members is incumbent on the leader, no matter his hurt. The life story of Josh McDowell, author and founder of Josh McDowell Ministries, a division of Campus Crusade for Christ, illustrates it best. The story was recounted in the movie, *Undaunted: The Early Life of Josh McDowell*. The film documented the effect Josh's lack of forgiveness of his father had on him as he was growing up. His father was a drunkard, and routinely beat Josh's mother and hurt the entire family, both physically and emotionally, in the process. Josh said that his father hurt him so much in life that he enjoyed hating him. Once, he feared he might forgive his father for all that he took him through. Josh, who was driven by the harsh reality of his life to prove that God did not exit, ended up proving the opposite to himself, and later had an encounter with the living Christ. In response to his father's curiosity as to why Josh had forgiven him for all he did to him, Josh said that, since Jesus forgave him his sin, he had to extend forgiveness to his father, who at the time was very sick in the hospital. Because of Josh's act of forgiveness, his father gave his life to Christ and was later healed. His father spent the rest of his life speaking about reconciliation, sharing how God had healed him physically and mentally from alcoholism, and healed him emotionally from his waywardness. His later focus in life was to reconcile with those he had hurt. That is a good example of an act of wholeness and healing-care, resulting from forgiveness and reconciliation. That was the example Jesus left for leader-servants to follow.

Acts of forgiving the self

The act of forgiving yourself is letting go of self-condemnation. Un-forgiveness of self is not letting go or emotionally keeping a record of your feelings for the hurt you've caused to others or the sin you committed. It is allowing the guilt of those sins to always be in front of you and condemning you. It is a sense of self-condemnation from the belief that you have done something unforgivably wrong to another or sinned against God. Those feelings and the associated guilt and shame have been shown to be stressful and unhealthy. You will not feel totally forgiven until you deal with those feelings.

The process of forgiveness of self is clearly stated in the Scriptures. We read about God's call for forgiveness: "My people, who are called by My name will humble themselves and pray, and seek My face and turn from their wicked ways, then I will hear from heaven, will forgive their sin, and heal their land" (2 Chronicles 7:14, NKJV). God was addressing His people to humble themselves, to pray, and to repent to reconcile to Him. If we confess our sins, He is faithful and just to forgive us our sins and to cleanse us from all unrighteousness (1 John 1:9). Here is a biblically-based process for the forgiveness of self and freedom from feeling of unforgiveness from God:

- Confess	Humble yourself; seek the face and relationship with God that was broken by that sin; State in specific terms the truth of what you did; acknowledge your sin and the unjust or hurtful actions of yourself or your group toward others.
- Repent	See yourself as a sinner and hate your sin the same way God hates it. Turn away from the sin or those actions with a heartfelt desire to change the behavior and attitude about what you did, forsake them, and return to loving actions, not to do them again by the grace of God through Christ.
- Reconcile	Free yourself from sinful condemnation and fully receive and accept forgiveness, and pursue new intimate fellowship with those you have offended, starting with God; Live and walk in the Spirit to sustain that relationship with God and others.

First, you must confess those sins before God and believe that He is faithful and just to forgive you of all sins, no matter how bad they are. Second, you must repent and forsake those sins. And third, you must begin to live and walk in the spirit of God. You must believe that there is no more condemnation on you now that you walk and live in the spirit of God (Romans 12:1-2). Of course, the process assumes that you are in Christ Jesus, that is, that you have accepted Him as your personal savior.

Cleansing and healing ourselves of these feeling goes together. Healing or restoration to wholeness is a process that starts with humility, confession, repentance, and reconciliation. In relation to the health benefits of self-forgiveness, Worthington et al (2007) hypothesized that "self-condemnation may impair self-care, produce depression and anxiety, and demotivate coping. That might result in more immediately apparent negative health consequences than would forgiveness of others" (Worthington et al 2007).

Forgiveness: Letting Go of Bitterness

What is bitterness? To be *bitter*, according to dictionary definition, means to be "sharp like an arrow or pungent to the taste, disagreeable; venomous," conveying the idea of something that is poisonous, with an overpowering taste, referred to in Numbers 5:18 as, "water of bitterness that brings the curse", a punishment given to women suspected of committing adultery. Simply put, bitterness is the act of being bitter—pungent taste, poison, sharp arrow to the heart.

The scripture gives us some other insights into the characteristics of bitterness and how to deal with it. Apostle Paul writes:

> "Therefore, putting away lying, "Let each one of you speak truth with his neighbor," for we are members of one another. "Be angry, and do

not sin": do not let the sun go down on your wrath, nor give place to the devil...Get rid of all bitterness, rage and anger, brawling and slander, along with every form of malice. Be kind and compassionate to one another, forgiving each other, just as in Christ, God forgave you." (Ephesians 4:25-32),

"Pursue peace with all people, and holiness, without which no one will see the Lord: looking carefully lest anyone fall short of the grace of God; lest any root of bitterness springing up cause trouble, and by this many become defiled." (Hebrews 12:14-15).

As a working definition, we can define *bitterness* as an emotional state of mind that intentionally holds on to angry feelings, offenses, and unforgiveness, and readily reacts in wrath at the slightest provocation. As an inner emotion, bitterness is an act of a poisonous spirit that holds on to unforgiveness and builds up anger inside, which externally explodes in wrath, "brawling," and malice (feelings of intense hatred toward another). Why does the Bible teach us to "get rid of all bitterness, rage and anger, brawling and slander, along with every form of malice"? (Ephesians 4:25-32).

Bitterness has a *source,* a *seed,* a *soil* (ground), and a *root.* How does the *source* provide the *seed* and how does *the* seed take *root* in the soil (your soul or heart)? The source of the seed in this context is the offender. The *seed* that grows into bitterness is planted by the nature of what the offender said, did, or took from the offended, which became planted in the soul (soil) of the offended. The offense often causes hurts, disappointment, and sometimes brokenness and suffering. It is often possible that the offender who caused the hurts did it unintentionally; other times they are deliberate, insensitive actions of the offender. Many things in our interactions with people can cause bitterness to take root in our hearts, resulting in deeply rooted resentment and lack of forgiveness. In any form it displays, bitterness is a negative energy of the offended expended in thinking about what the offender did to, said to, or took from the offended or what the offended perceives was done to him; sometimes the offended feels he or she has the right to be bitter.

When the seed of bitterness grows to maturity in the heart of the offended, it is reflected outwardly in negative reactions or effects such as outburst of anger, rage, animosity, malice, hostility, etc. In fact, anything that is the opposite of pleasure or better is bitterness. Bitterness is an inner emotion that negatively drives a person's emotional response toward anger and readiness to forgive. As a whole, bitterness:

- Deprives you of your peace of mind, joy in your life;
- Occupies your thought, thinking about the offender, how and why he hurts you, and sometimes how to get even;
- Saddens your spirit; bitter people are often miserable, negative people;
- Causes stress and makes your body sick;
- Defiles your character and others around you –your children, spouse, your friends, and God;
- Affects your relationship with others.

There are several lessons to learn from the above scriptures to help us fully understand what I will encapsulate in the word **BITTERNESS.** Specifically, bitterness is:

Bondage to unforgiveness. In this sense, bitterness is not only the result of unforgiveness rooted over a period of time but one's determination not to pursue peace, a refusal to forgive, resulting in the person being held captive by unforgiveness, poisoned in his heart, bound by iniquity to act wickedly toward the other person.

Intentional choice to poison your heart. In the words of Apostle Peter, the bitter person is "poisoned by bitterness and bound by iniquity" (Act 8:23). It starts with anger but when we choose to let that anger remain, in disobedience to "do not let the sun go down on your wrath," we "give place to the devil" (Ephesian 4:25), whose ultimate purpose is to destroy the relational tranquility between people. This is intentional because staying in a state of bitterness too long is a choice a person makes, purposely to be captive to unforgiveness. Hence, one can choose instead to let go of anger as soon as possible; the thought of what has generated the anger if not regulated can poison the heart, and the more it lingers, the sooner it reaches the level of bitterness.

Torment against your soul. The seed of bitterness when planted, gradually poisons and becomes a torment to the soul. Anyone who has been bitter against another person will agree that bitterness torments the soul. Bitterness kills whatever joy you had before in relating with the person and replaces it with provocations with the slightest disagreement; it sets the mind in constant battle with the other person as the love turns to hate. Most importantly, bitterness is rooted in un-forgiveness, the one condition under which God will not forgive our trespasses (Matt 6:14-15). Bitterness affects our souls by defiling all that makes the souls remain joyful, making the soul unholy before God and unpeaceable before men. The immediate result is that a defiled soul will likely pursue that which is evil. God may allow us the choice to the evil desires of our hearts, which invariably will decrease our willingness and capacity to respond positively to God and His ways.

Tool and Tactics of the devil against forgiveness. This is the very reason Paul said, "Do not let the sun go down on your wrath, nor give place to the devil." Bitterness resulting from unforgiveness is a tool the devil uses to defile our relationship with each other and with God. Hence, we are to "pursue peace with all people, and holiness, without which no one will see the Lord." He warns us to look carefully "lest anyone fall short of the grace of God." We must understand the full purpose of the devil here—uses bitterness as a tactics to keep us captive to unforgiveness —a clear tactics that is used to make us fall short of the grace of God, receive unforgiveness from God, and make us his follow candidate for hell.

Emotional response abound with iniquity. Bitterness is an emotional response that the devil uses as a vice for malice and hatred against another person. It thrives with wickedness. A person filled with bitterness against another is likely to intentionally act out wickedly against the other, even in cases where that other person makes unintentional mistake in situations not related to the past hurt.

Reinforcement of unforgiveness and malice. Although unforgiveness is the primary root of bitterness, bitterness when developed is one primary driver of unforgiveness and often becomes the root of unforgiveness in other interactions between the parties. The bitter person often finds himself easily angered by the slightest provocation. And the cycle continues!

Nurtured negative energy against your wholeness. Bitterness is negative energy nurtured over time against another person, resulting in defilement and brokenness of the relationship. Bitterness also works against restoring the wholeness of the relationship

Energy expended more against your wellness of the offended than the offender. Unforgiveness directly affects the physical, mental, and spiritual wellness of the forgiver more than the wellness of the others. Bitterness negatively affects our own physical health and relationships. I have had periods, where I spent days angry, in some cases bitter because of what someone did to me that hurts and wallowing in self-pity, only to realize that the offender either did not intend to cause any hurt, did not even remember, or was completely misunderstood. Bitterness in all of its forms defiles your love-base character in such a way that, in those states of bitterness, all that one sees is the negative aspects of the offender, and will never bring about the righteousness of God. When we fail to forgive the offender or focus on getting even, we miss opportunity for greater blessing that God gives to those who forgive. Bitterness can be conquered by compassion and act of love.

Springer of stronghold of trouble and defilement. Scripture above warns us that bitterness will give "place to the devil" (Ephesians 4:27), meaning that bitterness will give the devil legal control of our soul. From Paul's interpretation of his metaphor (*"For the weapons of our warfare...for pulling down strongholds, casting down arguments... thought into captivity to the obedience of Christ..." (2 Corinthians 10:4-6. NKJV)*, we can define stronghold as a human spiritual thought fortress (human false reasoning, pattern of thought, and imaginations) reinforced by logic and philosophy to resist the truth of God's word. By giving devil the control of our souls through bitterness, we also give him legal right to build strongholds for his evil operations and further torment our souls in other areas. The Bible also warns that we "do not let the sun go down on your wrath" before we forgive and let go of the anger. This is because when we allow the sun to go down upon our wrath, we give the devil more place, reason or "ground" to attack our soul (Eph. 4:26-27), creating stronger hold in other parts of our lives, and creating in us strongholds in the form of false pattern of thinking, vain philosophies, and imaginations. Such state of mind, which is contrary to Scripture, is likely to negatively influence our will toward godly decision. Bitterness produces negative emotions or reactions such as anger, depression, resentment, rage, animosity, and hostility. These emotions generate negative thoughts and imagination as strongholds. We can pull down these strongholds, because the weapons for such warfare are mighty only through the grace of God and are specifically designed to cast down every false philosophy and deceptive imagination, and bring every thought to the obedience of the truth of Christ's teaching God (2 Cor. 10:4-6). Bitterness as a stronghold can be seen in the offended feeling or imagining ways to "get even" or punish the offender. Yet, the

Bible teaches us not to repay evil with evil for "Vengeance is mine, I will repay, says the Lord" (Rom. 12:19).

$\underline{Sin}$ against God. The spirit of bitterness leads a bitter person to be resentful, harsh, malicious, and unpleasant to be around. Bitterness often yields the work of the flesh, such as "outburst to wrath…and those who practice such will not inherit the Kingdom of God" (Galatians 5:20-21). It is to be noted that this 'outburst to wrath' is listed among other sinful acts, equating it to all other sinful habits. These characteristics come from a defiled false mindset and such act is a sin against God. For that reason, we are warned not to allow the root and acts of bitterness in our hearts, as such acts can cause us to fall short of the grace of God and cause us trouble and defilement (Hebrews 12:15). Instead, we are to live out the fruit of the Spirit– love, joy, peace, holiness, etc. (Galatians 5:22-24).

Overcoming Bitterness

Ways to overcome bitterness is to forbear with and forgive one another. If any man has a quarrel against any, he must manifest patience to let go or forgive the other person's hurtful action. This patience makes it easier to surrender our rights to be able to forgive.

First, we must recognize that bitterness is a stronghold with two elements: imaginations and controlling thought patterns. Second, we must understand the tools the scripture provides for overcoming bitterness: *"For the weapons of our warfare are not carnal but mighty in God for pulling down strongholds, casting down arguments… bringing every thought into captivity to the obedience of Christ…" (2 Corinthians 10:4-6. NKJV).*

Forbearing and forgiving any offense resulting from a quarrel are intentional acts of love to God who readily forgave us and makes forgiveness the condition under which he will forgive our trespasses against Him. Thus, forgiving one another is an important act of compassion that frees you to let go bitterness and begin more wholesome method of resolving conflict.

Forgiveness helps us to triumph over the stronghold of bitterness (Luke 6:27; 1 Peter 3:9, Col 3:12-18). As will be discussed in the next section, forgiveness calls us to relinquish our right to get even by letting the person who has hurt you off the hook. Romans 12:19 says: "Never avenge yourselves. Leave that to God." After all, Jesus commands that you "Love your enemies, do good to those who hate you." (Luke 6:27). Peter reminds us of the same calling, "not returning evil for evil or reviling for reviling, but on the contrary blessing, knowing that you were called to this, that you may inherit a blessing." By letting go the person and the hurt and by appropriately answering the call for compassion by the Lord, we also become free from the captivity of unforgiveness and bitterness that results from it.

Focusing on the prefect love of God above all things can break the bondage of bitterness as we readily submit to nurturing each other above all things as bonds of perfection. As perfect love bears all things and counts no wrong of the other (1 Corinthians 13:4-8), we can forgive each other and work together to build each other's strengths in the areas of weakness.

Focusing on achieving peace together as one body can help to manage conflict (Hebrews 12:14-15) by letting the peace of God rule in your hearts; we must earnestly pursue peace and root out all bitterness as the only option. We need to correct each other firmly but with love and gentleness. Other ways of overcoming bitterness include:

1. **Breakthrough from the poison of bitterness (Eph 4:25-32, Heb 12:14-15).** Some other ways that we can adapt to help us breakthrough from the poison of bitterness are to:
   - Speak truth with each other ;
   - Forgive and not to let the sun go down on your wrath;
   - Being careful not to give a place to the devil…

- Identify and get rid of all root of bitterness (lying lips, rage and anger, brawling and slander, malice, unforgiveness);
- Be kind and compassionate to one another;
- Readily forgiving each other;
- 'Pursue peace with all people, and
- Be attentive and not allow any root of bitterness spring up.

2. **Admit that you have bitterness.** Because bitterness is a sin and stronghold against our lives, we must first admit that we have an anger and bitterness problems. "If we confess our sins, he is faithful and just to forgive us our sins, and to cleanse us from all unrighteousness (1 John 1:8-10) As those who live and walk in the Spirit, we must not allow any element of bitterness. ¹⁴But if you harbor bitter envy and selfish ambition in your hearts, do not boast about it or deny the truth.

3. **Realize that you are the primary beneficiary.** The sickness and hurts from bitterness are 100% curable by simply admitting it and choosing to let it go. Some challenges we face in admitting bitterness is the fact that the offended who is bitter feels that he is the victim without realizing that he is the one hurting and needs to let go of the bitterness

4. **Confess the sin of bitterness.** Once we have admitted our state of bitterness, we must confess it as sin and pray for forgiveness from God (Eph. 4:29-32).

5. **Forsake bitterness by regulating your emotions.** This means learning and adopting strategies to control your response to *bitter seed* and not allow it to grow; you can choose not to give it a place in your heart by intentionally taking the following other-centered actions for sustained breakthrough (cf Col 3:12-19):
   - Cloth yourselves with compassion, kindness, humility, gentleness and patience.

- Bear with each other and forgive one another as the LORD forgave you.
- Put on love to bind you all together in perfect unity.
- Let the peace of Christ rule in your hearts,
- Admonish one another with all wisdom from the Spirit of God with gratitude and thanksgiving in your hearts.
- Do whatever you do in the name and glory of the LORD
- Wives, submit yourselves to your husbands, as is fitting in the LORD.
- Husbands, love your wives and do not be harsh with them.

The 5 R's: Strategies for True Forgiveness

That you must forgive the person who has wronged you is a command that really requires absolute obedience as its primary benefit is for the forgiver. Your forgiveness and blessing from God are interwoven with your own forgiveness of the offender. I believe the choice is simply: Forgive! But how do you forgive—that unfaithful spouse that cheated on you, the friend that used you, the friend, brother or sister that said those lies against you, the boss that abused you, etc. Remember the following five stages, I have referred to as the 5R's: *Relinquish, Respond, Release, Refocus, and Reconcile.*

1. **Relinquish your right to get even.** The first step to forgiveness is committing not to take justice into your own hands. Let God be the impartial judge. This is one of the things I have learned in walking with God over the emotion of anger, especially toward my wife. I heard him telling me: "You have no right unless that which I gave you, no matter the right you think you have, or what you believe she is not giving you. What I have given you is to unconditionally love my daughter"; and so, in the process, I have learned that I must take Him more seriously than my wife, or even myself, and

love everyone unconditionally. As difficult as that was, especially when I felt disrespected and absolutely correct, that voice would remind me, "you have no right to be upset." Such an attitude regulated my emotions toward anger and allowed me to channel my thought toward taking God seriously. You have to start by letting the person who has hurt you off the hook. Romans 12:19: "Never avenge yourselves. Leave that to God, for he has said that he will repay those who deserve it." The first step to forgiveness is to commit to not take justice into your own hands. Let God be the impartial judge.

2. **Respond and overcome the hurt with good.** This means *responding* to the evil with good. The Bible says, "Don't be overcome by evil, but overcome evil with good" (Romans 12:21, NIV). You don't overcome it by criticizing the offender. You overcome it with good, a positive attitude toward the offender. How do you know you are working in true forgiveness? Let us look at forgiveness in the life of Joseph, in Genesis 37-45:1-15. To put this discussion in context, let us review the background. Joseph was the second to the last of the 12 sons of Jacob. The youngest was Benjamin. His father loved him and spent more time with him because he was the son of his old age (Gen 37.3). His brothers became jealous of him because he was seen as the favorite son. Joseph had two prophetic dreams: in one, he was the binding sheaf of wheat grain with his brothers, when his sheaf stood tall, and his brothers' sheaf bowed down to it. In the second dream, the sun and the moon and eleven stars were bowing down to him (Genesis 37.9). When he shared the dreams with his brothers, they were insulted and plotted to kill him. However, his oldest brother Reuben urged them not to kill him. His other older brother Judah suggested that they sell him into slavery, to merchants going to Egypt, and they did. In Egypt, Joseph prospered in every challenge he faced and everything he did, because the Lord was with him

(Gen 39.23). Eventually, he became second in command to Pharaoh in all the affairs of Egypt, including being in command of the management of food crops for the famine that came all over the land. So it was that Joseph's brothers also came to Egypt to buy corn, as "the whole world came to Egypt to buy corn from Joseph" (Gen 41.57).

Now, put yourself in the position of Joseph, in the presence of people who hated him enough to sell him into slavery, with clear intent to make him suffer. Could there be a worse enemy or better opportunity for revenge? Joseph had all the rights, power, and privilege to get even with his brothers. Nevertheless, he willingly chose to relinquish those rights to bring healing through forgiveness and reconciliation. Joseph, in dealing with his brothers, followed these paths, worthy of emulation by any leader-servant:

- *He was prepared and private for the pain of forgiveness* (Genesis 45: 1-2). Leaders must be prepared for the true pain of forgiveness—letting go. Joseph was not willing to see outsiders see him overcome by his feelings, but cried out because of the hurt and the compassion he felt. It is okay that he wanted to keep the sins of his brethren as private as possible, even as God forgives our own trespasses, casting them into the depths of the sea (Micah 7:19). When we tell people of others' trespasses against us, what do we become? We become the judge. We want them punished, thereby acting as God who said: "Vengeance is Mine, I will repay say the Lord" (Romans 12:19). We also become the jury, setting the standard as our own judgment. God's perfect love drives away fears of punishment. We are to be kind, loving, and forgiving to each other, as God forgives us (Ephesians 4:32).

- *He was genuine and authentic* (Genesis 45: 3-4). Joseph did not appear intimidating, and at the same time, he appeared to show the act of forgiveness, as some of us will be tempted to do to appear unapproachable. But Joseph approached his brethren with love and compassion (Love drives away fears) (1 John 4:18). Compare this with our usual approaches: we keep the offended at a distance, and we forget that God does not keep us at arm's length. God does not bring forth our past to make us guilty for the present. He did not give us the spirit of fear, but of sound mind and son-ship (Romans 8:15). Joseph could have easily been puffed up by his success, despite their sins against him; he could have with his power shown some vindictiveness. Rather, Joseph revealed himself and his brothers' sin to them without passing any judgment, excusing their actions, and relating what they did in a non-threatening way.

- *He avoided creating a guilt-trip for the offender* (Genesis 45:5). When we let the Holy Spirit work in the offender, it produces true repentance that helps in the forgiveness process. Joseph used the opportunity to honor God and give Him glory. His act of forgiveness made it possible for his brothers to forgive themselves. One of Paul's greatest burdens was self-forgiveness for beheading the Christians. He was now ministering to the widows of those he had killed. Your guilt and self-pity will drag you down with a bad taste; guilt can affect or even destroy your future relationships, steal your joy, and shorten your potential in some cases. Take, for example, Judas, Jesus' disciple who betrayed him for 30 pieces of silver; instead of asking for forgiveness, he committed suicide, due to guilt.

- *He saw the sovereign act of God in the wickedness without approving the action* (Genesis 45:5-8).God sent Joseph before them and saved him to preserve their lives. He saved them from shame by showing the act of God. This is true forgiveness with love expressed. God elevated Joseph and made him the agent with which to accomplish His will. We could see the same pattern in the life of Jesus. Judas betrayed Jesus, but God elevated Jesus above all names. Joseph forgave from the heart and with no place for self-righteousness because he saw God's hand at work in the bigger picture of things, and meant well when he said, "You meant evil against me but God meant it for God. This indeed is a true, total, and complete forgiveness. Forgiveness as a commandment from God needs to be done in the attitude of love of God. The process of forgiveness calls for us to have the mind of God and do it in the attitude of Love of God" (Romans 7:24; 1 Corinthians 13:4-7).

3. **Release it to God.** Our never-ending issues in life often make us ask, "How long, Lord?" Nevertheless, real peace comes from committing those worries and outcomes, and ability to overcome them to God. When Jesus cried, "Father into your hands I commit my spirit" (Luke 23:46, NIV), it was an act of complete trust whereby he surrendered total control to His father. His prayer was "not my will, but yours be done" (Luke 22:42, NIV). Jesus released it all to the Father. So, whatever we are facing today in life, in the face of despair and our deepest struggles, we must release all to God. Release it to God. Every time you remember how you've been hurt, release it. Jesus said: "Forgive 70 times seven" (Matthew 18:21-22, NIV). Does that mean 490 times? No, it means an unending number of perfections. In other words, we just keep forgiving each other, no limit intended. If a person slaps on one cheek, present the other cheek. If he slaps you on the second cheek, you still have the first cheek to present again. You will not run out

of cheeks. We are talking about surrendering your self-will/initiative as a process of forgiveness. You know you've totally released the pain when it doesn't hurt anymore. Even so, every time the pain comes to your mind, you say, "God, I give it to you again."

4. **Refocus on your servanthood.** Concentrating on the hurt takes you away from your purpose of serving others to focusing on yourself. A servant leader's purpose is to relinquish his rights to focus on serving others. He focuses more on the health of his relationship with the follower than the hurt. People are more likely to become what they focus on. You become a slave of what you make your master. Will you focus on the pain of the hurt or the purpose for service? You must refuse to be distracted and must focus on the purpose of your service, as we learned from Job: "Put your heart right, reach out to God...then face the world again, firm and courageous. Then all your troubles will fade from your memory, like floods that are past and remembered no more" (Job 11: 13-16). Your blessings depend on your intentional choice to forgive and put your heart right.

5. **Reconcile and reach out to others**. This final stage of forgiveness is what ultimately makes it true and whole. It calls us to reach out, reconcile or be reconciled for lasting peace of mind. Without reconciliation, forgiveness alone will not bring unity and prosperity in the work of God. Wholeness will not be completely restored without reconciliation: Jesus died to reconcile us to God and commanded us to do the same **(cf** Mt 5:21-24**)**; Joseph established lasting peace with his brothers through genuine reconciliation; good marriages last for a long time not because couples are perfect, but because, when in crisis, the couple is able to readily reconcile by working together to build emotional stability (See Genesis 11:1-9; Acts 4: 31-34).

Although Jesus could have focused on His own hurt and pain, on the cross, He chose to reach out in love as a fellow sufferer, and comfort others. "Today you will be with me in Paradise" (Luke 23:43). Job lost all his children and possessions, but found healing and greater things after he prayed for his friends, including those who despised him (Job 42:10, 16). My younger step-brother (of separate mother) and his mother hurt me greatly as we were growing up. His mother worked very hard, negatively, to cause me not to complete my high school education; she made sure I received little or no support from my father, which subjected me to extremely difficult challenges designed to discourage me from receiving my education. But God canceled all her negative plans, and I finished and moved on the greater things by God's grace. Out of jealousy and envy, my brother hated me and said so many hurtful things about me despite my love for him. Later, after several years, this brother became sick, and I was sought out to help, as I had the means to do so. This was an opportunity to either get even with him or help him. Despite many people's advice to let him suffer, remembering the wickedness my own mother and I suffered in their hands, I chose to reach out to him, and spent quite a lot of money on medical bills to bring healing to him. I learnt later, before his mother died, that she could not believe I did what I did for her son. She saw that God had blessed me, despite all they did. I forgave her, to bring healing to the relationships, without requiring her apology. As we look at Joseph in the Bible (Genesis 37-45:1-15), he had the opportunity to get even with those who put him through so much pain and suffering, but he chose to reach out to them with love and empathy.

Health Benefits and Effects of Forgiveness

One of the most comprehensive reviews of the health benefits of forgiveness can be found in the recent review article and other works of Worthington et al. (2007) and Toussaint et al. (2003). Included in the review are studies on forgiveness and peripheral physiology with a focus on the emotional processes, as potentially related to forgiveness, and physical health. In the study by Toussaint and Williams (2003) cited in the above review, the blood pressure of a diverse sample of 100 mid-western community residents was measured to determine the effect of forgiveness on blood pressure. According to these researchers, higher levels of total forgiveness were associated with lower resting diastolic blood pressure across participants. The study also revealed differences separated by socioeconomic status and race: among white participants of high socioeconomic status, total forgiveness and forgiveness of self were associated with lower resting diastolic blood pressure. Forgiveness of others was associated with lower resting diastolic blood pressure among black participants with low socioeconomic status, and forgiveness of others, total forgiveness, and perceived divine forgiveness, were associated with lower resting cortisol levels. The combined results, according to these authors, suggest that "chronic unforgiving responses could contribute to adverse health by perpetuating stress beyond the duration of the original stressor. By contrast, forgiving responses may buffer health both by quelling these unforgiving responses and by nurturing positive emotional responses in their place." (Worthington et al., 2006).

In addition to spiritual and emotional healing, and meeting the condition of answered prayers, forgiveness has some other research-based physical health benefits. We have learned from studies by Lawler et al. (2003), and other studies, that forgiveness can be associated with lower heart rates, lower blood pressure, and stress relief. These studies concluded that forgiveness can bring long-term health benefits for your heart and overall health.[45] Similar follow-up studies by the same group found that forgiveness can be positively associated with five measures of health: physical symptoms, use of medications, sleep quality, fatigue, and asthmatic complaints.[46] These researchers noted the importance of emotional forgiveness in reducing un-forgiveness.

Through forgiveness, one can experience a reduction in negative effect (depressive symptoms), a strengthened spirituality, improved conflict management, and stress relief. All of these qualities have a significant beneficial impact on overall health. Forgiveness not only restores positive thoughts, feelings, and behaviors toward the offending party, but it restores the relationship to its previous positive state (Karremans et al., 2005)

Reconciliation for Lasting Peace of Mind

Pursue reconciliation for lasting peace of mind. True reconciliation is an important dimension of wholeness healing. It is a process that starts with true forgiveness and ends with a total inside-out cleansing. To be free from accusation means to heal the hurting souls who have allowed their relationships to deteriorate to that of becoming enemies.

It is not the conflict or the sin that caused the deterioration of the relationship, but the lack of forgiveness. Reconciliation opens the door to love and be loved again without fear. Without reconciliation, forgiveness alone will not bring unity and prosperity in the work of God. Wholeness will not be completely restored without true reconciliation. These are the kinds of love and forgiveness that God wants us to show to others. Jesus died to reconcile us to God. Joseph established lasting peace with his brothers through genuine reconciliation. Good marriages last for a long time not because couples are perfect, but because, when in crisis, the couple is able to readily reconcile by working together to build emotional stability (See Genesis

11:1-9; Acts 4: 31-34). Several lessons from these scriptures can be noted: satisfied intimacy builds your strengths and reduces emotions; better understanding increases knowledge of each other; mutual emotional, physiological, and physical understanding yields more tolerance; evaluating the outcome of individual actions and making changes if necessary builds emotional stability.

How to Achieve Reconciliation

Apologize to reconcile

This is important if the offense was perpetrated by the leader-servant. What does the Bible say about apology or apologizing? It says nothing that directly addresses the method of apologizing! However, we learn about apologizing by studying the words "confession," "forgiveness," "repentance," and "reconciliation." We can also take a look at some situations in the Bible where elements of apologizing took place, and what the outcomes of apologizing were.

Real and meaningful apologies are a cry within us for reconciliation. Meaningless apology can actually make reconciliation, difficult and must be avoided. Meaningless apologies are often given to benefit the offender in some way, rather than helping the victim feel better. It may also be an attempt to blame the victim for the exploitation, or an attempt to turn around the situation and accuse the victim of causing the offence. Alternatively, an apology may be given because the abuser now wants or needs something from the offended, or can be offered simply to silence the victim, move on, and avoid anyone else learning about the offense or betrayal.

Some elements of a meaningful apology include ensuring that the words are genuine and heartfelt, and that the offender accepts responsibility for the wrongdoing. It is focused on the victim's feelings rather than those of the offender; it attempts to bring healing to the victim; it is delivered in a humble and non-patronizing way; the offended feels genuine commitment by the offender not to do the same thing again; and no excuses or attempts are made to make the offended feel guilty. A worthwhile apology must be concerned primarily with making right the wrong and to make it crystal clear that the victim's feelings are the offender's top priority. An apology can also show an understanding of and remorse for the pain the offense caused, the ramifications of the behavior, and how it affected the victim's life.

Apology is beneficial, but not a requirement

We can also recall Jonah's heartfelt apology to God for his disobedience. As a result, God had the fish spit Jonah out on dry land, and thus Jonah was given a second chance (see Jonah chapter 2). Joseph's brothers sold him into slavery. Instead of their intent, Joseph was favored by God and man; his brothers apologized for what they had done to Joseph. Joseph and his brothers were reconciled after some heartfelt apologies. We also see how God allowed the devil to inflict Job physically and financially. Job apologized to God for speaking about things he did not understand. It wasn't until this apology happened that God healed Job and restored his finances (Job Chap 42). In Genesis (32, 33), Jacob tricked Esau into giving him his birthright, and then stole his father's blessing. Jacob offered Esau a sincere apology along with many gifts. Esau forgave his brother and did not kill him like he had said he would earlier. Jacob received forgiveness and got to keep his life because he apologized.

Apology also helps the offended receive healing for the hurt, and a blessing from God for forgiving the offender. Both the offender and the victim (offended) are reconciled, and the relationship is restored and strengthened. Joseph's brothers' relationship with Joseph was restored.

Being accountable for what you have done is the true test of maturity in a leader-servant. Being accountable for your behavior means repentance, restitution, and personal responsibility. Some of the action promises you can make when you forgive someone include: I will be settled in my mind that the incident is over; I will not bring this incident up and use it against you; I will not allow this incident to stand between us or hinder our personal relationship and work for God.

In these actions, it is important to keep in mind what forgiveness is not: It is not an approval or to show that what happened did not hurt. It simply means that you can forgive an action without approving of it or denying the hurt (John 8:11).

Even with its benefits, why is apologizing difficult for some? When apologizing feels difficult to an offender, it may mean that the offender has not really owned up to the responsibility of the offense. The offender may not be caring or showing care enough for the feelings of the victim and subsequent reconciliation of the relationship, or the risk of being ridiculed for the offense; alternatively, there is the potential risk of rejection and humiliation if the other person rejects the apology and refuses to forgive. Apologizing, then, can require a great deal of courage. The risk of being viewed as the instigator of unpleasantness can initiate a feeling of guilt. I believe that pride, and arrogances, are the main reasons people find it difficult to readily apologize. Apology is God's command as part of repentance, forgiveness, and reconciliation to bring healing. This is an imperative call for action for healing of the victim and offender, and requires humility and boldness.

Humility from a servant's heart

Humility from a servant's heart initiates the acts of reconciliation. Only a heart of humility, like in the case of Jesus or Joseph, will allow an offended to relinquish his rights to see a broken relationship healed. I believe the relationship Joseph had with his father, his love for his family, and the authenticity of his brothers, drove his actions for reconciliation. Building authentic relationship is an important element of effective leadership. Looking at Joseph's life again, as an example with respect to reconciliation (Genesis 45:9-15), we can learn the following lessons:

Offended helps the offender deal with the regret, repentance, and forgiveness (Genesis 45: 9-15). Joseph helped his brothers deal with the guilt, regret, and self-forgiveness; Joseph chose to dwell only on the positive work of God in the situation; and Joseph's complete forgiveness is exemplified by his unconditional reinstatement of their relationship.

Offended and offender work together to build each other's strength. Lasting relationships work together to build each other's strength (spiritual, emotional, and physical strengths) by adopting a good character; increasing security in the relationship builds trust and confidence.

The offended empties the hurt to reconcile and bond again with the offender. The hurt breaks the bond that holds relationships together. In order to reconcile, we must empty the hurts and clean ourselves inside-out to bond and relate again. True reconciliation takes place when the two begin to enjoy intimate fellowship with each other, which is made possible only through the cross of Jesus Christ. At the cross, Jesus healed the broken hearts of His followers and mankind through reconciling humanity to the Heavenly Father. He also commissioned His followers to the ministry of reconciliation in the world.

The primary lessons learned from the Calvary cross is that the offended bears his cross and expends himself toward the offender. Jesus expected his followers to bear their own crosses. He said, "Take up your cross and follow Me" (Matthew 16:24, NKJV) as a way of empowering His followers to be healers and reconcilers by enduring any pain for the sake of service toward others. To quote Pastor Lance, "Leaders must commit to spending themselves instead of spending on themselves." This means acts of reconciliation begin with God. We must invest in the health of others more so than in ourselves. If we are not fully reconciled to God, we cannot accommodate others. Our relationship with others is as healthy as we make our relations with God. When the relationship is in good condition, it empowers and secures us to heal other relationships. To be reconciled to God, we must openly acknowledge and confess our sins to be cleansed and forgiven; indeed, covering up the sins brings down judgment. A leader-servant's responsibility is to lead his followers to follow James 5:16: "Confess your faults one to another that you may be healed."

In all of these examples, Joseph, who was the offended in being sold into slavery, initiated the acts of reconciliation. He gave up his rights for apology. Rather, he saw the hand of God in the offense. That is an essential action expected by a leader-servant as demonstrated also by Jesus through our ministry. Joseph was a good reconciler, and we must be humble enough ourselves to emulate his examples to bring healing to others.

Be the reconciler to reconcile

As I was looking for good reconcilers in our world today, I came across an article by John Dawson of International Reconciliation Ministry. In his book, *What Christians Should Know about Reconciliation* (Dawson, 1998), he recounted how to "walk out" of reconciliation. He had to move his Anglo family into an African-American community in Los Angeles. He identified with the struggles of this community and developed meaningful friendships there. In one of his travels, he sat next to an African American grandmother on an airplane, and took the opportunity to ask for forgiveness for the sins of his people. The grandmother was cool to him early on in the flight, but later opened up and shared how her own great-grandmother had been sold at age 8 at a slave auction in Richmond, Virginia. Eventually, they fully connected, and the conversation changed when she heard that John had lived for 20 years in an African community, and realized how they shared many things in common through this community. This is an outstanding example of an authentic reconciler. Obviously, it took commitment and conviction to make such a move. John wrote,

> *As Christians, it should be our hope that our children will not have to deal with the hatred and alienation that have marked these and previous generations because of devilish strongholds rooted in history. Let us identify the ancient and modern wounds of injustice, pride and prejudice in our world and heal them in a biblical way, without self-righteous accusation or dishonest cover-up.*

A leader-servant is called to be a reconciler of his followers not only to God but each other, confessing faults one to another to bring healing and wholeness to the body. The Scripture says to "Make every effort to live in peace with everyone and to be holy; without holiness, no one will see the Lord" (Hebrews 12:14, NIV). We are called to make every effort, and that includes taking intentional steps to forgive and be forgiven, renew relationship, and be at peace with people.

Be an Intercessor to Reconcile

During the darkest days of the American Civil War, we read that Abraham Lincoln summoned the people. He proclaimed the following words (Lincoln Library, speech he gave in 1863):
:

> *"... recognize the hand of God in this terrible visitation, to remembrance of our own faults and crimes as a nation and as individuals, to be humble ourselves before Him and to pray for His mercy - to pray that we may be spared further punishment, though most justly deserved... it is the duty of nations as well as of men, to own their independence upon the overruling power of God; to confess their sins and transgressions in humble sorrow; however, with assured hope*

that genuine repentance will lead to mercy and pardon." (President Lincoln gave this warning in his proclamation of March 30, 1863)

This is a president who is acting as an intercessor. These words could as well have come from the notes of a preacher. Just like John the Baptist, he was saying 'confess, repent, and be healed.'

Be an Imitator of Christ

Leader-servants can emulate the ultimate leader-servant: Jesus Christ. The purpose of His Calvary Cross is the reason for your existence to be used to reconcile others. Your Calvary cross is any state of suffering and distress you experience as a child of God. He was an empathetic healer through reconciliations. Five lessons from Calvary's Cross are on helping the Leader-Servant heal others:

He suffered for the remission of our sins. He "gave himself for our sins, that he might deliver us from this present evil world, according to the will of God and our Father" (Galatians 1:4). So, as a leader just like Jesus, you must be humble yourself and endure an insult from a friend or a family member, or forgive a family member of that BIG sin? His Calvary cross must yield in us a mind to suffer any hurt and be an example for others. He suffered to demonstrate His love in that "...for when we were yet without strength, in due time Christ died for the ungodly...But God commended his love toward us, in that, while we were yet sinners, Christ died for us" (Romans 5:6-8). This challenges us to see love as a covenant commandment that we must demonstrate to all people regardless of the response or action of the receiver. We must be able to demonstrate that to others through examples.

He suffered for our reconciliation, to bring all to God since he "... made peace to reconcile all things unto himself; to present you holy and blameless in his sight" (Colossians 1:20-22). This means that there is no limit to the extent that you must go to in order to bring peace into any

Godly relationship, especially to those in the household of God, beginning with your family. We must triumph over the devil's stronghold that affects our peace, for at Calvary cross, Jesus "…spoiled principalities and powers, he made a show of them openly, triumphing over them in it" (Colossians 2:15).

CHAPTER 12

COMPASSION: A CALL FOR SELFLESS LOVE

In the context of the Leader as Servant Leadership Model, service leadership was defined as "a process in which a leader engages and empowers followers for maximum productivity or fruitfulness in others-centered services."[1] Within that framework, the act of compassion is an intentional and others-centered service motivated by selfless love of others. The husband with his wife, as joint-leaders, seeks to transform their family by developing the mindset of a servant toward all in the family who follow in his leadership. As a leader-servant, he pushes for the rights of others more than his own rights, and inspires them to grow to follow his example, as Jesus here demonstrated. "…But whoever desires to become great among you, let him be your servant. And whoever desires to be first among you, let him be your slave—just as the Son of Man did not come to be served, but to serve, and to give His life a ransom for many". (Matthew 20:26-28). You are not ready to be a great husband and a father until you are prepared to lay down your life and rights, and serve your wife and children as a servant. At the heart of such a mindset is love and compassion toward them.

Love of your followers in your immediate family (wife, children, and servants, etc.) is the starting and ending point of the act of compassion in service leadership for a family. First, God's love of mankind was the attribute that defined the work of salvation and His reconciliation of mankind to Himself (John 3.16). Peter demonstrated how we can show love in our attitude of service to each other (1 Peter 3: 8-13). We are to be of one mind, and unified in purpose, just as Jesus and the Father God are unified in purpose; we are to be compassionate with one another as one way of bearing and empathizing with one another, and showing practical love to each other; we are also to be tender-hearted, which allows us to forgive each other readily and repay evil with blessings. These positive attitudes are direct manifestations of the fruit of the Spirit, and a measure of the quality of the spiritual work of a leader toward others. Paul wrote, "But the fruit of the Spirit is love, joy, peace, forbearance, kindness, goodness, faithfulness, gentleness, and self-control. Since we live by the Spirit, let us keep in step with the Spirit. Let us not become conceited, provoking and envying each other. (Galatians 5:22-26). This means that the Spirit of God in a leader should yield the fruits of the Spirit. This, in turn, should produce fruit and affect the people served. A leader can only produce in others the identical fruit he has inside and can display outwardly. In other words, the amount of love, joy, and peace your work brings to others, in some measure, is how much of the same you can demonstrate. Are you joyful in your work? Do the people you serve feel loved and joyful? How forbearing and kind are you when you serve others? What level of goodness and faithfulness does your work show to others? In rendering your service, how much gentleness and self-control do you show? Your love of others is defined by what your acts of love do. How are you doing in each of the attributes of love delineated in I Corinthians 13:4-8?

The unconditional love of your family should be at the core of what drives your work as the leader of your family. To discuss this last point fully, I state here the law of conservation of God's love:

GOD'S LOVE IS CONSERVED EVEN IN OUR SUFFERINGS.

The three dimensions of this law are that a model of the acting out of the love of God is unconditionally LOVING, CONSERVING, and even in our SUFFERING. The first is very much known to us through the things it does (1 Corinthians 13:4-8).

God's Act of Loving is Unconditional.

God's love is unconditional, and the characteristic of His Divine love are shown by what love does (by the act of loving), as in 1 Corinthians 13:4-8:

1. **Patience.** Love suffers long. Patience is the ability to endure waiting, delay, or provocation without becoming annoyed or upset, or to persevere calmly when faced with difficulties. "But you, O man of God, flee these things and pursue righteousness, godliness, faith, love, patience, gentleness". (1 Timothy 6:11)

2. **Kindness.** Love is kind. Kindness is the practice of being or the tendency to be sympathetic and compassionate (to show consideration and caring). "For whoever gives you a cup of water to drink in My name, because you belong to Christ, assuredly, I say to you, he will by no means lose his reward" (Mark 9:41).

3. **Generosity.** Love is generous. Generosity is the willingness to give money, help, or time freely. David said, "The generous soul will be

made rich, and he who waters will also be watered himself" (Proverbs 11:25).

4. **Humility.** Love does not parade itself. Love is not puffed up; humility is the quality of being modest or respectful. "Remind them to be subject to rulers and authorities, to obey, to be ready for every good work, to speak evil of no one, to be peaceable, gentle, showing all humility to all men. For we ourselves were also once foolish, disobedient, deceived, serving various lusts and pleasures, living in malice and envy, hateful and hating one another." (Titus 3:1-3)

5. **Courtesy.** Love does not behave rudely. Courtesy is to be polite and considerate, to display behavior-consideration for other people or good manners; "Nevertheless, not to be tedious to you any further, I beg you to hear, by your courtesy, a few words from us" (Acts 24:4).

6. **Unselfishness.** Love does not seek its own but the good of others; unselfishness is putting the general good or the needs or interests of others first. "Let nothing be done through selfish ambition or conceit, but in lowliness of mind, let each esteem others better than himself." (Philippians 2:3)

7. **Good Temper.** Love is not provoked and never resentful. Having a good temper is an emotional condition, predisposition, or tendency not to get angry either easily or suddenly. "And everyone who competes for the prize is temperate in all things. Now, they do it to obtain a perishable crown, but we for an imperishable crown." (1 Corinthians 9:25)

8. **Godliness.** Love thinks no evil; it is always gladdened by goodness to others; love does not rejoice in iniquity; godliness is in right moral standing with God, fit for or having the divine qualities of God. "For bodily exercise profits a little, but godliness is profitable for all

things, having promise of the life that now is and of that which is to come." (1 Timothy 4:8)

9. **Truthfulness.** Love rejoices not in iniquity, but in the truth; truthfulness is the act of telling the truth or having the tendency to tell the truth. "The truthful lip shall be established forever, But a lying tongue is but for a moment." (Proverbs 12:19)

10. **Forgiveness.** Love bears all things; forgiveness is the act of pardoning someone for a mistake or wrongdoing, or the tendency to forgive offenses readily and easily. "And whenever you stand praying, if you have anything against anyone, forgive him that your Father in heaven may also forgive you your trespasses." (Mark 11:25)

11. **Trustworthiness.** Trustworthiness is the capacity to trust someone or be trusted by the same. Trustworthiness is the worth of the trust someone places in us, or that we place in someone else. The worth of our trust in something or someone is measured by the value we place on that person's character, such as in honesty, integrity, truthfulness, and so on.

12. **Long-suffering.** Love endures all things. Love believes all things, and hopes for all things. Long-suffering means being patient or tolerant despite many difficulties. "Or do you despise the riches of His goodness, forbearance, and longsuffering, not knowing that the goodness of God leads you to repentance?" (Romans 2:4-5) Eternal love never fails.

God's Love is Conserved

A leader's sense of knowing that God's love is conserved and never changes reassures him to know the nature of God's love to mankind, and the leader's love for others must be conserved even in that state of suffering, persecution, conflicts, and rebellious state, in which a person seems to be far from God . In reality, His position never changes. In

Romans 8:28, we read, "Know that all things work together for good to them that love God, to them who are the called according to his purpose...and in all these things, we are more than conquerors through him that loved us..." This means that God's love for each of us is conserved—if not in allowing us what we requested of Him, it may be in refusing, He knows that it was not expedient; if it is not in healing those infirmities we wanted healed, like in the case of Apostle Paul, it will be in making us see His strength in our weakness. There is no fear in suffering, for He will take the hardship and bring good out of it. The scripture did not say that suffering would not come, but that suffering would be transformed into good within God's purposeful will. When conflicts arise in your service toward others, leading your family, finding the purpose of God and teachable moments in those conflicts, you need to allow God to use those lessons for His glory and the good of others.

Transform those conflicts, as God would, into the good of the other person. Thus, God's pre-ordained plan is not for me to suffer, but to be conformed to the image of Jesus Christ. My suffering only preserves me more for Him, because it teaches me more about me, Him, and others.

God's Love is Perfected in Suffering

In the context of conserving God's love, we need to always remember, though, that hardships or suffering may all come, even as you yield to the will of God and determine to do right. But in the midst of them all, we must remain undaunted and have the mind to delight in the suffering for His sake as according to the Scripture "...But if, when ye do well, and suffer for it, ye take it patiently, this is acceptable with God. For even hereunto were ye called: because Christ also suffered for us, leaving us an example, that ye should follow his steps." (1 Peter 2:19-

21). "For it is better, if the will of God be so, that we suffer for well doing, than for evil doing." (1 Peter 3:17).

Leader-servants must emulate the three parts of love described above. Your love for others must be measured to the extent that it follows the Divine nature of God's love as modeled in Figure 12.1.

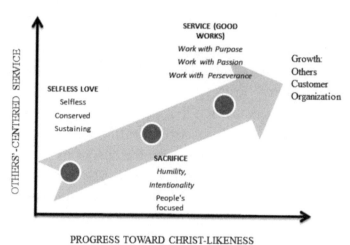

Figure 12.1. Service Leadership Process Model

Acts of Compassion from Spiritual Leaders

Jesus and the Apostles demonstrated that compassion is an integral part of any ministry that wants to care for the needs of people. Compassion is the inner strength quality that comes from the heart of a spiritual leader who is centered on people. Spiritual leaders in this sense must desire and possess the heart of compassion to the highest extent possible. Here are some key distinctive characteristics that identify most spiritual leaders:

Influence Transformation of Individuals

The purpose of helping individuals be transformed is so that they can develop the characteristics that God can use. Jesus taught his followers that they are the light and salt in the world. Thus, maintaining their shine and flavor was a necessary spiritual conditioning for the Kingdom's servants. Jesus said, "Let your light so shine before men, *that they may see your good works and give glory to your father who is in heaven*" (Matthew 5:14). This means that the life of spiritual leaders in God should have their good works and the power to transform others' hearts stand as a testimony for them to see and give glory to God. A father is the spiritual leader of his family. One result of a father's spiritual leadership is to transform the attitude of his children toward good works to each member of the family, and so extending such attitude to others outside. The transformation also includes leading the family to the part of righteousness and wholesomeness, or influencing spiritual growth. Spiritual leaders are intimately connected with God.

Impact their community

By their representation of godliness, spiritual leaders transform the transcendent presence and interaction in their environment. Most spiritual leaders experience this effect. For example, when a spiritual leader works himself into a gathering of people or joins a meeting, immediately an aura of influence and spiritual light appears in the room because of the respect and anointing of God in that leader. People's language and behaviors change just through the mere presence of the man or woman of God in the room. It's similar to an officer being in the room. As a leader, you are the steward of the truth of God in the life people see. In the presence of danger, people look to a spiritual leader for care and comfort. Think of how Jesus stilling the storm transformed the immediate environment and atmosphere; it manifested God's love, joy, peace, and patience. If you consider yourself a spiritual leader, and you find yourself in an environment where people are not influenced by your presence, you should question whether you are carrying the life of God that you are supposed to be reflecting. Spiritual leaders, with the real anointing of God, have the power to influence all people everywhere, both believers and unbelievers.

Love all humanity

Loving humanity is the single-most important element in spiritual servant leadership. This is the work for which Christ came and died. This is the work of salvation that is so important to God the Father that He allowed His only-Begotten Son to die. Jesus said, "For even the Son of Man came not to be ministered unto, but to minister, and to give his life a ransom for many." (Mark 10:45). The spiritual leader lives to reflect God's intentional love and care for everyone, no matter who they may be—unbelievers, friends, or enemies, as Paul writes, "But God demonstrates his own love for us in this: While we were still sinners, Christ died for us" (Romans 5:8, NIV). The basic elements of forming the character of a spiritual leader include interest and love to serve all men as Christ did and seeking nothing in return. Christ gave His life so that many could have abundant life (Luke 19:10, Mark 10:45). Clearly, His aim was first to love and serve humanity. He did it with humility and did not show His superiority. Hence, the basic qualification to do God's work is the heart to serve all. Paul further demonstrated this by his passion, discipline, and commitment to the mission to serve all men: "For though I am free from all men, I have made myself a servant to all, that I might win the more... I have become all things to all men that I might by all means save some." (John 10:10). All leader-servants are to embrace the same principle as the Apostle Paul demonstrated throughout his ministry: "Now this I do for the gospel's sake, that I may be partaker of it with you" (1 Corinthians 9:19-23, NKJV),

Provide spiritual care

We address this point last because its importance requires more attention. In your work or ministry, have people asked difficult questions about what they are going through at a particular point in their lives? On various occasions, I have heard questions such as, "Why should this happen to me? Why should God allow my husband to die? Why am I still in this situation?" People have also expressed helplessness in emergencies and disasters, and all people displaced and affected both spiritually and emotionally often ask such questions. Even when they do not openly ask questions, you must listen to their hearts, and you will see their helplessness and their need for healing. These are spiritual needs and concerns, and require immediate spiritual care. Spiritual needs differ from emotional needs, but can result in emotional and more serious needs if not handled with spiritual care.

Spiritual care can be defined as "any service or act that helps an individual, family, or community to draw on a spiritual perspective as a source of strength and healing."[37] In a disaster, anything that nurtures the human spirit in coping with the crisis is spiritual care. Everyone has had one form or another of spiritual need at some point in his or her life. Some spiritual needs are out there ready to emerge, and a leader-servant must be sensitive and spiritually equipped to provide spiritual care as part of his leadership function. Churches and community faith leaders are usually spiritually equipped to handle these situations.

In Stephen's Ministry, which is dedicated to caring for hurting people, I came to realize the prevalence of spiritual needs and the imperative nature of spiritual care in the care-giving ministry. It appears in almost all the challenges people face every day; care receivers usually have more spiritual questions than any other concern.

We need to understand how to engage people intentionally in the spiritual aspect of compassion to help the care-receiver find healing, rest, reconciliation, and affirmation in God.

Providing Compassionate Spiritual Care

Here are a few suggestions on how to provide spiritual care:

1. **Walk along in the experience with the care-receiver.** Because the spiritual need is not an emotional need, spiritual care is not therapy. It is a leader walking along the valley of the experience with the care-receiver, but allowing God to provide the cure and the healing.[38]

2. **Foster the appropriate situation for God to work.** Spiritual leaders prepare the ground for God to cure the need by creating the appropriate situation and waiting for God the Caregiver to introduce the cure, whether it is an emotional, mental, physical, or spiritual resolution. Fostering the appropriate situation could mean taking the care-receiver to be prayed for, to receive special delivery ministry, or praying along with the care-receiver for the expressed need.

3. **Provide the correct perspective.** In a state of suffering in which a person has earnestly prayed over an issue for an answer, doubt sets in and develops wrong perspectives of God's providence. Spiritual care relates the answers a care-receiver has to God's perspectives, which allowed the event to happen, but without passing any judgment.

4. **Build up the faith of the hurting person.** It is about building the hurting person's faith in the midst of suffering. In certain situations, the faith of even the strongest of us all can falter, especially in an extended period of suffering. The caregiver positions himself or herself to build up that person's faith.

5. **Provide the listening ear.** It is about providing the hurting person the opportunity to share his or her stories and experiences. It is about someone just listening rather than trying to fix their problems.[38]

6. **Share your presence and loving affection.** It is not about judging right or wrong, but about fostering the right atmosphere to edify one's spirit. Just being present with the person is a strong expression of affective and loving care. People in need of spiritual care need to feel loved and nurtured.

CHAPTER 13

COMPASSION: A CALL FOR ENCOURAGEMENT

Compassion-encouragement is an act of encouraging someone who is in a state of emotional despair or suffering. A case study of the characteristics of Barnabas or leaders like him could provide teaching tools in developing leaders' attitudes for compassion through encouragement. We read that Barnabas was named "Son of Encouragement" or "Son of Consolation" by the disciples (Acts 4:36). Barnabas was a Levite whose family came from the Island of Cyprus, where some of the Jews of the Diaspora had settled. His Hebrew name was Joseph ("may God increase") or José ("He that pardons"). Only later was he called Barnabas by the apostles. All three names reflect the attributes of God, but the most important characteristic was encouragement. He was an encourager. What did they see in him? Obviously, he must have impacted them with his acts of encouragement, and his example is a good reference point for emulation. He clearly inspired all of them. They saw him as an encourager by his courage to inspire them at a time when they desperately needed to move the ministry forward. Courage, as we have seen before, is an inner strength quality of a person's mind. Thus, a leader's act of encouragement to inspire a person in a lower emotional state comes from the leader's inner strength and self-security. You can only be an encourager as based from the strength of your inner personality. The act of encouragement is mostly expressed, such as in words, endorsement, and praise. In such a case, it is purely an inside-out strength of a leader, expressed outwardly to strengthen or inspire others. In others, it serves as a completely outward attribute, but most of the time it is expressed from the inner strength of a leader.

Encouragement can also be given outside of expression, such as through fostering an environment to inspire growth or applying a spiritual gift to serve others, or as a direct act of compassion. As Paul reminded us: "We have different gifts, according to the grace given to each of us; if it is serving, then serve; if it is teaching, teach; if it is to encourage, then give encouragement..." (Romans: 6-9). The same was referred to by Peter when he said, "Each one should use whatever gift he has received to serve others, faithfully administering God's grace in its various forms... If anyone serves, he should do it with the strength God provides, so that in all things, God may be praised through Jesus Christ" (1 Peter 4:10-11, NIV).

Research has shown that people can be encouraged to perform by fostering positive relationships in organizations and by modeling and providing acts of compassion, collective forgiveness, and expressions of gratitude, as well as by fostering the formation of friendships at work. Studies by Heaphy & Dutton (2004) showed that such acts of encouragement produce physiological effects, which motivate people toward higher performance, as well as fostering virtuous cycles of enriched relationships. What motivates someone to encourage another? How is encouragement an inner strength attribute?

Most encouraging leaders are internally enthusiastic and passionate about their mission, and they affect their followers with the same enthusiasm. An enthusiastic leader naturally has a positive perspective and will see the cup as half full rather than half empty. Encouraging leaders also readily look for ways to appreciate their followers for their efforts, especially those efforts which they see as having potential for the follower's greatness. Such leaders usually follow up with the follower with mentoring to encourage further growth.

The characteristics of Barnabas as an encourager were identified through his inspiring acts of service in *kindness, generosity, courage, compassion, reconciliation, and commitment*. A leader's acts of service go to the heart of the followers. The impact the followers experience often emerges from their feelings toward their leader.

The Principle of Encouragement Attribute

Encouragement was identified as a dimension of empowerment in the Leader as Servant Leadership Model (Wosu, 2014a). Encouraged followers are more likely to feel empowered for higher productivity; they will have a greater sense of accomplishment and meaningfulness in an organization. Based on these characteristics, my working definition in the context of the LSL model is as follows:

> *The servant leadership encouragement attribute is the combined acts of enthusiastically inspiring and affirming others with the courage to follow a new course of action for growth or uplifting the spirits of others with compassion to persevere in life challenges.*

The life challenges in the definition include states of trials, suffering, impending danger; and emotional lows and highs due to such things as losses, health, marital issues, and others. Life challenges could also mean career issues, promotion issues, difficulties in repositioning to a new career, extended family issues, and others. Uplifting someone's spirit is a product of the act of exaltation or praise.

An act of compassion, or any of these four characteristics (*enthusiasm, affirmation, exaltation, and compassion*) in service to others, can easily differentiate a person as a caring and encouraging leader if the leader's impact resulted in any of the following elements:

(1) Inspired courage and confidence for a new course of action.

(2) Brought some hope or promise.

(3) Uplifted a spirit to persevere.

Developing Encouragement-Compassion

Encouragement-compassion is a leader's acts of compassion that encourage others. An act of compassion is the highest level of encouragement where practical care or service is rendered in serving others, including caring that inspires courage, hope, or promise, and an uplifting of the spirit of another person. Typical examples of such acts, as we learned from Barnabas, manifest as generosity to meet needs, courage to stand behind followers in challenging times, kindness, compassion for reconciliation, commitment to mentoring others, and consolation:

Be generous to meet the needs of others

The scripture recorded that Barnabas was a landowner who sold his land, and willingly and generously donated the proceeds for the Apostles' upkeep in Jerusalem (Acts 4:36-37). Now, imagine the impact that that action by today's measure would have had on the Apostles' courage and confidence to continue in the ministry, and the impact on their hopes in God for providence. If they were fearful as to how they would survive, as is usually the case in such ministries, imagine how they would have felt with Barnabas' gift. They were definitely so encouraged that they agreed to change his name from 'Joseph' to "Son of Encouragement."

Be courageous for challenging times

Be courageous to stand behind the followers at challenging times. In the very early days of Saul of Tarsus, people in Jerusalem, especially the disciples, feared Saul as a persecutor of Christians. Some were casting stones at him. But not Barnabas; we read that several years after he donated the proceeds of selling his land to help the Apostles, God appointed Barnabas as an apostle to the gentiles, and he was to accompany Saul, now renamed Paul after his conversion (Acts 13:2-3; 14:14). Barnabas remained very courageous to stand by all the messengers in a time of tumult, including believing in Paul's authenticity and standing by him. If you were in Paul's shoes, how would you have felt? Paul definitely felt more confident and more courageous because the encourager "had his back."

Be committed to building up others

Be committed to the mentor and show positive attitudes to build up others. In the midst of fearing Saul (later Paul), Barnabas was the first person to show a positive attitude toward Paul by extending intimate warmth and the hand of fellowship at his home (Acts 9:26-31). He extended himself, showed great kindness, and committed himself to mentoring Paul to greater prominence, while he remained in a supporting role. Paul gained more clarity in his next course of action because Barnabas showed him the way.

Barnabas was a man who exemplified servant leadership in his commitment to mentor Paul. In fact, Barnabas showed the four unique aspects of commitment—dedication, sense of security, self-effacement, and sense of sacrifice—to servant leadership:

- His *sense of dedication to serve*. Barnabas showed dedication to service, leading, and mentoring others by serving them. Because of Barnabas' contagious humility and witness, others came to believe in the Gospel message.

- His *sense of security*. He showed that he had nothing to lose in serving. Barnabas was people-centered, which enabled him to sell the fields he owned and present the money to the apostles for their use (Acts 4:37). He could rejoice with others' victories (Acts 11:23) and never wondered about his own fame.

- His *self-effacement*. When everyone still had reservations about Paul and his conversion, Barnabas showed conviction and belief in Paul's potential, and encouraged him and others to remain faithful to the calling (Acts 11:23). He showed that he had nothing to prove by glorifying in his own limelight, but instead committed to mentoring Paul, even if it meant Paul rising above him. To Barnabas' sight, this young apostle must grow in his new faith. Barnabas had self-worth, but he did not see mentoring Paul as a means to prove himself to anyone.

- His *personal sacrifices to grow others*. He nurtured and encouraged other apostles to grow; it inspired the growth of the others; built up, encouraged, and further developed John Mark, who showed weakness in their earlier missionary trip. Barnabas saw an opportunity to develop John Mark to his fullest potential. John Mark was later confirmed by Peter and Paul, when they acknowledged how he had become useful to them.

Bring comfort and consolation

Bring comfort, hope, or relief as acts of consolation, as a move to compassion. Consolation is the act of bringing comfort, hope, or relief to someone in a state of pain, trial, or suffering. The word "encouragement" has been translated by scholars as consolation, comfort, and exhortation (Acts 4:36), all of which can be seen as characteristics of encouragement. Some believers scattered due to the persecution that broke out when Stephen was killed, and some traveled as far as Phoenicia, Cyprus and Antioch, spreading the word only among Jews (Acts 11:20). Many believers were added. When the news reached the church in Jerusalem, they sent Barnabas to Antioch.

Bring hope to others. The reason Barnabas was sent can be debated. However, there is no debate that he was a man who set himself apart as an encourager. One possible reason for sending him was because he was the most likely to bring comfort and hope to the disciples amidst the mix of the progress and pain due to the death of Stephen. Barnabas came onto the scene immediately, and during the turmoil. Barnabas was a minister sent "to establish and encourage the believers concerning their faith" (I Thessalonians 3:2-3), as Luke described him as a good man of faith.

Share in other people's suffering to comfort. Consolation is an important element of encouragement because of the continued trials and sufferings of those under us. To encourage people under some suffering is like sharing the suffering of Christ. The Bible shows that it involves comforting others, drawing on the comfort and consolation we received from God. Barnabas was to help the Christians in Antioch triumph over their trials, even as they made more progress. We see that he did just that, bringing them together first in fellowship as Christians. Paul wrote about this when he said, "Now may our Lord Jesus Christ Himself, and our God and Father, who have loved us and given us everlasting consolation and good hope by grace, comfort your hearts and establish you in every good word and work" (II Thessalonians 2:16-17).

Engage in conflict management

Engage in conflict management as an act of compassion and reconciliation. As new relationships were formed after Christ's resurrection, especially among fresh converts, with brand new and exploratory teaching, and with little to guide their leadership except what they learned from Christ and the Holy Spirit, disagreements were inevitable. Conflict resolution, however, is part of the leadership process. Barnabas and Paul experienced a period of conflict, possibly due to tensions over John Mark, who was Barnabas' cousin (Acts 15:36-41). John Mark's decision in Pamphylia to leave them and their work created the conflict, and resulted in Paul and Barnabas heading separate ways—Barnabas moved on with John Mark to Cyprus, and Paul chose to continue with Silas to Syria and Cilicia. Even so, all focused on the same mission agenda. Paul and Barnabas later reconciled and talked about supporting the work of God and the ministry to which they were called, and which they saw as much bigger than both of them combined (1 Corinthians 9:6).

In summary, Barnabas was kind and generous in his acts of service; he demonstrated a positive attitude to forgive and reconcile with Paul. Luke summarized it this way: "When he came and had seen the grace of God, he was glad, and encouraged them all that with purpose of heart they should continue with the Lord" (Acts 11:23, NKJV). Luke further portrayed the character of Barnabas as "A good man, full of the Holy Spirit and of faith" (Acts 11:24), and noted that "a great many people were added to the Lord" (Acts 11:24b).

Barnabas' acts of encouragement were instrumental in the first gathering of believers in Antioch, and in their being named Christians: "And when he had found him (Saul), he brought him to Antioch. So it was that for a whole year, they assembled with the church and taught a great many people. And the disciples were first called Christians in Antioch" (Acts 11:26). His acts of kindness and generosity, and his forgiving nature, helped pull the disciples together, consoled in the death of Stephen, and encouraged them with a course of action. All the members in Antioch, he "encouraged . . . that with a purpose of heart, they should continue with the Lord" (Acts 11:23). In the words of the Apostle Paul, Barnabas consoled the believers in Antioch with the knowledge that "as the sufferings of Christ abound in us, so our consolation also abounds through Christ" (II Corinthians 1:5).

CHAPTER 14
COMPASSION: A CALL FOR GENEROSITY

Generosity is an outward measure of the level of sacrifice, what is shared, or the impact a giving makes, not just the size of the giving.

Generosity can be defined as "the *habit of giving* without expecting anything in return. It can involve offering time, assets or talents to aid someone in need."[21] Such habits can include spending your personal money, time, and/or labor for the welfare of others, or expending (suffering or being consumed or spending) for others' well-being. How is this applied to leadership? We can say that it is definitely not included within the general sense of today's self-centered leadership. When political leaders or Board members 'vote their conscience' on important issues that affect others, what is that conscience and how do such leaders contribute to the welfare of others? How could they display the heart of generosity or open-handedness to the less privileged? Hanson (2003), in his article, "Make the Offering," recounted the story of Nkosi Johnson, a South African 12-year-old boy born with HIV who became a national voice for children with HIV/AIDS. Before the boy died, he summed up some elements of generosity when he said: "Do all you can, with what you have, in the time you have, in the place where you are."[22] I just cannot say it better than this boy did!

In the phrase of this dying boy, what distinguishing characteristics do leaders have to make impact with their time, money and authority in the places where they are? All giving to help humanity is crucial to help meet the needs of the most vulnerable of God's children. A $100 gift, for example, can be a big sacrifice to a giver who has only thousands to spare, when compared to $1000 given by a giver who has millions to spare. But can we define generosity in terms of the size of the gift?

One of my unusual Scriptures among others to define generosity in servant leadership is in relation to salvation is God's generous acts. The Scripture says, "For God so loved the world that He gave His only-begotten Son, that whoever believes in Him should not perish but have everlasting life" John 3.16, NKJV). When you look closely at what humanity gives back and what God has promised (His only son and everlasting life), there is absolutely no comparison. Generosity is not an attribute seen in most leaders; however, it is an attribute of God, and one major example set forth in the Scriptures. In this chapter, we will explore what distinguishes a leader's acts of giving, as in the Scripture above, from his inside intentions. We will identify the key leadership characteristics of generosity and frame functional definitions of the servant-leadership generosity attribute and principle. The chapter presents in details how a leader-servant can develop these characteristics, and with them, effectively practice service leadership.

Characteristics of Generosity Attribute

Paul, writing to Timothy, instructed him: "Command them to do good, to be rich in good deeds, and to be generous and willing to share" (1Timothy 6:18). Generosity is a necessary attribute for today's leader-servants in a suffering global world, and displays a leader's intentional efforts to look out for the welfare of others and desire to spend and expend from the heart.

The emphasis of giving without expecting anything in return is demonstrated in the Bible in God's salvation to man: "If any of you lacks wisdom, you should ask God, who gives generously to all without finding fault…" (James 1:5, NIV). It is also to be done happily: "If it is to encourage, then give encouragement; if it is giving, then give generously; if it is to lead, do it diligently; if it is to show mercy, do it cheerfully" (Romans 12:8, NIV). The Bible uses the word 'generously' interchangeably with 'sharing' in love. We read: "And though I have the gift of prophecy, and understand all mysteries, and all knowledge; and though I have all faith, so that I could remove mountains, and have not charity, I am nothing." (1 Corinthians 13:2, KJV). What Paul is saying in this Scripture is that having all the knowledge in the world, without the desire for charity or sharing with the suffering or needs of others, is nothing as far as service and extensions of love to people are concerned. This is particularly important in the context of servant leadership that focuses on the use of spiritual qualities to serve others.

The Bible also compares the works of the unwise to those of benevolent men. "The foolish person will no longer be called generous…But a generous man devises generous things, And by generosity he shall stand" (Isaiah 32:5-9). This passage teaches that a generous heart stands on principled leadership to devise good things for others. It is impossible to be a serving, other-centered leader without the generosity attribute. The leadership benefits of the generosity attribute includes encouraging the followers' engagement for greater fruit bearing. Paul encouraged generosity among Christian leaders: "Whoever sows sparingly will also reap sparingly, and whoever sows generously will also reap generously" (2 Corinthians 9:6). So generosity is the direct opposite of being sparing or stingy. A generous leader, accordingly to Apostle Paul does not grudge or complain in giving. Rather, he gives very cheerfully.

The Principle of Generosity Attribute

Based on these scriptures, the key characteristics of leadership generosity are a leader's acts of sharing with others, giving and showing kindness to others. We state the following:

The servant-leadership generosity attribute is the combined acts of freely sharing with and giving to others as an act of kindness, without expectation of reward or return to him.

In today's America where people get tax deductions from their charitable donations, it is common to give generously without a good measure of love for the recipient. Nevertheless, it is impossible to love the recipient without intentionally giving to meet his or her need. The giving of such an offering is not always measured in terms of the pocketbook, but in the sacrifice and intentionality as relative to the potential of the giver. The last statement and the identified characteristics lead to the following principle:

Servant leadership generosity principle: Generosity is an outward measure of the level of sacrifice, what is shared, or the impact a giving makes, not just the size of the giving!

This principle can also be restated to show that generosity can be measured not by the size and abundance of the gift offered, but by the intent and sacrifice of the giver. This is what Jesus was appreciating about the widow's mites: "Truly I say to you that this poor widow has put in more than all; for all these out of their abundance have put in offerings for God, but she out of her poverty put in all the livelihood that she had" (Luke 21:3-4, NKJV). This widow made more sacrifice than those that gave out of their abundance and had still more left; she had none left.

The principle of servant-leadership generosity attribute is modeled in Figure 14.1 and it shows that all acts of sharing, giving, and kindness are funneled toward others' needs as the primary focus, and can be expressed as:

GENEROSITY = SHARING + GIVING + KINDNESS

Figure 14.1: Servant leadership generosity-attribute model of sharing, giving, and kindness are funneled toward others

Developing the Acts of Generosity-Sharing

Generosity-sharing actions are to freely and liberally apportion as much as possible of what you have (your personal money, time, and/or labor) with others without expecting a reward or return. To the Thessalonian believers, Paul shared his life: "For you remember, brethren, our labor and toil; for laboring night and day, that we might not be a burden to any of you, … how devoutly and justly and blamelessly we behaved ourselves among you who believe… how we exhorted, and comforted, and charged [a] every one of you, as a father does his own children" (1 Thessalonians 2:9-11, NKJV). His labor and hardships, working night and day, are sacrifices as measures of his generosity. He showed them how he devoutly and uprightly and blamelessly behaved toward believers. Sharing yourself may involve defending, dialoging, or reasoning with the disciples or your audience. On several occasions, Jesus had to reason with disciples, and they sought to know more about Him, such as Whom He was and why He did what He did. Paul exemplified the same throughout his ministry, especially in his missionary activities in Acts. He went about with his disciples as a training for them to teach, witness, dialog, and persuade people to believe the Gospel. The Bible says, "He witnessed to them from morning till evening, explaining about the kingdom of God…he tried to persuade them about Jesus (Acts 28:23-24).

Share your time and delights

Paul was very generous with his time, words of affirmation, and visitation with his followers. He delighted in seeing them progress and was happy to expend himself to witness the growth in them. He told them, "I will most gladly spend and be spent for your souls. If I love you more, am I to be loved less? (2 Corinthians 12:15, ESV). He made time to visit and bear with them in their states of suffering, and celebrated in helping them bear their sorrows.

Share with those in need

This is a critical part of the generosity attribute. Leader-servants must be highly committed to meeting followers' needs. The leader demonstrates this by actually sharing in the suffering and well-being of the followers. In the case of Jesus, He did not just share in the need; He completely took on the suffering of humanity from God's wrath and died to reconcile man to God. He also demonstrated His compassionate heart for the people's needs, as shown in His feeding of the four and five thousand. Paul practiced the same principle of sharing in people's needs though his ministry. He wrote, "For Macedonia and Achaia were pleased to make a contribution for the poor among the Lord's people in Jerusalem… For if the Gentiles have shared in the Jews' spiritual blessings, they owe it to the Jews to share with them their material blessings" (Romans 15:26-28).

Share freely without grudge

The disciples showed practical love toward each other through their magnanimous acts of giving: "For all who were possessors of lands or houses sold them, and brought the proceeds of the things that were sold, and laid them at the apostles' feet; and they distributed to each as anyone had need" (Acts 4:35). Other ways we can be generous and other-centered include intentionally making sacrifices to forego certain comforts so that others can have some. We can share thoughts, words, deeds, and emotions, developing a sense of what others desire and offering to meet those needs as much as possible; developing a sense of the impact of sharing with people without expecting a reward; and committing daily to relating actions as offerings. This yields a sense intimacy with your followers and a sense of importance of kind affection. Think of things you can express to make someone improve their day. Do control your emotions, as you share testimonies with others in a state of suffering to encourage them.

Developing the Acts of Generosity-Giving

Generosity-giving is the act of liberally giving to meet another's needs. It is a leader's act of sowing bountifully in the lives of his followers for their spiritual growth. Paul encouraged generosity-giving. He wrote, "Whoever sows sparingly will also reap sparingly, and whoever sows generously will also reap generously" (2 Corinthians 9:6, NIV); and to the Galician's Christians, he made the same point that; "A man reaps what he sows" (Galatians 6:7).

Jesus taught His disciples the principle of generous giving: "Give, and it will be given to you . . . With the measure you use, it will be measured to you" (Luke 6:38, NKJV). This means that you can purely harvest in proportion to your planting. Alternatively, you can harvest to the extent to which you are willing to plant. This principle can also be applied to the extent to which we invest time in the discipleship of those we lead. Jesus invested time with his disciples. The world reaped great and committed leaders who followed to change the world with His Gospel message.

We learn several lessons from Paul's teaching on the generosity-giving habits of the Corinthians church (2 Corinthians 9:7-15). Paul made three important points about charitable giving:

1. Giving is a personal matter to be settled in the individual's own heart. "Each should give what he has decided in his heart to give" (2 Corinthians 9:7), and the "How much?" is a question that each person must answer for him- or herself, and not in comparison to what others have given.
2. Giving is what the individual deliberately decides in one's mind to give, not impulsively, but in purposeful decision. This disputes telethons or preachers who play on people's emotions to solicit contributions.
3. Giving is a private matter, not a community decision, made in the heart, and not for public honor, praise, or recognition. The real reason should be to give because God first gave His son out of love for humanity.

Although the purpose of generosity-giving is not to expect reward, Paul makes it clear that indeed God's response to generosity is to make all grace abound to the giver; that is, God extends to the giver His unmerited favor in the form of spiritual and material blessings. Paul goes on to point out several benefits to giving generously (2 Corinthians 9:9-15):

- The righteousness of the liberal giver will endure forever. (v. 9)
- The generous giver, like the farmer, will receive from God (who supplies seed to the sower and bread for food), Who will also supply and increase stores of seed and will enlarge the harvest of your righteousness. (v. 10)
- God provides not only for his immediate physical needs in the form of a harvest for his daily bread, but also for his future needs as seed for next year's planting (He supplies seed to the sower). (v. 10)
- The more we give, the greater we will receive from God. And the further we receive, the more we are expected to give. "You will be enriched in every way so that you can be generous on every occasion, and through us your generosity will result in Thanksgiving to God." (v. 11)
- God supplies the giver's seed and even increases it so that he can be generous on every occasion (vv. 10-11) when we show we have good intentions. The primary act of generosity-giving is to supply the needs of God's people. (v. 12)
- The primary benefit of generosity-giving to the receiver is meeting the immediate need of the receiver. Paul says: "This service that you perform, supplies the needs of God's people." (v. 12)
- The specific help rendered by the offering is that of supplying the needs of the Judean Christians. So, the help offered through the Corinthians' contribution is by way of need and necessity, not wants.
- Offering not only meets a real need, but it's an expression of thanks to God (v. 12) and many heartfelt prayers for the Corinthians (v. 14).

The primary lessons here relate to charitable generosity, and the principles can be applied to the giving attitude in the generosity attribute. Leaders are commended if they live a lifestyle of generosity. For those who give cheerfully and willingly, the promise is that God will provide all they need to continue doing good deeds.

The benefit of generosity-giving to God includes Thanksgiving to God. Paul says, "This service is also overflowing in many expressions of thanks to God (2 Corinthians 9:11-12). Another important benefit to God is praise, as Paul illustrated, "Because of this service, men will praise God for the obedience that accompanies your confession of the gospel of Christ" (2 Corinthians 9:13). And, second, for your generosity in sharing with them and with everyone else. God is also praised for the givers' generosity in sharing with others. The recipients will also praise God, not merely for any material gift (including money), but will praise the generosity of the heart as an expression of God's ultimate supreme example of giving: "Thanks be to God for his indescribable gift!" (2 Corinthians 9:15).

To what extents are leaders able to extend themselves in giving liberally to others? Indeed, God is the supreme example that cannot be matched. He gave beyond humane comprehensions; He gave what Paul calls an indescribable gift, a gift that is beyond human description: that is, Jesus Christ. He so loved the world that He gave the ultimate sacrificial and unmatchable gift—the gift of His only Son.

Developing Generosity-Kindness

Generosity-kindness is an act of good-hearted affection whereby you extend yourself and readily do all you can to offer what you have to care for others' needs. It means showing gentle action toward caring, comforting, and extending emotional healing to others, especially the fainthearted. Kindness is the practice of being or the tendency to be sympathetic and compassionate (show consideration and caring). "For whoever gives you a cup of water to drink in My name, because you belong to Christ, assuredly, I say to you, he will by no means lose his reward." (Mark 9:41) The giver of generosity-kindness expects nothing in return.

Act according to your obedience to God

As spiritual leaders, we often act according to our obedience to God. This is especially true with the generosity attribute, which requires making sacrifices to extend yourself, sometimes living below your means to create room to help someone else. When was the last time you skipped a lunch or a comfort to send money in response to a global need? Or when did you last respond to a call for an offering for a mission project? Have you ever imagined yourself in someone else's situation and extended an act of kind affection based on being sensitive to the person's need, or responded to the Lord's leading to help someone in need? The following example helps answer these questions.

A Case of Generosity-Kindness

Mr. Gaylord Wilkerson was a very generous man who always found ways to respond to the needs of others. To put this in context, Gaylord was a faithful man of God, a Christian Brother, who would not allow anything to stop him in his quest to help someone else. Gaylord was in a wheelchair for most of his adult life after serving in the military. He was 65 years at the time of this testimony. We were attending the same church during the later days of my wilderness walk of faith as a graduate student. I was nearly ready to complete my studies.

An announcement came that my wife and I were qualified to apply for a green card (U.S. permanent residency). We were overjoyed, and shared the testimony with Brother Gaylord. He was very happy with us; the thought of us becoming American citizens gladdened him, as it did most members of our small congregation of less than 250 people.

My wife and I wasted no time in getting to the immigration office to complete the application. As we completed the paperwork, we were disappointed to learn that the application fee was $600 for both of us. In our financial state at the time, it would take us until the next year's tax return—if not longer—to save $600. However, we did not despair. We knew we could save the money and apply again next year. We were just happy that we were finally qualified to be U.S. citizens in a matter of a short time.

One Sunday after church, we were happy to share with Gaylord, and he couldn't wait to hear the good news. "Brother Sylvanus," he said, with his usual high tone, "did you get it?!"

"No, Brother Gaylord, we did not. However, we'll go back and get it next year," we told him.

"Why, Brother Sylvanus? Why next year? Are you not qualified?" He just kept asking us questions in rapid succession. We could sense his concern. He really took personal ownership of this need, because he knew all that we had endured to survive in the U.S. as students with a large family. He wanted the suffering to end.

I smiled and replied, "We are qualified, but it will cost us $600, which we do not have. We will get it next year when we get our tax return."

"Is that all?" he asked. "Come to the house this evening, and I will give you the $600."

At first, I did not quite hear what he said, because I was laughing at myself about how I was going to raise $600. He repeated himself, "Brother Happy, do not worry, come to the house this evening, and I will give you the $600."

I was shocked and overjoyed when I finally heard his offer, and for his readiness and ease of generosity. That evening, we went to Brother Gaylord's. With a loving heart, he handed me $650. "This will serve the need," he said. "Go back Monday and get it," he said as if giving a loving command.

I looked at the money and said, "Brother Gaylord; the fee is $600 not $650."

His very confident response was this: "The Lord impressed upon my heart to make it $650. I believe you are going to need it. Now go, and let me know how it goes."

In obedience, the next Monday morning, we went to the immigration office to pay the fee and complete the application process. To our great surprise, when the fees were computed for payment, it was exactly $600 plus a $50 agent fee. My first response was tears—tears of how God works, how He always has a way of caring about my affairs beyond myself, and tears of joy and love for this Brother who had extended himself generously to obey God, despite his own needs. It was moving to see a person who needs so much, and yet can love others so much regardless! To me, Gaylord's act of generosity to me and to so many others is indelible to our hearts.

Of course, the rest is history. We applied, and a few months later we received permanent residency status, and then citizenship a few years afterward.

CHAPTER 15

THE PATHWAYS TO COMPASSION

What are the pathways to compassion which we should follow to bring wholeness within and outside of the family or fellowship? What is the nature of the type of ministries we should invest in that will be most effective in bringing wholeness to the fellowship or church to which we belong? James, addressing the plight of the widows and orphans in the church, wrote: "Pure and undefiled religion before God and the Father is this: to visit orphans and widows in their trouble, *and* to keep oneself unspotted by the world" (James 1:27, NKJV). This means that a good measure of the undefiled fellowship is the ability to consider the needs of the most vulnerable of God's children in the fellowship. Can a community thrive when some of its members are left out of the functioning of the organization? The pathway to create or model the type of compassion that will reach out, build, and sustain a thriving community is described in this chapter.

Pathway of Faith through Actions

The Apostle James asked some very critical questions about the relationship between faith and deeds: "What good is it, my brothers and sisters, if someone claims to have faith but has no deeds? Can such faith save them? ...faith by itself, if it is not accompanied by action, is dead....Show me your faith without deeds, and I will show you my faith by my deeds" (James 2:14-18). A pathway for compassion from this Scripture is faith through works. The faith we have in Jesus and His ministry means nothing unless it is demonstrated through our works of compassion. That faith saves or brings wholeness to people only when accompanied by works or actions that meet specific needs. For example, providing clothing, sustenance, or anything done to meet the physical needs of people demonstrates our faith more than just the commitment to pray for someone for healing.

Pathway of Attentiveness to Community Needs

A leader-servant is accountable for the community he or she serves. Equipping a follower for service must also include the knowledge of how to manage the community. Here are some strategies:

Integrate individual with community

Integrate individuals' needs with the community's mission. Since the community is made of diverse needs, we must, by the collective actions, see to the need of the community of brethren as a whole, and also oversee specific challenges of the individuals in the community. Three possible behaviors can occur as the leader tries to manage the community:

First, he can overemphasize the group's diversity and minimize the assets (strengths, interests, and uniqueness) of everyone. For example, we can focus only on the collective ministry of the fellowship, the dominance or control of one particular group, the mission agenda, the growth of the children, etc. The mostly likely outcome of this scenario is fragmentation or conflicts as individuals whose assets are neglected will feel less valued and empowered. Such individuals will not be fully engaged in their growth and will develop a sense, of feeling "there is nothing for me here."

Second, the leadership can overemphasize unity or the needs of individuals, and minimize the collective needs of the community. For example, we can focus on a doctrine or one major aspect of Jesus's ministry, some individual leader-servants' agenda, or the children ministry alone, etc. The most likely outcome in this case will be conformity, as individuals strive to submit to whatever is prevalent in the community. This leads to a mono-culture or unity of purpose. This is good if the organization is performing at its highest level. However, it does not allow for innovation and integrating new ideas in managing skills. In this case, individuals will not grow beyond their talents, which will lead to stagnation. If the desired goal is to develop a leader-servant of high repute and upright standing, neither of these two extremes leads to the sought-after goal.

Third, instead of any of the first extremes, we can integrate unity with diversity for increased innovation and growth. By merging its diverse community goals with the assets of its individual members or potential leaders, the community will thrive internally and externally, and be known for its integrated inclusiveness and relationship toward service to others. Both the individuals and organization grow together.

I can state with a good degree of confidence, based on my years of experience, that you cannot expect a strong fellowship or organization when there is no maximum use of the individual assets or when there is no relationship between the members. You cannot expect to build excellent relationships when the individuals harbor anger and are unforgiving. Nor can you expect a thriving organization that caters to the community it serves when individuals who make up that community are not fully committed to or engaged in the collective mission of the organization. The whole is as important as the individual units that make up the whole! In discipleship of potential leaders, the leader-servant must focus on the community as one body (one whole) with many members and gifts. Such gifts include wisdom, knowledge, faith, healing, working miracles, prophecy, and the ability to distinguish between spirits, tongues, and interpretation of tongues.

All of these skills are empowered by one and the same Spirit who apportions to each person individually as He wills. The success and effectiveness of a community to accomplish its God-given mission can be measured by the strengths and commitments of each member of the community, to the shared vision of the organization. By the collective act of compassion, no member can be left out for being weak because "God has so composed the body, giving greater honor to the part that lacked it… that the members may have the same care for one another. If one member suffers, all suffer together; if one member is honored, all rejoice together" (1 Corinthians 12:24-25, NIV). This oneness within the whole is a mindset and a principle that, when applied to organizations in general, will yield a culture of excellence in which the least and the greatest reach beyond their potentials—just by share use and distribution of the strength of the community.

Pathway of "Iron Sharpening Iron"

A pathway for compassion is discipleship and peer mentoring that capitalizes on maximizing the strength of the community through the assets of individuals or a group.

Methods of maximizing the strength of the community include:

- Create and encourage participation in group activities, building consensus among individuals.
- Create peer mentoring between individuals. Let "iron sharpen iron" by creating one-on-one mentoring relationships.
- Create a community of leaders and members who desire to be leaders rather than followers.
- Create a community vision shared by individuals.
- Use a culturally relevant communication strategy such as celebrating a compassion mission day.

- Weave partnerships and networks with similar organizations with related mission connections.
- Foster a culture of compassion leadership where leaders demonstrate, in their own lives, a pattern of the acts of compassion.

These activities call for leaders to know about the people and how they can best serve them. Leaders as influencers of the attitude toward compassion must be capable of identifying the need, and capitalizing on using the assets (gifts, strengths, talents, interests, and uniqueness) of each person, subsequently enhancing their ability to grow in their primary talent. The influence attribute allows a leader to consistently assess his followers, and to understand how they think as part of their accountability to the growth of each person.

The diversity of each individual's assets defines the strength of the organization. For example, knowing each person's gifts and talents helps the leader better customize the approach that maximizes talent. Needs are deficiencies and weaknesses that must be addressed in training a disciple. Some members may appear talented and mature in skills they have, but are empty spiritually; indeed, that is then their weakness. Some may be spiritual in the wrong doctrine and teaching. Some may confuse religiosity with real Christ-likeness. These flaws must be identified and corrected through sound teaching. How do leaders maximize the followers' talents within a code of conduct that projects a positive reputation to outsiders? The imagery of the flock of God is that of sheep needing care and guidance by the shepherd. The leader must see that the herd is complete, expending 100% effort to ensure that none are lost. This simply means overseeing the work and growth of others as a shepherding leader.

Former President George H. W. Bush (Papa Bush) will remain in my mind as a leader who counted the value of every nation that mattered when planning the Gulf War with Iraq to build one of the most powerful coalitions since World War II. He built a consensus among 34 nations, with differing agendas and desires, into one with a unified mission and focus to drive the Iraqi army out of Kuwait. President Bush proved to be an excellent influencer. He lobbied nations, one-by-one, according to their interests and security in the area, their regional aggression in the Middle East, shared concerns for the European NATO allies, and conflict on the doorsteps of Eastern Asian allies. By every account, the coalition-building efforts were considered very successful because by the time the fighting operations began on January 16, 1991, naval forces had been sent by 12 countries to join the regional states of Saudi Arabia and the Persian Gulf states, as well as the might of the U.S. Navy, ground forces from 8 countries and seventeen heavy and six light brigades of the U.S. Army, and nine Marine regiments. Every military arsenal that was needed was provided by collective cooperation of the coalition.

Pathway of Inclusivity and Trust

A culture of inclusivity is one that values, respects, includes, and trusts the people. When people feel valued, included, and empowered, they can trust and engage with others to build relationships in which they work interdependently and synergistically. Valuing diversity of both people and perspectives increases trust and productivity. Here are some ways to achieve this goal:

- *Explore, identify, and value the group differences.* Listen actively, openly, and respectfully to others. Show that you understand the key challenges your followers are facing.
- *Manage cultural differences as a joint trust-building opportunity.* Be open to other people's ideas and perspectives by fostering a respectful environment in which ideas flourish, and the structure has the flexibility to accommodate new ideas and provide regular opportunities for collective action.

- *Increase cultural competence and sensitivity.* Recognize multiple perspectives on an event or behavior, identifying one's own cultural values and those of others, and develop a positive attitude toward understanding and appreciating the cultural difference that promotes appropriate behaviors.

- *Foster links between the mission and the practices of the group community.* This requires the ability to speak the language of others in the community; that is, get to know the people, understand their culture, and how they discuss ideas differently. Capitalize on the diverse strengths that differentiate each member of the community, understanding how everyone can work together in the various spheres of responsibility to translate ideas into action.

- *Develop a community-wide culture that supports free-flowing ideas.* This encourages collective efforts within the community and recognizes the need for ongoing reflection and renewal. Make intentional efforts for people to collaborate around a common goal, and show that you value others' contributions through an effective reward system.

Pathway from Growth Opportunities

We live in a world where the majority if its inhabitants are in a state of suffering. We are limited, but our self-centeredness, especially in those that have the capacity to help, hinders progress. If you have traveled to any part of developing or underdeveloped countries, you have readily found opportunities for compassion everywhere, from the observed hardships in health, sanitation, poverty, homelessness, on, to mention a few. We can grow in compassion leadership based on these opportunities—beginning with our local churches, fellowships, or organizations. Here are some few thoughts:

Be sensitive to the needs of the members. Church or organization leaders need to pay attention to situations that current members are going through and provide services to meet those challenges. There is an absolute need for leaders to be personally involved in the lives of the members of the congregation. Membership sensitivity also means being aware of the composition of the congregation. Taking sides on national issues, merely for reasons of political alliance, can be interpreted as insensitivity to political diversity, and has no place on the pulpit. However, churches and leaders should not shy away from engaging in such dialogue purely on sound biblical teaching, not motivated by politics.

Be sensitive to the need of the external community. Churches must recognize where and how the Kingdom's business needs to be positioned by examining what and how God desires the Church to respond. Outreach sensitivity could be in church planting in order to respond to gospel or outreach need in a community. Outreach could be to a community turned apart by poverty, mass unemployment, or drug infestation; it could be an attack on the basic biblical teaching to which the congregation is exposed. Churches cannot afford to be passive, but must move the congregation along with teachings for or against the trend.

Some years ago, our church was involved in outreach ministries to the homeless and drug addicts in the community. Some of these individuals were picked up from the streets and bused to church on Sundays. The senior pastor devoted one Sunday, before the outreach started, to teach on the subject of sensitivity and love beyond outward appearances. His purpose was to prepare the congregation for their new visitors the next Sunday. He warned that some would not look or smell like what members were accustomed to, but they desired to be loved, even as filthy as they might appear, just as Christ loved us.

Enlarge your vision-tent and be ahead of others– Your vision-tent is the spread of the foundation of your mission purpose, and provides the size and extent of your vision. Churches and Christian organizations must readily reexamine their current vision-tents with respect to the growths of the internal and external communities; they must project that vision to an imaginary larger future, and identify potential opportunities for breakthrough ideas for growth. Here are other actions they must take:

- Identify with the community to which they belong by creating a sense of place in the community and promoting an individual's sense of well-being.
- Assess and understand what the community needs now and in the future; plan towards the future while addressing the present.
- Be the first to be innovative and ahead of others. One example, in the Monroeville Assembly of God, is the creation of a free medical clinic on one day per week, where low income community members come to receive medical attention.

Identify and respond to the gaps in mission–Just as in a secular business, a ministry that has remained stagnant in growth for three or more years, or in which members of the ministry are not growing spiritually, or where the ministry cannot quantify its accomplishments, must need to reexamine gaps in its mission or strategies for growth. Churches must learn to identify gaps in the current ministerial model and the changing demography of memberships they serve, the diversity of membership they serve, or support services that hold value to attract more members to the gospel message, all and any as growth opportunities. A possible gap in the church ministry could be in children ministry, or in mission works with the poor and homeless in your community to the neglect of other ministries and their need.

A case in point: one organization that I have served under was started by students in their late 20's. In over 40 years of the existence of the organization since then, so many opportunities were missed in not only identifying the gaps that needed to be filled in the outreach to the youth and the young adults of the original membership, and in adequately responding to their needs. The result was that this second generation of membership was quick to find out that there was really nothing for them, and the majority of them disengaged themselves. This was a missed opportunity for greater growth, and if only there had been compassionate leadership!

Pathway of Nurturing a Sense of Identity

A sense of group or community identity is a feeling of satisfaction that one belongs to a particular community. A sense of community drives a person's motivation to share and engage in the work of compassion of that community. A community can be defined as a group of people with diverse characteristics, but unified in common interests, identity and values. According to John Gardner in *Reading, Leading, and the American Dream*, a community is characterized by "wholeness incorporating diversity", and may include people of different ages, ethnicities, educational backgrounds, and incomes" (Gardner, 2003). A community is built or created intentionally, and the relationships within the community are nurtured by caring leaders. Community members balance diversity, within the community, with a vision; they will bring together people of good faith, so as to create something new. The goal of a strong community is to foster a respectful environment in which ideas flourish, where unity creates focus, and diversity provides opportunities for innovation and collective action.

The feeling or satisfaction that one belongs to a particular group can motivate a person to emulate others in the group who have excelled. Such groups are defined by shared cultural norms and people are motivated by the excellence of those who belong to the group. Group members' accomplishments tend to set the group's standards. The five things needed to nurture and promote a sense of community for compassion include:

1. **Community identity** relates to creating and having a clear sense of place in the community. It promotes an individual's sense of well-being, and a level of personal satisfaction and engagement in the work of the community. Each of Jesus' eleven disciples had a sense of identity within Jesus' mission, and they moved on with the same compassion to continue in the work.

2. **Community interaction** among members of the community allows for sharing of ideas and concerns, strategic engagement, and sharing of information that helps members to get to know each other. As Jesus commissioned them, His disciples encouraged each other, and shared what they had, to assist in spreading the gospel. There was no record in the scriptures that these twelve men, while they met with Jesus, interacted without any conflicts. That is an effective leadership process worthy of our emulation.

3. **Community involvement**, which is more than just interaction or identity, means individuals actively caring about what happens in the community. It includes loyalty and concern that comes from having a sense of ownership and control over the group's decisions and direction.

4. **Community climate for change.** Each step in the leadership process for change is seen as an inevitable and logical next step to achieve global community goals. All the eleven disciples of Jesus were collectively committed to the ministry, despite the danger that they faced.

5. **Community assets to empower change** (strength, vision). The leader nurtures and promotes a sense of community for compassion by capitalizing on the collective resources and diverse strengths that different members of the community bring to the group (PKAL, 2004).

CHAPTER 16

SUMMARY AND PRACTICE

CHAPTER 1

    A. Identify the key elements of wholeness compassion.

    B. In ways did Jesus' demonstrate Wholeness-Compassion?

    C. What are the five tests of Authenticity in Compassion?

CHAPTER 2

    A. What is the human nature of the nature of compassion?

    B. How is humility an intrinsic driver for compassion?

    C. How can we develop the heart for compassion?

CHAPTER 3

    A. What are the five levels of the call for compassion?

    B. How does each differ from the other?

CHAPTER 4

    A. What are the key characteristics of the Empathy-Compassion Attribute?

    B. Discuss the two key barriers to Compassion.

    C. How can you overcome these barriers of outward Compassion?

CHAPTER 5
  A. How is humility, wisdom (similar to awareness or knowledge), and empathy related to compassion?
  B. Define self-awareness... How does it determine the core qualities of the empathy attribute?
  C. How does correct self-perception increase a leader's understanding of his or her character in relation to followers' feelings or difficulties?
  D. How can you Develop self-awareness; self-assessment?
  E. How do you develop the following:
      a. Sympathy?
      b. Empathy-Self-Regulation?
      c. Empathy-Compassion?
  F. How does your humility maximize empathy-compassion?

CHAPTER 6
  A. What is wholeness-healing compassion?
  B. Identify the characteristics of the healing-care attribute.
  C. State the principle of the healing care attribute.
  D. How can we develop the following:
      a. Acts of wholeness-self-healing?
      b. Empathy-healing-care?
      c. Healing-care comfort?

CHAPTER 7
  A. What are the key elements of developing Listening-Concentration?
  B. How can we develop the following:
      a. Listening-Hearing?
      b. Listening-Understanding?
      c. Active Listening Skills?

C. What are the elements that hinder Listening-Communication?

CHAPTER 8

A. What is the Purpose of Unity in marriage?
B. How can one sustain and strengthen Unity?
C. What is Wholeness-Communications between Spouses?
D. What factors affect marital Wholeness Communication?
E. What the key roles of the Husband in Wholeness Compassion?
F. Compare the key roles of wives to husbands in Compassionate oneness.
G. How can communication between spouses be improved in the areas of sex and finance?

CHAPTER 9

A. How is covenant marriage different from contractual marriage?
B. What are the Major Sources of Disunity and Conflicts?
C. How do spouses manage the following conflicts:
   a. Financial issues?
   b. The innate differences in the sexes?
   c. List the Six Stages of Conflict Resolution.

CHAPTER 10

A. How can you be what you wish your child to be?
B. What are some of the key strategies of dealing with Intergenerational Realities?
C. What are some of the broader impacts of failure in dealing with these realities?
D. How good is your parenting as a father? Answer YES/NO.

a. Are your children feeling your fatherly impacts in their lives?

b. Are you representing Christ-likeness in the lives of your children?

c. Do your children see you in the Word or praying?

d. Do you use curse words in front of your children, especially against God?

e. Do you drink, smoke or use substances that you would not want your children trying?

f. Do they hear you talking badly about someone you are friends with (gossiping)?

g. Are you living a life in Christ that you hope for your children to follow in?

h. Do you communicate and work things out with your spouse?

i. Do you provide for their physical, financial and emotional needs?

j. Do you instruct the children in words and in examples?

If you answer NO to two or more of these, I suggest you review these principles and information in the text to help your in you parenting. Note, these are just examples; the Bible is your best resource.

CHAPTER 11

A. How is God's love unconditional?

B. How is God's Love conserved?

C. How is God's Love perfected in Suffering?

D. List some Acts of Compassion of Spiritual Leaders.

E. How can leaders provide compassionate Spiritual care?

CHAPTER 12

A. What is wholeness reconciliation?
B. How can we achieve reconciliation?
C. How does total forgiveness drive true reconciliation?
D. How do you forgive those that have hurt you?
E. List the key strategies for true forgiveness.
F. What are some of the health benefits and effects of forgiveness?

CHAPTER 13

A. What is compassion-encouragement?
B. State the principle of the encouragement attribute.
C. How can we develop the acts of encouragement-compassion?

CHAPTER 14

A. How do you define generosity and how is this applied to leadership?
B. How could they display the heart of generosity or open-handedness to the less privileged?
C. What are the key ccharacteristics of Generosity Attribute

CHAPTER 15

A. What are the five key pathways to compassion?
B. How can the pathway of "iron sharpening iron" yield compassion?

Personal Audits: Pride/Humility, Love, Communication

	Table 16.1. 12-Point **Love Actions audit** 1= Always; 2= Frequently; 3= Sometimes; 4= Almost Never; 5= Never					
	Self-Assessment Question on Love to Others	1	2	3	4	5
1	I can endure waiting, delay, or provocation and persevere calmly when faced with difficulties.					
2	I am tenderhearted, sympathetic and compassionate (showing consideration and caring) to others.					
3	I am willing to expend my time & money freely with others.					
4	I act with humility and do not parade myself to people; rather I show modesty and respect.					
5	I am polite and show courtesy and consideration to others					
6	I do not seek my own interest, but put the good or the needs or interests of others first.					
7	I am not resentful or provoked to anger easily or suddenly.					
8	I am always gladdened by goodness to others and moral standing with God.					
9	I do rejoice in telling the truth or the tendency to tell the truth.					
10	I do bear with people in all things and have a tendency to forgive offenses readily and easily.					
11	I have the capacity to trust someone or be trusted by the same, with value on my character and those of others.					
12	I am long-suffering, endure all things, and am patient or tolerant despite many difficulties.					
Score	*Total Score in each column*					
12-21	Outstanding acts of love for a great leader-servant					
22-31	Above Average, excellent leader-servant potentials					
32-41	Average; developing potential for love in service					
42-51	Below Average; deficient in most areas					
52-60	Little or no Love in you					

	Table 16.2: 20-Item Pride Test (Be true to yourself and take this test) Insert: 5=Always; 4=Frequently; 3=Sometimes; 2=Almost never; 1=Never	Insert Number 1-5
1	I am more likely to set my mind on my rights and desires above the needs of others.	
2	It is hard for me to evaluate people without projecting my self-worth.	
3	I do not think or recognize others to be at equal level.	
4	I feel very low when my ego is hurt by someone.	
5	I sometimes believe that my perspectives and ideas are better than others.	
6	I like to get recognition that comes from my accomplishments, degrees, or position.	
7	It is a challenge to see others as better than myself.	
8	I have the tendency to quickly judge those who have different gifts or strengths from mine.	
9	I expect praise from the help I give people.	
10	It is a challenge to submit to anybody for any reason.	
11	I want to be seen as the best in what I do and better than most people.	
12	I choose to control others rather than develop self-control.	
13	I have a strong sense self-worth and desire to do my will.	
14	I feel ashamed and demeaned by the action of serving somebody lower than I am.	
15	I work more to protect my position than focus on others' growth.	
16	I can't remember the last time I demonstrated a compelling modesty and shunning of public adoration.	
17	I am more likely to channel ambition to myself than greater success for others.	
18	I believe it is sometime acceptable to be boastful of my achievements and accomplishments.	
19	I have little self-interest for recognition in my service to make my organization great.	
20	I get defensive when criticized by others, especially telling me what to or not do.	
Total Score: Humble: A score >70%; Proud: A score <70%		/100

Item	Listening and Communication Check 1=Always; 2=Frequently; 3= sometimes; 4= Almost Never; 5= Never	1	2	3	4	5
	Table 16.3. Listening/Communication Attribute Audit Understanding the Health of your communication Assess the quality of your acts of listening communication. Please check insert an X below the number that best describes your response to each statement.					
1	I empathetically listen to understand and be understood.					
2	I reflectively Listen carefully to understand and be understood.					
3	I Use positive words to help others build self-confidence.					
4	I Show interest in listening and looking directly at others as they speak to me.					
5	I pay careful attention to what is being said.					
6	I listen to the expressed feelings even when I disagree.					
7	I Look for the unspoken words when I listen.					
8	I am aware of my own weaknesses when listening to people's concerns.					
9	I Avoid interruption and respond only when necessary.					
10	I am always willing to avoid factors that may hinder my communication.					
11	*Add up your rating in each column*					

Score Range	Guide and Explanation of Score: understand the areas you need to develop (Total Score =)
10-17	Great Listener; keep it up!
18-25	Above Average listener; need to work on 25% of the areas
26-33	Average listener; need to work on 50% of the areas
34-41	Below average listener; need to work on 75% of the areas
42-50	Not a listener; Seek help in all the areas

REFERENCES

Adler, R., Rosenfeld, L. and Proctor, R. (2001). *Interplay: the process of interpersonal communicating (8th edn)*, Fort Worth, TX: Harcourt

Boyatzis, R., Goleman, D., & Rhee, K. (2000). "Clustering competence in emotional intelligence: insights from the emotional competence inventory (ECI)". In R. Bar-On & J.D.A. Parker (eds.): *Handbook of emotional intelligence* (pp. 343-362). San Francisco: Jossey-Bass.

Bradberry, T. and Su, L. (2003). "Ability-versus skill-based assessment of emotional intelligence, Psicothema", Vol. 18, supl. pp. 59-66. (PDF). Retrieved 2014-03-11.

Chapman, Gary (2015). The Five Love Languages: The Secret to Love That Lasts. Northfield Publishing

Clark, Arthur J. (2010). "Empathy and Sympathy: Therapeutic Distinctions in Counseling". *Journal of Mental Health Counseling* 32 (2): 95–101.

Coleman, D (1997). *Emotional Intelligence*. New York: Bantam Books, 1997.

Covey, S. (2004). *The Seven Habits of Highly Effective People*. New York, NY: Free Press.

Dawson. J (1998). *What Christians Should Know about Reconciliation*, Published by International reconciliation coalition.

Djiker, A. J. M. (2010) "Perceived vulnerability as a common basis of moral emotions". *British Journal of Social Psychology* 49: 415–423.

Fieldham, Shauti (2004). *For Women Only: What You Need to Know about the Inner Lives of Men*, Multnomah Books

Fieldham, Shauti and Fieldham, Jeff (2006), For Men Only: A Straightforward Guide to the Inner Lives of Women, Multnomah Books.

Gardner, John W., *Living, Leading, and the American Dream*. Jossey Bass, 2003.

Gulf War Wikipedia. http://en.wikipedia.org/wiki/Desert_storm

Haughk, KC. *Christina Caregiving: a Way of Life*, Augsburg publishing house, Minneapolis 55440, 1984, p 19-29.

Heaphy, E.D. & J.E. Dutton (2004) "Embodied connections: Understanding the physiological effects of positive connections at work." Working paper, Center for Positive Organizational Scholarship, University of Michigan Business School.

Hudson-Smith, A, Robert, J, Coulton (2013). "P. Digital Personhood: Creating and Exploring Digital Empathy, in a Grant submitted by Engineering Physical Science Research" Council, EP/L003635/1. http://gow.epsrc.ac.uk/NGBOViewGrant.aspx?GrantRef=EP/L003635/1

Hunt, J. C (1998) *"The Servant"*, Prima Publishing Roseville, CA, p. 30.

Kanov, J.M., S. Maitlis, M.C. Worline, J.E., Dutton, P.J. Frost, & J.M. Lilius (2004). "Compassion in organizational life." *American Behavioral Scientist"*, 47, 808-827.

Karremans JC, Van Lange PA, Holland RW. "Forgiveness and its associations with pro-social thinking, feeling, and doing beyond the relationship with the offender." *Personality and Social Psychology Bulletin*, October 2005.

Kernaghan, K. (2003). Integrating values into public service: The values statement as centerpiece. *Public Administration Review, 63*, 711-719.

Lawler KA, Younger JW, Piferi RL, Billington E, Jobe R, Edmondson K, Jones WH (2003). "A change of heart: cardiovascular correlates of forgiveness in response to interpersonal conflict." *Journal of Behavioral Medicine.*

Lawler KA, Younger JW, Piferi RL, Jobe, RL, Edmondson, KA, Jones, WH (2005). "The unique effects of forgiveness on health: an exploration of pathways." *Journal of Behavioral Medicine.*

Lincohn Library," (President Lincoln gave warning in his proclamation of March 30. 1863).

Lingren. H. G

http://ianrpubs.unl.edu/family/g1392.htm#top#top.

Lynn, Adele (2001)..."*50 Activities for Developing Emotional Intelligence*" HRD Press, Amhest MA.

Martinuzzi, Bruna (2009). "The Leader as a Mensch: Become the Kind of Person Others Want to Follow," Six Seconds.

Maxwell, J. (2007) *The 21 indispensable qualities of a leader: Becoming the person others will want to follow.* Thomas Nelson Inc.

Maxwell, JC (2007).*Talent is Never Enough.* Thomas Nelson

Mayer, J.D. Salovey, P. Caruso, D.L. & Sitarenios, G. (2001). "Emotional intelligence as a standard intelligence." Emotion, 1, 232-242.

MCDowell Ministries (2014). *Undaunted: The Early Life of Josh McDowell DVD*, Josh MCDowell Ministries

Mehrabian, Albert (1971). *Silent Messages* (1st ed.). Belmont, CA: Wadsworth. ISBN 0-534-00910-7

Mehrabian, Albert (2009) "'Silent Messages' – A Wealth of Information About Nonverbal Communication (Body Language)". *Personality & Emotion Tests & Software: Psychological Books & Articles of Popular Interest.* Los Angeles, CA: self-published. Retrieved April 6, 2010

Missler, N (1998), "Practically, How Do We Renew our Minds? Attitudes - (Part 2), http://www.khouse.org/articles/1998/155/

Nancy Missler (1998), "Practically, How Do We Renew our Minds? Attitudes - (Part 2)

Nee, Watchman. *The Character of God's Workman*, Christian Fellowship Publishers, Inc. New York.

Nelson Mandela (1994). *Long walk to Freedom*, Little, Brown and Company, New York.

PKAL (2004). Project Kaleidoscope), "Leadership Investing In The Future Building Institutional Leadership For Natural Science Communities: What works, what matters, what lasts" 2004-2006, Volume, Iv: http://www.pkal.org/template2.cfm?c_id=1040

Remen, Rachel Naomi. "Culture of Empathy", Retrieved July 30, 2014 http://cultureofempathy.com/References/Experts/Ot hers/Rachel-Naomi-Remen.htm

Slamka, S (2010). "Humility as a Catalyst for Compassion The Humility-Compassion Cycle of Helping Relevance to Counseling", College of St. Joseph In Vermont. http://compassionspace.com/sg_userfiles/revised_humility-compassion.pdf.

Smalley, G and Trent, J (1991). *The Language of Love*, Focus on the Family Publishing.

Smith, C (2005) Servant-Leadership: The leadership theory of Robert K. Greenleaf Paper for Info 640 – mgmt. of info. Orgs *www.carolsmith.us/downloads/640greenleaf.pdf*, Retrieved Dec 12, 2012

Toussaint, L. L., & Williams, D. R. (October, 2003). "Physiological correlates of forgiveness: Findings from a racially and socioeconomically diverse sample of community residents. "Presented at 'A Campaign for Forgiveness Research' Conference, Atlanta, GA.

U.S. Army Handbook (1973). *Military Leadership*

Undaunted: The Early Life of Josh McDowell DVD

Warmerdam, GV. Self-Awareness: Pathway to Happiness, http://www.pathwaytohappiness.com/self-awareness.htm, Retrieved July 10, 2013

Worthington Jr, E.L, Witvliet, CVO, Pietrini, P. and Miller, AJ. "Forgiveness, Health, and Well-Being: A Review of Evidence for Emotional Versus Decisional Forgiveness, Dispositional Forgivingness, and Reduced Unforgiveness". *J Behav Med* (2007) 30:291–302.

Worthington, E. L. Jr. (2001). "Unforgiveness, forgiveness, and reconciliation in societies." In R. G. Helmick & R. L. Petersen (Eds.), *Forgiveness and reconciliation: Religion, public policy, and conflict transformation* (pp. 161–182). Philadelphia: Templeton Foundation Press.

Worthington, E. L. Jr. (2006). *Forgiveness and reconciliation: Theory and application.* New York: Brunner-Routledge.

Worthington, E. L. Jr. (Ed.). (2005a). *Handbook of forgiveness.* New York: Brunner-Routledge.

Wosu, SN (2014). *Leader as Servant Leadership Model: An Integrated Transformative Leadership Model*, Xulon Press, Florida.

Wosu, SN (2014). *The Authentic Leader as Servant Part I: The Outward Leadership Attribute, Principles, and Practices*, Elohiym Publishing House, Maryland.

Wosu, SN (2014). *The Authentic Leader as Servant Part II: The Inner Strength Leadership Attribute, Principles, and Practices*, Elohiym Publishing House, Maryland.

INDEX

OTHER PUBLICATIONS BY THE AUTHOR

Any of these books can be purchased from: www. amazon.com
or http://www.kanmasleadership.com/book_Publications.html.
For speaking engagement and consultation, contact
Prof. Sylvanus N. Wosu, email: swosu@kanmas.com

Leader as Servant Leadership Model: The Laws of Integrative, Transformative Leadership
Sylvanus N. Wosu
Pages: 458
ISBN: 978-1-4984-0381-8
Xulon Press FL 2014

In today's global world, there is no better time for servant's heart of service to reach people seeking authentic leadership. The *Leader as Servant Leadership Model* is for anybody who aspires to be a leader in service of others and organizations. The books guides you through four integrated dimensions of transformational leadership processes: personal, spiritual (relational), empowerment, and service. With this foundation and for the leadership process to be effective for growth of others and organization, the leader must be more centered on people than organization. Whether you're serving your church, business, institution, organization, or community, this book will guide you in a far-reaching, biblically-based dialogue on the role of the leader as servant. If you're serious about making a lasting and positive impact on others' lives, *The Leader as Servant Leadership Model* is for you. You are not ready to lead until you are willing to selflessly serve others.

The Authentic Leader as Servant Part I: The Outward Leadership Attributes, Principles and Practices

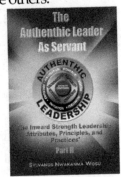

Sylvanus N. Wosu
Pages: 386
ISBN: 978-0-9746364-4-3
Elohim House, Maryland 2014

The Authentic Leader as Servant Part I: The Outward Leadership Attributes, Principles, and Practices looks at leadership from a perspective proposed thousands of years ago: A leader who is also a servant is, for the most part, qualified to lead when the individual is ready to carry out their assignment as a servant while pursing the growth of others... The book describes the leaders' outward attributes using comprehensive, irrevocable facts and principles. The author Dr. Sylvanus Wosu describes the exemplary leader-as-servant outward attributes, including servant-hood as trust, influence, generosity, and persuasion, among many others, especially how to apply these qualities when serving others. The book focuses on the Biblical model of leadership that engages studies from the secular, sociological, and business perspective, and explores how leader-as a servant relationship to followers can be productive and nurturing.

The Authentic Leader as Servant Part II: The Inner Strength Leadership Attributes, Principles, and Practices looks at leadership from a perspective proposed thousands of years ago: A leader-servant is most qualified to lead when most ready to serve as a servant for the growth of others.. Describing the leadership outbound attributes using comprehensive, irrevocable facts and principles,  author Dr. Sylvanus Wosu explains exemplary leader-as-servant leadership inner strength attributes including empathy, courage, responsibility, initiative, and listening/communication, among many others. Importantly, Wosu describes how to develop and apply these qualities when serving others. The book focuses on a Biblical model of leadership that engages studies from secular, sociological, and business sectors to explore how leader-follower relationships can be productive and nurturing. Wosu argues that nothing is as authentic, other-centered, and service-oriented as a leadership modeled after the ultimate authentic leader-servant, Jesus Christ.

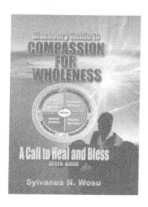

Discovery Guide to Compassion for Wholeness: *A Call to Heal and Bless Workbook*

Sylvanus N. Wosu
Pages - 137
Elohiym House
ISBN: 978-0-9746364-8-1
Published 2014
www.amazon.com

This guide-book is a discovery teaching workbook or study guide for anyone desiring deeper understanding of how to develop a heart for compassion that heals the broken hearted, restores and sustains relationships within and outside families, and leads others effectively as a servant. The guide uses exploratory self-discovery method to help the reader better understand and retain the content through intentional conversation and challenging critical thinking questions. The guide can be used for individual study, small group study, training workshops, or a combination of the above. Some biblical teaching moments and readings are used to guide the reader explore the text and meaning in the book and to lay his or her own foundation and understanding of the key elements of compassion for wholeness

RELATIONAL SERVICE LEADERSHIP

Relationships and interactions between a leader and followers are intricately linked to leadership. Relational leadership is an interpersonal process through which the interactions of values, attitudes, behaviors, and beliefs are nurtured, constructed, and practiced to connect with respect to empowering productive ser vice. In this context, *Relational Service Leadership* model focuses on the integration of relational and service leadership concepts to transform 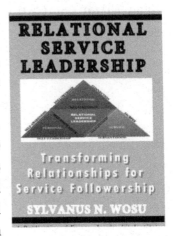 and interconnect relationships for effective others-centered service. The thesis of the book is that great leaders relationally touch the hearts of their followers as a pathway through which they influence and impact them for service; relational leaders are transformational as they positively impact the emotional, spiritual, and psychological wholeness of the people with whom they serve or come in contact. This is a new kind of mentor-leadership in which a leader nurtures personal relationships that transform and empower followers for service. This book will benefit students of leadership who desire to understand the ways in which interpersonal connections, services, and sacrifices are integrated as a strategic process of transformation, growth, and empowerment for greatness in today's emerging global world. It is a must-read for all leaders that aspire to lead extraordinary change!

.

Transformative Personal Leadership

In this book, *Transformative Personal Leadership*, we focus attention on the process of leaders developing high moral standard and becoming forces for change, transformative figures for themselves, their followers, and their organizations to lead extraordinary change. By taking a broad view of the understanding of what a leader can be, and should be, the book details a progression of self-study, and other-centered work and thought. The book serves as an excellent resource for both followers aspiring to be leaders and practicing leaders who aspire to be great transformers of followers and organizations, whether in their churches, businesses, corporations, institutions, or communities. Detailed discussions of the key elements of effective transformative leadership process. Leadership characteristics, core foundations of personal leadership are presented. The subjects of Transformative Change Management and Leading and Executing Change are discussed in greater details as the over-arching applications of transformative personal leadership as a whole, *Transformative Personal Leadership* provides leaders, managers, employees, and followers with a framework to embrace a leadership process of becoming an excellent and transformational change agent. The book is an inspiration for anybody that aspires to be a better version of self— personally, organizationally, and professionally— with a far-reaching impact on the followers and organizations with which he or she serves

Relational Mentorship in Higher Education

Relational Mentorship in Higher Education explores various models for mentorship as developed for undergraduate students, graduate students, and faculty. It presupposes two critical pillars for effective mentorship—mutual trust and relational connection. By framing mentorship as personal service, followership, and leadership processes, this book presents a  unique perceptive of the mentoring process that puts emphasis on goal-oriented relationships and mutual trust that benefit both mentor and mentee, along with their communities and organizations. With this focus, the book gives attention to strategies for all parties involved—faculty mentors, student mentees, and universities—in a manner that not only gives guidance to each individual involved but also provides each party with a view into the mind of the other parties. The text provides an extensive foundation for members of higher education who want to implement mentorship opportunities and work to make the process an attainable and positive goal within their communities and organizations. Relational Mentorship in Higher Education is a must-resource book for student-mentees to learn how to develop and be engaged in their personal growth plan, for faculty-mentors desiring to develop more mentorship skills, especially in cross-gender or cross-racial setting, and for academic administrators planning to develop effective mentoring or faculty professional development program.